The *Scudamores*
of Kentchurch *and* Holme Lacy

The *Scudamores*
of Kentchurch *and* Holme Lacy

HEATHER HURLEY

LOGASTON PRESS

FRONT COVER: *(top)* Watercolour painting of Kentchurch Court, ?1869 *(Kentchurch Archives)*; *(bottom)* Oil painting of Holme Lacy House, English School, date unknown, discovered at Coleshill Park, Warwickshire *(by kind permission of Mr K.E. Wingfield Digby, Sherborne Castle)*. BACK COVER: Stone bears, originally from Holme Lacy House, being taken by Roy Lane to Kentchurch Court in 1952, where they were erected at the entrance *(Kentchurch Archives)*

First published in 2019 by Logaston Press
The Holme, Church Road, Eardisley HR3 6NJ
www.logastonpress.co.uk
An imprint of Fircone Books Ltd.

ISBN 978-1-910839-38-6

Designed and typeset by Richard Wheeler.
Cover design by Richard Wheeler.

Printed and bound in Poland

Logaston Press is committed to a sustainable future for our business, our readers and our planet. The book in your hands is made from paper certified by the Forest Stewardship Council.

FSC
www.fsc.org
MIX
Paper from
responsible sources
FSC® C105618

British Library Catalogue in Publishing Data.
A CIP catalogue record for this book is available from the British Library.

CONTENTS

ACKNOWLEDGEMENTS   *vi*

INTRODUCTION   *vii*

1 Origins of the Scudamores at Kentchurch   I

2 The Dissolution and Effect of the Reformation   17

3 Civil War and Aftermath   31

4 Colonel John Scudamore and Keck's Remodelling of
Kentchurch Court   45

5 John Lucy Scudamore, John Nash's Legacy and
Thomas Tudor   61

6 Laura Adelaide, the Lucas Family and the Colourful
Twentieth Century   79

7 The de Lacys and the Early Scudamores at Holme Lacy   101

8 John Scudamore, Sir James and Sir John Living at
Holme Lacy House   113

9 Sir John 1st Viscount – Civil War, Holme Lacy,
Dore Abbey and Hempsted   129

10 The Restoration and Remodelling of Holme Lacy
House, 2nd & 3rd Viscounts   145

11 The Heiresses Lady Frances Scudamore and her
Daughter the Duchess of Norfolk   161

12 Scudamore-Stanhope, the Earls of Chesterfield
and the 1909 Sale   177

APPENDICES   197

BIBLIOGRAPHY   205

ENDNOTES   207

INDEX   225

ACKNOWLEDGEMENTS

The acknowledgements are numerous for producing this book, with many thanks to those who assisted with the archives, helped with the research and made their work available to enable writing this intricate history of the Scudamore family. I am most grateful to the Lucas-Scudamores of Kentchurch Court, who allowed access to their archives, house and grounds, with special thanks to Rosie Watts for her cataloguing, cooperation and photography; also to Jan Lucas-Scudamore for her encouragement and enthusiasm. Equally important for the research was the friendly service of Rhys Griffith and his experienced staff who willingly handled masses of documents at Herefordshire Archives. Works available either in a printed or digital format by the late Warren Skidmore with later papers, edited by Linda Moffatt, were an invaluable source, as were the surveys and writings of David Whitehead, and the digital images of maps and archives provided by David Lovelace. Then there was Joan Fleming-Yates who helped with her knowledge of both ancestry and of the Monnow valley.

Apart from the documentary research there was a certain amount of fieldwork carried out at Kentchurch, Holme Lacy and the surrounding area, exploring the highways and byways, following riverside paths along the Monnow and Wye and investigating places of interest accompanied by my husband Jon. My thanks therefore also go to Holme Lacy House Hotel for allowing access to the house and grounds, mainly accompanied by Jon and occasionally by Julie Balsom. At Kentchurch such walks were often also made in the company of Rosie Watts and Tristan Gregory.

Guidance was given from Robert Walker about dovecotes and from Brian Robbins regarding cider making. Thanks are extended for assistance received from Hereford City Library, Hereford Cathedral Archives, Monmouth Museum, Ann Smith (archivist at Sherborne Castle), Brenda Ward (archivist at Belmont Abbey), the Landscape Origins of the Wye project and lastly to Andy Johnson and Richard Wheeler of Logaston Press for editing and publishing *The Scudamores of Kentchurch and Holme Lacy*.

INTRODUCTION

This is the story of two different branches of the Scudamores, a prominent and important family domiciled in the shadow of the Welsh borders at Kentchurch in the Monnow valley, and at Holme Lacy in the Wye valley in the county of Herefordshire. The challenging task of researching over a thousand documents, maps, papers, photographs, paintings, books and journals relating to the Scudamores has revealed a fascinating account of the two families. The senior ones of the eleventh century still reside at Kentchurch Court, whereas the Holme Lacy branch of the fourteenth century ran out of heirs and resources by the end of the nineteenth century, though managed to remain at Holme Lacy until the early twentieth century. The two contrasting families reflect their own personalities and characteristics, with the more liberal 'quiet and home-keeping people' who took little activity in national affairs at Kentchurch becoming overshadowed by the prominence of the ambitious and powerful family at Holme Lacy.

Although the book is primarily about the Scudamores it has also been written as a local history, introducing people and places set against a background of both national and local events that occurred in Kentchurch and Holme Lacy throughout many turbulent and intriguing times. The history, traditions and legends of the present family have been honoured and put into the context of the chronological documentation. The majority of the research was undertaken at Herefordshire Archives, searching through their collections, including the Kentchurch Court Papers and Documents deposited by Sybil Lucas-Scudamore in 1942 with the National Library of Wales and later transferred to Herefordshire Archives. These findings were supported by archives held at Kentchurch Court, catalogued by Rosie Watts (née Lucas-Scudamore), a most supportive and encouraging assistant. Other sources of importance were the papers produced by the late Warren Skidmore and those edited by Linda Moffatt, the park surveys of Kentchurch and Holme Lacy by David Whitehead Associates and a series of the Duchess of Norfolk's deeds at the National Archives, digitally reproduced by David Lovelace for the Landscape Origins of the Wye project.

The Scudamores have produced many male characters of fame, fortune and failure, some strong and flamboyant, others quiet and reflective, but the women have formerly been overlooked, even though they played an important and sometimes a dominant role in the history of the family. It was also due to two women that the portraits, photographs, letters, maps, furnishings and carvings were acquired from Holme Lacy House and conserved, together with the archive and collections at Kentchurch Court. At the time of writing it is interesting to note that both Kentchurch Court as a country house and garden, and Holme Lacy House as a hotel are open to the public.

Rosie and Heather at Kentchurch Court

During my years as a guide at Kentchurch Court I was often asked by visitors to write the history of the family, my reply being that it would be a lifetime's work! But I was persuaded by Andy Johnson of Logaston Press to undertake this project with the full support of the Lucas-Scudamore family at Kentchurch Court.

Heather Hurley
Bridstow, 2018

Origins of the Scudamores at Kentchurch

> That this Family, variously written in Records, de Eskidemore,
> Esquidmor, Escuedmor, Schidemore, Skydmore, &c. was vary
> anciently of a plentiful Estate And great Esteem, evidently
> appears from their early Benefactions to the Abbey of Dore, and
> other Authorities.
>
> *reprinted from an ancient book, Kentchurch Archive*

THE name Scudamore – also recorded as Skidmore, Scudemer and Escudamore in addition to those mentioned above – is traditionally believed to be derived from 'shield of love' or alternatively 'low moor'. The family origins were equally traditionally obscure until it was revealed recently that one Ralph, born around 1040, was ancestor to the Scudamore family'.[1] Under Alfred of Marlborough, the Domesday Book records Ralph as one of nine knights at Ewyas Harold in Herefordshire as well as holding Upton Scudamore in Wiltshire. The unnamed land held by Ralph at Ewyas was considered to have been Corras in Kentchurch held later by 'Reginald de Scudemer'. Upton Scudamore lies nearly two miles north of Warminster in Wiltshire and was known as Upton Escudamore before 1150, implying by the place-name that members of the Scudamore family were previously living there.[2]

Corras was a small medieval settlement situated near the river Monnow opposite the present Great Corras Farm. In 1988 archaeologists discovered a quantity of stone lying on the surface, and evidence for a small pond, a well and several house platforms, together with that for a larger building which may have represented a barn or manor house. Another investigation discovered a structure and finds with documentary evidence to support the site of a chapel that had been in use from the end of the eleventh century until around 1400, but considered to have been ruined and decayed by 1607. Nearby, and standing hidden in a defensive position above the steep banks of the Monnow, is a castle motte rising steeply to a height of 12 feet with a flat top measuring 12 feet across.[3] There was also a ford across the Monnow which is still in use, and at the beginning of the fourteenth century a mill with a weir.[4]

Looking over Kentchurch Court and Park from Garway Hill (*Heather Hurley*)

The River Monnow at Kentchurch (*Heather Hurley*)

There are many examples of the Scudamore coat of arms described and illustrated in the past by members of the family and in publications. Heraldry first appeared in Western Europe in the early twelfth century, the date when the Scudamores acquired their coat of arms. It has always been understood that a cross similar to the Maltese cross was the coat of arms of ancient origin before the adoption of the three stirrups 'leathered and buckled, which have been borne without change ever since by all branches of the family'. The Kentchurch Scudamores' ancient coat of arms was a 'cross patée fitched in the foot gules' – considered to be 'extremely early in date' – coupled with the motto 'Scuto Amoris Divini' (By the Shield of Divine Love). The crest is a 'bear's paw issuing from a Ducal Coronet – borne from an early date, but the precise origin is unknown'.[5]

RIGHT (*from top*): The Scudamore coat of arms as shown in G. Strong's *Heraldry of Herefordshire* (1848): the arms associated with Holme Lacy, the shield on the left being those of the Lacy family and on the right of the Stanhope family; the ancient arms of the Kentchurch Scudamores on the left and the modern arms on the right. Sir John Scudamore's coat of arms (Alice, the daughter of Owain Glyndwr, here being called Elizabeth as was sometimes the case). (*Kentchurch Archives*)

In the twelfth century, Harold of Ewyas gave the tithes of St Keyne of Kentchurch and the chapel of Corras held by an elderly Ralph to St Peter's Abbey in Gloucester. Ralph was followed at Corras by 'Reinaldus de Scudemer' and his brothers Walter and Hugo, as recorded in the abbey cartulary.[6] In 1149, during the reign of Stephen, Sir Walter Scudamore of Corras gave parts of his land called Fulk's Mead to Dore Abbey in 1149.[7] His successors included several Walters, a Ralph, John and Vincent of Abergavenny.

This Glebe terrier of 1607 states: 'We have a Chapell within our said parish called the Chapell of Cawrosse now ruynated and decayed with a Churchyarde therunto belonginge and now in the occupation of the aforesaid John Scudamore esq. but Whether it be a member of our said church or noe we knowe not.' (*Herefordshire Archives*)

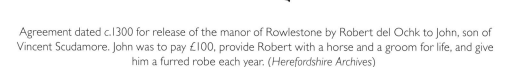

The 1257 grant of Corras (*Herefordshire Archives*)

Agreement dated c.1300 for release of the manor of Rowlestone by Robert del Ochk to John, son of Vincent Scudamore. John was to pay £100, provide Robert with a horse and a groom for life, and give him a furred robe each year. (*Herefordshire Archives*)

In 1257 the widow of one of the Walters and known as 'Ysenda, Lady of Kaueros' granted the manor of Corras to William de Tregoz, rector of Kentchurch, for an annual rent of a pound of cumin. A few years later the rector granted the manor to the Knights Templar at Garway.[8] Ralph (*see timeline on p. 197*) may have been the first Scudamore to settle at Poston in Vowchurch, where he or his family built a fortified house in the early thirteenth century. Vincent married into the Wroth family of Abergavenny, where he lived as a wool merchant and acquired a meadow situated below a pond belonging to a vinery at Abergavenny, a grant that was witnessed by the Wroth family.[9] Ralph's son Walter de Scudamore of Poston must have been the father of Matilda 'for which a Welsh arrow ought to be rendered to her yearly' for a tenement at Puddlestone near Leominster in Herefordshire, binding herself to him yearly for a seam of corn and one of oats in 1264.[10]

Before the end of the thirteenth century, Vincent Scudamore's son John became the first of a sequence of John Scudamores who are not easy to identify individually. The first John was granted a capital messuage (a dwelling-house with outbuildings and land) in Rowlestone, and in 1299 his other son Robert acquired lands and tenements in Rowlestone formerly belonging to Peter de Oka from his daughters Agnes and Gladys.[11] A well-preserved document of 1307 records the release of the manor of Rowlestone from Robert de Oka to John Skydmore in consideration of several payments, as well as providing Robert with a horse and groom for life and giving him a 'furred robe yearly for a free man', as indicating a man not tied to a Lord.[12]

The second of these John Scudamore was to become known as John Scudamore of Abergavenny and Rowlestone, and was followed by his son, the third John Scudamore, and two great-grandsons: Richard of Rowlestone, who served five times as Mayor of Hereford, and John the fourth, who became Sir John of Kentchurch after acquiring lands in Kentchurch and Thruxton. He or his son was known as Sir Jenkin, lord of Rowlestone, who married Alice, daughter and coheir to Sir Robert Ewyas, Knight. He was remembered as 'a stout fellow who had all the rule of the country thereabouts'.[13]

By the end of the fourteenth century the settlement at Corras, with its chapel and motte, had become redundant in an area of the remote and wild Welsh borders known to be inhospitable, unlawful and irreligious, and where friendship was unsure. The area's depopulation was partly due to the Scudamores, who were increasing in importance, having left Corras and established themselves at Kentchurch.[14] Here, in a secluded and almost hidden site, Sir John Scudamore (the fifth in the line of Johns), appointed Mayor of Hereford in 1386,[15] built a fortified house later known as Kentchurch Court. To existing buildings Sir John added a thick-walled rectangular tower using some of the good stone from the chapel and buildings at Corras. The tower of five storeys contained a garderobe and a stair within the walls – all built of local sandstone, rubble and ashlar – which formed part of a fortified enclosure with a two-arched gateway flanked by buttresses and featuring a draw-bar hole.[16]

The fourteenth-century tower at Kentchurch Court (*Heather Hurley*)

THE SCUDAMORES OF KENTCHURCH AND HOLME LACY

A fourteenth-century gateway at Kentchurch Court (*Heather Hurley*)

Life on the Welsh borders during this period was dangerous, unstable and subject to cross-border raids. With violence, intimidation, robbery and ransom causing fear and uncertainty, the important families protected themselves against attack by constructing strong defensible homes.[17] Within its fortified enclosure Sir John's home would have consisted of a great hall, a chapel, bed chambers, servants' quarters and stabling. There was adequate fresh water nearby, and plenty of timber for building and firing the hearth.

In the village of Kentchurch in the 1380s a new rector was appointed by the name of John Kent,[18] possibly the character better known as Jack of Kent whose life was surrounded by myth and legend. As a lad he worked in the stables at Kentchurch and was noted to be bright and

A room inside the tower in 2017 (*Heather Hurley*)

quick to learn so was sent to Oxford to be educated and then ordained as a priest. On his return he served as the rector at Kentchurch and as the Scudamores' family chaplain, but according to folklore he showed extraordinary supernatural powers in league with the devil. Amongst the many tasks attributed to Jack of Kent and the devil were building a bridge in one night across the Monnow, keeping the crows from eating the corn, thrashing a whole bay of corn in one day, and flying through the air carrying rocks, but throughout his life he always outwitted the devilish spirit. Jack had reputedly made a pact with the devil that he could have his soul when he died, whether he was buried inside or outside a church, so it is said his body was interred within the thick walls of the church so as to be neither inside nor outside.[19]

It has been suggested that his popular reputation as a wizard was owed to the credulity of the clergy of the day, for he was known as a Lollard. Saying that a man had sold himself to the devil if he disagreed with your theological opinions was not uncommon in clerical circles during the Middle Ages.[20] A Commission on Information, signed by John Scudamore and others, stated that some of the king's subjects commonly called Lollards were captured, because the king had taken against them and their opinions, which included traitorously planning his death and doing things to the destruction of the Catholic faith. In the county of Herefordshire, those who were found guilty were arrested and imprisoned until orders were given for their punishment.[21]

At Kentchurch the supernatural life of Jack of Kent as a wizard was never forgotten. At Kentchurch Court, a ghostly fifteenth-century portrait, painted in the Flemish style on a wooden panel, is reputed to represent Jack of Kent appearing in front of a walled medieval building understood to represent the Court. A seventeenth-century barn constructed of timbers from an earlier building was known as 'Jack O Kent's barn', and had a beam inscribed 'Io Kent',[22] and in the park a magnificent veteran oak bearing the name 'Jack O Kent' certainly dates from this period. Folk-tales originating from the late fifteenth century have been continuously recorded over the centuries, and the legendry building of the bridge over the Monnow is illustrated on the local inn sign.

The sign relates to the story of Jack asking the devil to build a much-needed bridge across the Monnow to connect Kentchurch in England with Grosmont in Wales. The devil agreed on payment of a soul from the first to cross the bridge, which he promised to build overnight. In the morning the parishioners were delighted to see the bridge, but Jack, already prepared to outwit the devil, picked up a bone and threw it to be chased by a dog across the bridge – so the devil was never repaid by a human soul! With changing innkeepers the inscription on the sign altered from:

This bridge was built without a hammer or trowel
Come in and take a glass with D. Powell

to:

This bridge was built without hammer or addis
Come in and take a glass with R. Harris[23]

LEFT: A painting at Kentchurch Court said to be of Jack O'Kent, but which some believe shows Owain Glyndwr in old age when possibly in hiding with the Scudamores (*Kentchurch Archives*) BELOW: Kentchurch Court as depicted in the fifteenth century in the background to the same painting

The Jack O'Kent Oak in Kentchurch Park (*David Lovelace*)

The former sign for the Bridge Inn (*Heather Hurley*)

During a turbulent period of unrest and lawlessness in the Welsh Marches, Scudamore entered the royal service as a 'King's esquire' by September 1396, and in November he obtained custody of an outlaw's lands in Dorstone, Herefordshire. A year later he was accompanied to his first Parliament by one of Richard II's household knights, Sir Thomas Clanvowe of Hergest and Yazor in Herefordshire.[24]

An unfortunate incident occurred at Dore Abbey in 1398 when the abbots had problems with the local population. For some reason, maybe reflecting the Welsh-English tensions, armed members of the Scudamore family went to the abbey and assaulted the abbot, chased him away from his abbey, threatened him, his monks and his servants with death, and took away 8 horses, 30 oxen and 30 cows to the value £100. They also took the common seal of the abbey, £20 of money, and other goods and chattels to the value of 1,000 marks, together with charters and other muniments. The abbot was followed to Grace Dieu, at Llangattock-Vibon-Avel in Monmouthshire, where the Scudamores continued their plunder.[25]

From 1396 Sir John Scudamore the sixth of Kentchurch received the 'wages and fees' belonging to the office of constable of Goodrich Castle, an office he held until

An idealised portrait of Owain Glyndwr based on the image on his seal (*Rosie Watts*)

at least 1413. The security of Goodrich castle came under threat in 1402 from the rising of the Welsh in support of Owain Glyndwr, when it was reported that 400 Welshmen had captured and robbed many men and beasts in the county of Hereford. As the king's steward in 1401 at Kidwelly in Carmarthenshire, and custodian in 1405 of the three castles of Skenfrith, Grosmont and White Castle on the Welsh borders, Henry IV refused to believe any charges of disloyalty against Scudamore for secretly supporting Glyndwr, as accused by John Oke. The outcome was that Scudamore was knighted, and Oke, a convicted cattle thief, was hanged before Sir John left for France and served in the Agincourt campaign. On his return he was reinstated as steward of Kidwelly in 1423 and appointed steward of Monmouth and the three castles in 1425.[26]

Owain Glyndwr, 'Prince of Wales' spent his early life educating himself in London where he acquired some of the social graces of the courtier. He became a soldier, served the Crown in several campaigns and at his home he led life as a normal Welsh gentleman. His quarrel with Lord Grey of Ruthin led to serious uprisings against

alien rule, in liberating the Welsh race from the bondage of their English neighbours, but after his last raid on the Shropshire borders in 1410 his efforts failed.[27] Glyndwr is remembered as 'the greatest Welshman of all time: the man who never bowed the knee to the conqueror, and conceived the idea of a national university of Wales'.[28]

As a young attorney, Sir John Scudamore first married Margaret Brut of Britte Court, Kingsland (its location now unknown), and after her death, Alice the daughter and heir of Owain Glyndwr. This placed him in an awkward political position. Sir John, although an opponent of Glyndwr, held Welsh sympathies during these turbulent times and was recorded as the receiver of £6,870 collected from Owain's English friends in support of the uprising. With Glyndwr still on the loose, John Scudamore, the Herefordshire squire who held Carreg Cennen Castle in Carmarthenshire, visited the rebel to seek safety for his wife Alice and his mother-in-law, but his request was refused. The custody of Carreg Cennen had been transferred to Sir John from his brother Philip who had deserted the position to support Glyndwr.[29] By 1412 Glyndwr 'was heard of no more' and by tradition when his cause was hopelessly lost and his own people had turned against him he sought shelter in the home of his daughter Alice at Kentchurch. His final resting place is still unknown but is believed to have been either at Monnington Straddle in the Golden Valley or at Kentchurch Court.

Similar to Jack of Kent of the same period, many legendry stories surround Glyndwr and his many escapes from being captured, including disguising himself as Jack, and shoeing his horse back-to-front in order to throw those chasing him off his trail. It is said that Glyndwr's spirit haunts the tower, since referred to as 'Glyndwr's Tower', at Kentchurch Court.[30]

The plaque in Llandovery commemorating the execution of Llewelyn ap Gruffydd Fychan in 1401 (*Heather Hurley*)

Owain's escape was partly due to an ultimate sacrifice made by Scudamore's kinsman Llywelyn ap Gruffydd Fychan who was married to his daughter Jennet. Llywelyn was a landowner from Caeo in Carmarthenshire, described as a man of gentle birth and bountiful, who yearly used 16 tuns of wine in his household.[31] In 1401 he was press-ganged by Henry iv to find Glyndwr's base.[32] However, he led the English king through the uplands of Deheubarth for several wasted weeks on a wild goose chase to allow Owain the chance to make his escape. Henry lost his patience with Llywelyn and, maddened with anger and frustration, he had Llywelyn publicly executed in a barbaric manner at Llandovery.[33] The site of the execution is marked by a plaque in the Market Square at Llandovery.

In July 1415, Sir John prepared to join Henry v's first expedition to France, with a personal party of four men-at-arms and twelve archers, but did not accompany the king on his famous march to Calais. Instead he stayed behind to garrison the con-quered stronghold at Harfleur in Normandy with a retinue of ten lances and thirty archers under the captaincy of Thomas Beaufort, Earl of Dorset. Alternatively it has been recorded that Sir John did serve with the king at Agincourt where he may have been wounded and where his eldest son died on the field.[34] Sir John was known to have been someone to whom the king pawned his plate and jewels to pay for the wages of the expedition.[35] In 1432, due to a previously forgotten statute of 1402 which forbade any Welshmen or supporters to carry weapons or become a government official, and his marriage to Alice, Sir John was removed from the bench in Herefordshire and was no longer considered to be eligible to hold office in South Wales.[36] As a result his offices as steward of Kidwelly, Iskenny, Monmouth, White Castle and Grosmont, and as constable of the castles of Monmouth, Grosmont and White Castle in South Wales, were taken over by Edmund de Beaufort, Earl Montaine.[37] Sir John Scudamore died in 1435 and was succeeded by his son Sir John the seventh, who married Joan, daughter of John Parry of Poston.[38]

MEMBER	YEAR	REIGN
Johannes Skydemore de Kenchurche	1397	Richard II
Johannes Skydemore, Chivaler	1413	Henry V
Johannes Skydemore, Chivaler	1414	Henry V
Johannes Skydemore, miles	1425	Henry VI
Johannes Skydemore, Chivaler	1429	Henry VI
Johannes Skydemore, Chivaler	1433	Henry VI
Johannes Skudamour, miles	1448	Henry VI

Table showing the Scudamore family members who represented Herefordshire in various Parliaments spanning the reigns of Richard II to Henry VI

According to family papers, many of the Scudamores between 1397 and 1448 served as Members of Parliament for Hereford.[39]

Hereford played a key role in advancing the Yorkist cause during the Wars of the Roses which developed into a long struggle for the Crown of England. Sir John the seventh earned a reputation as one of the most stalwart and consistent supporters of the Lancastrian cause.[40] In 1451 there were disturbances along the Welsh Marches, resulting in an agreement being drawn up by gentlemen commoners, tenants and residents of several lordships to keep the peace. They agreed that if a thief stole any goods from one lordship and took them to another, then the lordship where the thief was apprehended bound him to redeliver the goods or pay to the owner the price he made upon oath, under penalty of 1,000 marks. This was signed and sealed by Sir John Scudamore on behalf of all parties.[41]

Sir John and members of his family, together with 30 retainers, fought for the Lancastrian cause at Mortimer's Cross in 1461 when, according to William of Worcester, James the son of Sir John was slain and his brother Henry was beheaded. William, Sir John's brother, died in his bed and Sir John, the most valiant of them, later also died in bed. John fought alongside Jasper Tudor, a relative on John's mother's side, and after the Lancastrian defeat they both managed to escape, with Sir John fleeing to Pembroke Castle and Jasper living to take revenge in supporting the campaign of Henry Tudor in 1485. Jasper's father, Owen Tudor, was captured and taken to Hereford where he was beheaded. It was a tragic end for Owen who came from an influential Welsh lineage and was known to have been a tall and attractive man living a notorious life. He secretly married Catherine of Valois, the widow of Henry V, got into serious trouble with the authorities and was deprived of the custody of their children, but was restored into favour and made a royal pensionary.[42] After Owen's execution in the market place, his body was buried at Greyfriars, where his grave was in a chapel or chantry on the northern side of the friary church, but since the Dissolution the site has been lost.[43] His son Edmund fathered the future King Henry VII.

One of the properties that Sir John Scudamore had acquired was a tenement with a garden and meadow adjoining Blackmarston just outside the city, along with other lands in Hereford. This was in 1451, the same year that Richard, another member of the Scudamore family, was serving as Mayor of Hereford.[44] In 1457 a grant was made to Sir John's son James for messuages and lands in Corras, which was witnessed by William, the rector of Kentchurch, and Thomas, the vicar of Grosmont. Dating from this period are a number of stories, rumours and legends relating to the Scudamores but not easy to authenticate. For instance, son James had served in France supplying six mounted archers and wearing the livery of the Duke of York. He married into a Carmarthen family and his father-in-law was arrested and charged for 'greatly grieving' the king's subjects, but was released through the influence of Sir John. The slaying of James, recorded by William of Worcester, apparently took place at a certain manor house at Kingchurch, understood to be Kentchurch. In 1456 a document records that a bond slave with all his goods and offspring was granted by John Dansey to Nicholas Skydmore of Rowlestone.[45] Dating back to these turbulent times, there is reputed to have been an underground passage available to those who needed to flee from the house, which led to the church where horses were kept ready-saddled in stables hidden under the building.[46] At nearby Llanithog, an extra-parochial place in Kentchurch, a chapel once existed even more ancient than the parish church.[47]

As Sir John's son, James, had died within his father's lifetime, and in anticipation of Sir John's death, a prenuptial settlement was made in 1473 between his grandson Thomas Scudamore and his wife Margaret, daughter of Morgan ap Jenkyn ap Phillips, to convey in trust the manor of Kentchurch and lands and tenements in the lordship of Grosmont to their only son James. Thus it was that in 1489 James became son and heir of Kentchurch whilst still a minor.[48] In 1505 he held lands, tenements, and appurtenances without any right or title, and was expected by custom to pay a rent of 25s, instead of the earlier rent of 13s, for Llanithog in Kentchurch, a rental paid to the Knights Hospitallers in Garway. Amongst the 52 items recorded in the Rental were three messuages, lands and tenements with appurtenances at Corras belonging to the Knights Hospitallers that abutted Garway Hill.[49]

The previous year (1504) the Lord of Abergavenny granted to James a pasture and meadow near Grosmont Bridge, a curtilage at Corras with two meadows, a field called Churchfield, a cottage where the smith dwelt and two other cottages. The grant also mentioned 'le Churche Way', 'le home Feld de le Olde Court' and 'Pistilbrook' all in the parish of Kentchurch.[50] In 1521, Johane, one of the daughters and heirs of this James Skydmore, married Philip Skydmore a cousin, related to the Holme Lacy Scudamores, whose family had been established at Hollington in Holme Lacy, possibly through marriage, for at least 100 years. This formed the first known link between the two main branches of the Scudamore family,[51] and through Philip the Scudamore holdings at Rowlestone and Llancilio were united with those at Kentchurch.[52]

RECTORIA DE KENCHURCH.

WILL'M'S MOTLOW CL'IC[s] RECT' IB'M.

VALET IN

	£	s.	d.		£	s.	d.
Decimis granoȝ viij[li] v[s] viij[d] & feni xij[s] v[d] iƀm cõibȝ annis - -	viij	xviij	j				
Decimis lactual' iƀm cõibȝ annis - -	—	xxv	vij				
Decimis agnoȝ & lani iƀm cõibȝ annis - -	—	viij	—		xij	—	ij ob'
Aliis decimis minut' iƀm cõibȝ annis - -	—	vij	ij				
Oblacõibȝ iƀm iij[bz] tempiƀȝ anni ufualibȝ - -	—	xv	ix				
Terris glebat' iƀm p annũ -	—	v	vij ob'				

Inde in

REP'IS' VIȝ

	£	s.	d.		£	s.	d.
Penc̃on' an[l'] aƀƀi Glouc' -	—	xvij	vj		—	xxviij	—
P'cur' an[iibz] ecctie Hereff' -	—	x	vj				

Tithes in 1535 as shown in the *Valor Ecclesiasticus* (*Herefordshire Archives*)

2

The Dissolution and Effect of the Reformation

The dissolution meant the end of monastic communities,
a particularly medieval phenomenon, characterised by a
combination of piety, learning, and economic energy. The
dissolution also meant the destruction of some of the finest
medieval buildings in Britain, and it saw the breakup of
immense estates and the redistribution of land on a scale
unknown since the Norman Conquest

Trevor Rowley, 1988

THE Dissolution of the Monasteries led to the Reformation which dramatically
changed the political, social, economic and religious way of life, and perhaps provides a better terminal date to the Middle Ages than the conventional political date of
1485. The Dissolution caused the destruction of some fine medieval buildings, the breaking up of estates, redistribution of land and 'secularisation of life and society'.[1]

From the early sixteenth century, documentation regarding the Scudamores remains
sketchy, but it has been established that James Scudamore of Kentchurch was married
to Joan, daughter of Sir James Baskerville of Eardisley. When James died he was followed by his daughter Joan and her husband Philip Scudamore (now of Rowlestone
and Kentchurch), a distant cousin from Burnham in Buckinghamshire. They were
certainly head of the household in 1535 during the reign of Henry VIII, when William
Motlow, the rector at Kentchurch, was receiving the tithes of grain, hay, milk, butter,
cheese, lambs, wool, other small tithes, and offerings from the glebe.[2] It was around
this time that the east and south wings were added to the free-standing tower at
Kentchurch. The walls of the range running south from the tower's south-east corner
were possibly contemporary with it, in which case they would have formerly belonged
to stabling or other buildings.[3]

From 1536 hundreds of religious houses, monasteries, nunneries, friaries and houses of
the Knights Hospitallers, previously belonging to the Knights Templars (an order which

itself had been suppressed in the early fourteenth century) were suppressed at the Dissolution. The Knights Hospitallers were a military order taking their name from a hospital dedicated to St John the Baptist, built at Jerusalem for the use of pilgrims going to the Holy Land. They were soon established in England and took over many Templar manors and estates where they placed small societies of their brethren, under the government of a Commander. The Order's lands in Herefordshire were under the overall charge of the Commandery at Dinmore, and included Harewood with its chapel and 200 acres,[4] and land at Garway.

The lands at Garway had been leased in the past to a number of tenants including James Scudamore (the father of Joan), William Capell and Richard Mynors with rents ranging from 1s to £8 6s 8d, including a high payment of 73s 4d paid by the curate or chaplain for the tithes of sheaves within the parish of Garway.[5]

A Knight Hospitaller as depicted in *A History of the Order of St John of Jerusalem* by W. Rees (1947)

In 1544 John Scudamore, son of Joan and Philip, was recorded as having use of the pasture in Kentchurch late of the Knights Hospitallers, probably referring to land forming the park. It appears from some sources that James instigated the acquisition of the parkland from the Knights Hospitallers, which was purchased by his elder brother John Scudamore of Kentchurch, Rowlestone, Llancillo and the title to Nuneham Courtney in Oxfordshire through marriage to Margaret Pollard.[6]

In 1546 all the hilly pasture land, with appurtenances then called Kentchurch Park and which was estimated at 110 acres and 4 lawns adjoining part of Garway Hill, was granted to Robert Thornehill and Hugh Thornehill (among others). The boundary recorded in 1546 is difficult to interpret accurately, but stretched from the lands of Corras to Llanithog and below Garway Hill lately in the occupation of John Scudamore or his assignees.[7] Set on an elevated site, the park is very typical of medieval deer parks, which were often well away from the centres of cultivation. 'This may well have formed the rump of John Scudamore's purchase in 1546, to which he added the former agricultural holdings further down Garway Hill, in the parish of Kentchurch' (rump referring to the upper slope of land).[8]

Possibly dating to the time of this purchase is a feature known as the Moat situated near the present entrance to the Kentchurch estate and just 100 yards south-east of the church, and which is believed to be of medieval or late medieval date. Traditionally, it has been understood to be an earlier site of Kentchurch Court and was identified by archaeologists in 1908 as a fine and perfect homestead moat, and recorded as a rectangular island surrounded by a shallow moat in 1926. Recent surveys and archaeological

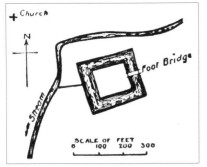

TOP: Kentchurch Park in the foreground as seen from Garway Hill (*Heather Hurley*)
MIDDLE: Deer in Kentchurch Park (*Heather Hurley*). BOTTOM LEFT: Plan of the moat near the
entrance to Kentchurch Court, as shown in the *Victoria County History* of 1908.
BOTTOM RIGHT: The moat site in 2017 (*Heather Hurley*)

investigations however now suggest the moated site could be a post-medieval folly or a pleasuance.[9]

The Holme Lacy branch of the Scudamore family also profited at the Dissolution, in their case from the suppression of the nearby Abbey of Dore. John Scudamore of Holme Lacy was appointed as the Particular Receiver by the Crown in 1537, and purchased building materials, household goods and other assets that led to many disputes and enquiries. In 1540 the abbey's estate was granted by the king to John Scudamore who eventually acquired the rectory and tithes plus a pension of 50s per annum awarded by the Crown, which he used to pay a priest-in-charge.[10]

In 1560 John Scudamore issued a Covenant (a formal document intending to give as strong a title as possible) to levy fines and ratify portions of many manors and rents of several thousand acres in Herefordshire, the Welsh Borders and along the Wye and Monnow valleys. The extent of the Scudamore holdings can be appreciated by the numerous places named at Kentchurch, Llanithog, Corras, Garway, Kilpeck, Bredwardine, Moccas, Bacton and Cusop. Other parties paying money or benefits as tenants were Watkyn and Rowland Vaughan together with their wives Johan and Elizabeth.[11]

1334	John de Healey
1348	William de Foye
1381	– Chandos
1411	Reginald Lane
1417	John Hales (*retired on pension*)
1419	John Henbergh (*died*)
1420	Hugh Carpenter
15--	Richard ap Howell
1516	Hugh ap Howell
153-	William Mutlow
1539	George Piers
	John ap Jenkin
	The Crown
1552	Simon Gilbert, Prebendary
1568	David Evans
1587	Roger Bradshaw
1591	John Gibson
159-	Simon Grover
	John Baguely (*died*)
	Thomas Barrett
1638	Richard Hawes

Rectors of Kentchurch, taken from notes by W.C. Cooke (*CF50/105*)

Despite the Reformation and the 1552 Act of Uniformity making Catholics liable to fines, John Scudamore at Kentchurch remained with the old faith, as recorded in a schedule of Catholics in England and in a report made by the Bishop of Hereford accusing John Scudamore, his wife and son, Thomas, of refusing to attend church. It was understood that John had made over his lands and goods to his son, possibly to avoid being fined.[12] As the pre-Reformation rector, William Motlow, had been replaced, it is most likely that the Scudamores worshipped secretly in their own chapel at Kentchurch.[13]

Those inhabitants who refused to attend Church of England services at their parish church under the Act of Uniformity were called Recusants and were mainly Catholics. Amongst the hills and valleys of the secluded Monnow Valley, where the river forms the boundary between England and Wales and the counties of Herefordshire and Monmouthshire, the Recusants found refuge. The remote and difficult terrain with its thick woods enabled them to continue practising their faith in secret places without being hounded by the authorities.[14] If evidence of recusancy was reported, the offender was liable to various penalties, land seizure and fines levied by the Exchequer. One such fine levied on John Scudamore was to supply one lance and a light horseman as a soldier if required.[15] Despite his Catholicism during the reign of Elizabeth I, John of Kentchurch served as High Sheriff of Herefordshire in 1565, as a Member of Parliament in 1584, and a Justice of the Peace in Hereford.[16]

As Catholics, the Scudamores would have been subject to harsh and cruel penalties for refusing to abandon their faith. After 1570 the Catholic subjects of Elizabeth I found themselves in a very different position due to the Papal Bull of Excommunication issued against the queen. Strict obedience to the Pope now meant treason against the realm of England and was punishable by the State with utmost severity. To avoid being discovered, secret places were created in houses and woods where Catholics could worship. Even so, in 1577 George Catsby of Grosmont was accused for not attending church and for having an altar erected in a wood; whilst John Thomas, a clerk (priest) from Llanarth in Monmouthshire, was presented at Quarter Sessions for not going to church and for wandering from place to place without having a living.[17] At nearby Treago Castle, passages and steps led to chambers used to secrete a Romish priest, which was known as the Pope's Hole; and at Alterynys, in the Monnow Valley, a narrow flight of steps led to a cul-de-sac amidst the open timbers of the roof, once used as a secret chamber.[18] At Kentchurch a Priest Hole has never been recorded or discovered, although one may have existed in the earlier building; however, could the hidden passage between the present library and drawing room remain as a reminder of the family's traditional story of concealing priests?

In 1562 John's son and heir, Thomas, had married Johan, the daughter of William, the eldest son of John Scudamore of Holme Lacy. Through marriage this formed another family link between the two branches of the Scudamore family. Johan bore no children and died early in life[19] and by 1582 Thomas was married to his second wife Agnes, daughter and coheir of Henry White.[20] Thomas and Agnes were based at Howton in Kenderchurch when he leased two meadows to a Garway yeoman. During the following three years Thomas granted a capital messuage and 15 acres of arable land in Corras to his father John of Kentchurch, who was listed as holding certain lands in Garway at a yearly rent of 40s in an inquisition made into the dissolved estate of Garway.[21] In 1590 John was recorded in an Ewyas Harold Rental for rents concerning certain lands in Kentchurch and Rowlestone.[22]

During the last decade of the sixteenth century John Scudamore was involved in disputes over rights and leases to the mills which were almost facing one another on the banks of the Monnow in the parishes of Kentchurch in Herefordshire and Grosmont, Monmouthshire. These disputes included 'Trespass on the River and Interruption of the Watercourse' of a grist mill at Kentchurch, and of 'A Water Corn Mill or Grist Mill, Wears, Watercourses, Fishings, Suits, Soke, Mulcture [miller's toll], and Profits with the Watercourse of the River, the Mill, Pounds and Mill Cawl [basket] at Grosmont

The weir on the Monnow at Kentchurch in 1900 (*Herefordshire Archives*)

and Kentchurch'. Also recorded at this date was the Queen's Mill at Kentchurch, leased to John Thomas, and a grant of a weir and a watercourse leading to Kentchurch Mill.[23]

Following the death of John Scudamore in 1593, his son and heir Thomas sought to recover lands that had been taken from his father as a result of his recusancy. It becomes clear from the case that Thomas lodged with the Exchequer that in 1584 his father had been in lawful possession of the manors of Kentchurch, Llanithog, Rowlestone and Llancillo, but was suspected of being a Recusant and refused to conform. He was therefore committed to prison where he stayed for a time until he was freed after entering into a bond for £300; however, as he did not put in a personal appearance at court he was apprehended in the county of Herefordshire as a prisoner under the ecclesiastical writ of *excommunicato capiendo*. His manors of Kentchurch, Llanithog, Rowlestone and Llancillo were seized by the Crown and granted to Thomas Brabone. Thomas Scudamore already possessed the manors of Howton in Kenderchurch and Gwerngenny in Kilpeck before he too was convicted as a Recusant and these manors were seized and leased to Edward Redhid.

If his request for the return of the estates was granted, Thomas reluctantly agreed to reform from his former recusancy and of his disobedience to the queen's laws and statutes. As a conforming Recusant Thomas had to obtain a certificate of compliance and take it to the bishop to show that he had heard a divine service, attended a sermon,

1602 Rental of Thomas Scudamore (*Herefordshire Archives*)

and received communion in the Church of England. Upon the return of the estates he discovered that the tenants had committed wilful waste and destruction including the

> cutting down of great timber trees and carrying away, selling and burning and spoiling the same and digging them up by the roots and in converting the timber trees to stack and suchlike wasteful uses and cutting down and burning of the hedges and damage of the premises and throwing down of the ditches … and in decaying and suffering the houses, edifices and buildings in their several occupations and possessions to go to utter ruin and decay for want of reparations and in setting up gates in unaccustomed places and in stopping or turning of usual highways and passages which of ancient times have been used … and carrying away of the corn, grass and hay growing upon the said premises without right or tithe either from her majesty or from myself.

Thomas also complained that the tenants had withheld from both him and the queen sundry heriots, rents, profits, duties, customs and services, which they denied and refused to recompense.[24]

Throughout this difficult period Thomas had lost his second wife Agnes, and took as his third wife Anne Middlemore. Both women produced sons.[25] With his estates

TOP: Part of Speed's 1610 map of the county showing Kentchurch – Kynechurch – near the centre (*Herefordshire Archives*). BOTTOM: John Scudamore's will of 1616 (*Herefordshire Archives*)

restored, Thomas, together with a relative, Phillip Scudamore of the City of London, granted a messuage and farm in Corras to his son and heir John Scudamore. The farm bordered both sides of the highway leading from the parish church to the towns of Monmouth and Hereford, a meadow called Broadholme, lands called the Lakes near the river Monnow and Corras Wood. He was also provided with an annuity of £80 out of the lordships of Kentchurch and Rowlestone.[26]

Despite Thomas's pledges to the state, there is evidence from the Scudamore family papers that his children remained as Catholics, with two daughters serving as nuns, another living as a Recusant, and a son ordained as a priest. Meanwhile, his heir John was imprisoned for his beliefs in 1592 and sent to the Tower of London in 1603 for his association with the Bye Plot. This was a conspiracy by Catholic priests and laymen to kidnap King James and hold him a hostage as a guarantee against religious toleration and the removal of unsympathetic councillors.

The young John Scudamore was caught, identified and restrained by the Sheriff of Hereford for entertaining a priest called Watson. It was only whilst he was on the road to Hereford under armed guard that he discovered that his former guest was wanted for treason. His father Thomas accompanied his son to London and pledged that he would give security for John if they were allowed to return to the Welsh borders to track down Watson. As a result John Scudamore was discharged from the Tower upon payment of a £500 bond and official caution.[27]

Throughout, Thomas Scudamore in fact remained true to the Catholic faith and in 1605, with his wife Ann, was listed amongst the most dangerous Recusants in the Diocese of Hereford.[28] Possibly due to the religious climate and a fear of his imminent death he produced a Rent Roll in 1606 naming all farmers and freeholders in Rowlestone and Llancillo. A year after his death in 1607 his widow Ann surrendered her interest of an award executed by Sir Herbert Croft and Sir Phillip Scudamore of the manors of Howton and Gwerngenny to John, her stepson and Thomas's heir, and the release of manors and lands in Kentchurch, Llanithog, Llancillo, Rowlestone, Corras and Llangua in defeasance of a statute merchant (a bond for securing the payment of money from debtor to creditor) from Thomas Scudamore to Richard Middlemore, the deceased father of Ann.[29]

Perhaps due to the growing anti-Catholicism after the failed Gunpowder Plot, John thereafter conformed in matters of religion. This ended the many difficulties that had beset his family at Kentchurch. John had married Amy, daughter of John Starkie of Darley Hall, Cheshire, where she had practised as a former Recusant, and the couple produced a large family.[30] Despite his attempt at settling his family's religious beliefs he would have been appalled at an incident caused by religious intolerance that occurred between John Baguley,[31] the local rector, and Thomas Cavendish on the road to Hereford from Kentchurch. Cavendish was charged with treason, destruction of a pew and a resistance to taking tithes.[32]

Church vandals shock villagers

BY VERONICA GOOLEY

PEOPLE in a Herefordshire village are shocked and angered by a theft and an act of vandalism in their beautiful church.

A churchwarden at St Mary's, Kentchurch, has admitted that she wept after discovering the theft of a unique brass plaque and finding the decapitated figures on a tomb group of praying children.

A woman parishioner said: "When they removed the plaque they would have had to kneel on the floor and the cross would have been in their eyes. It is not a Christian thing to say, but I hope their sight gradually dims."

The brass plaque, in the shape of a shield bearing the heraldic coat of arms of the Lucas Scudamore family, was prised from the floor, and the heads of two of the ten children were broken off and removed.

Both the plaque and the group of children, also Lucas Scudamores, were saved from the old church, which was burned down in the 1860s.

The fine tomb group of the praying children dates back to 1616. They were the children of John and Amy Scudamore, whose alabaster figures also stand in the church. The broken heads were those of two of the boys.

One of the two churchwardens, Jean Mauruschatt, confesses that she cried when she saw the vandalism.

Mrs Mauruschatt told The Hereford Times that the theft and vandalism took place between July 12 and 19.

AREA SEARCHED

"The police came out and had a look, but said this sort of thing is happening all the time," she said.

A search of the immediate area, including the churchyard and brook below the church, had revealed no sign of the missing heads.

Mrs Mauruschatt appealed to anyone who may notice anything resembling the heads on the roadsides or verges to let the police know. She believes that those responsible may have thrown them from the windows of a car.

"The parochial church council wants the heads to be repaired, because it can't bear to see the decapitated children, but we are not sure if that would be ethical," she added.

Mrs Mauruschatt said the church was locked at night, and sometimes during the day.

"But I have a set of keys and if people want to see the church I go with them and tell them about its history," she said. Only one other set of keys was owned, and the holder is abroad, so it is not known if the church was locked when the vandalism took place. But there had been reports of a man in the church on the Saturday, taking photographs of the windows.

"A car with Gloucestershire number plates was seen nearby, and the local policeman also noticed a car with foreign number plates outside the church on the Thursday before this happened," said Mrs Mauruschatt.

ABOVE: Part of the monument of 1616, to Amy and John Scudamore in Kentchurch church (*Logaston Press*).

LEFT: An article in the *Hereford Times* of 1 August 1991 recording vandalism to the Scudamore monument

John died in 1616 and part of his will states:

> I give and bequeath to my beloved wife Amy Scudamore and my worthy & loving
> kinsman Sir James Scudamore knight the manor of Rowlstone & Landsillow
> with their appurtenances in the county of Hereford To have and to hold the said
> manors with their appurtenances to them & their heirs for the use benefit &
> behalf of my younger sons – Philip Scudamore, Richard Scudamore, Ambrose
> Scudamore, Humphrey Scudamore, James Scudamore and Jonatas Scudamore
> to be equally divided between them for & during their natural lives. And if any
> of them shall happen to die then the part or portions of him do dying shall come
> & descend to my eldest son John Scudamore & his heirs forever. And whereas
> my wife Amy Scudamore is now pregnant my will is if it be a male child that
> he shall have his full part in the said manors proportionally with the rest of his
> brothers as aforesaid And if it be a female I leave the preferment of her to the
> discretion of my said wife.

John bequeathed to his wife, Amy Scudamore, and to Sir James Scudamore of Holme
Lacy all his tenements with their appurtenances in Howton, Gwerngenny, Kentchurch,
Corras and Garway mentioned in a lease dated 29 November 1607.[33]

John was buried at Kentchurch church where an alabaster monument was later
erected to him and his family by his wife Amy. The monument originally stood behind
the altar with iron palisades surrounding 'a man in armour & his Wife in Dress of
Time, both recumbent & reclining their heads on their left arms, each a book in their
right hands, on the base of the Tomb, below them kneel 8 Boys in black Gowns ... a
Girl also kneeling at prayer before a desk, a child (which was posthumous) in swad-
dling Clothes at Mother's feet'.[34] When the church was rebuilt the monument was
moved into the north wall of the chancel, together with tablets commemorating that

A lease of Llancillo forge in 1637 (*Herefordshire Archives*)

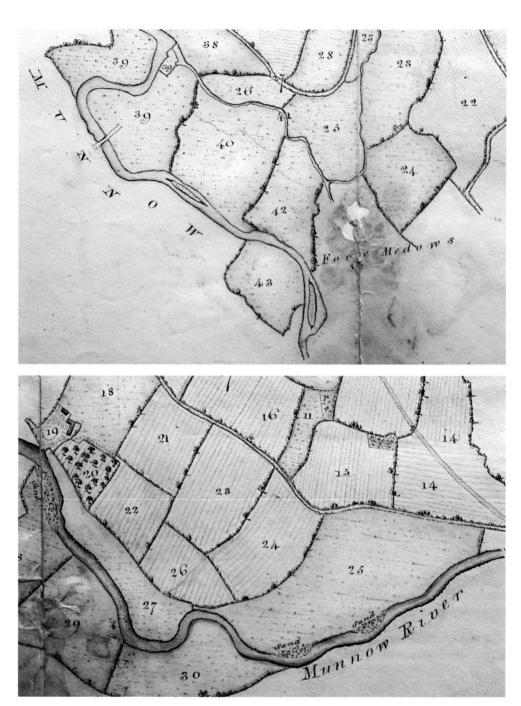

TOP: Llancillo forge meadows, where the forge was located, shown on Joseph Powell's map of c.1790 (*Kentchurch Archives*). BOTTOM: No. 19 (*top left on map*) is 'Forge Old Homestead' on Joseph Powell's map of c.1790 (*Kentchurch Archives*)

John was 'Worthy in Blood & Worthyer in Minde that Settled Bothe Religion & Peace Amongst Us', and another tablet names his wife, Amy, and their nine children; John, Philip, Richard, Ambrose, Humphrey, James, Jonathan, Edward and Marie. The unborn child was named Martin, and later became rector at Kentchurch and married a distant Scudamore relative.[35]

Amy's eldest son, John, married Elizabeth, the eldest daughter of Sir William Cooke of Highnam, Gloucestershire. The marriage settlement of 1621 between this John Scudamore and Elizabeth's brother listed manors and messuages at Kentchurch, Llanithog, Gwerngenny, Carross, Howton and included a valuable asset of a water corn-mill on the Worm Brook in the parish of Kenderchurch. This was a short-lived mill in Howton, which was only remembered in subsequent years by the fields named Lower, Middle and Upper Mill Meadow.[36] This marriage settlement was disputed by Amy's second husband Thomas Cavendish in 1624 (probably the same Thomas Cavendish who had earlier been charged with treason), but was resolved the following year in a General Release. This document appears to be the first known reference to Kentchurch Court.[37]

John attended Gray's Inn and, in complete contrast to his father and grandfather, was known for his antagonism to the Catholic Church. In south-west Herefordshire he was living in the midst of popular recusancy at its strongest in the Monnow Valley, which formed both the county and Episcopal boundary. With Charles 1 on the throne there was a fear that the Catholic religion would be restored, which led to John becoming an even more zealous activist. His wife Elizabeth produced at least seven sons and three daughters. The eldest son, William, failed to outlive his long-lived father. Four sons were to attend colleges at Oxford before, during or after the Civil War.[38]

Apart from the water corn-mills already mentioned, the early sixteenth century saw the establishment of water-powered iron forges in a burst of industrial activity in the Marches, starting from the river Severn and spreading westwards. This industry was based on charcoal blast furnaces, generally sponsored by local landowners. John Scudamore was one of those who joined the industry, and in 1637 he leased an iron work or forge at Llancillo for three years from Cavendish. In the mid seventeenth century a schedule was recorded of the materials, instruments and implements that this forge produced.[39] A bleak stone building and a large pile of slag, stone and cinders are all that now remain of this forge on the banks of the Monnow, which operated for nearly 200 years.[40] The charcoal was produced from wood of up to 20-years growth, obtained from the local coppices, which may have included wood from Gilbert's Wood in Abbey Dore where three cords of wood were taken to make a load of charcoal.[41] There was also a forge at Pontrilas on the Monnow, which had been founded by Benedict Hall, who hailed from the Forest of Dean. During the 1630s Viscount Scudamore of Holme Lacy produced figures that showed the cost for making 'one tunn of barr iron' totalled £11 16s 5d, out of which a profit was made of £1 13s 6d. Although clearly marked on later maps, this mill appears to have had a shorter working life than the forge at Llancillo.[42]

Kentchurch and its surroundings as shown on Isaac Taylor's map of Herefordshire of 1754

3

Civil War and Aftermath

> The Kentchurch branch ... have always been active in county
> affairs and often represented the city and county of Hereford in
> Parliament, but have been content to leave to younger branches of
> the old stock the task of achieving prominence in matters of wider
> importance. In the great civil war, for instance, while Sir Barnaby
> Scudamore, of Ballingham Hall, held Hereford City for the King,
> his kinsmen of Kentchurch did not in any way make himself
> conspicuous on one side or the other. It is, of course, just possible,
> that Kentchurch in that day was so remote from the world that he
> did not dream of the civil war until after the restoration.
>
> *Revd S.C. Watkins, 1912*[1]

In the early 1640s, nine of John and Elizabeth Scudamores' ten children had already been born, and the impending threat of a civil war did not cause any alarm to those living so far west in Herefordshire. As a lawyer, John quietly continued managing his estate, dealing with transactions of copyhold land and leases of properties in Howton.[2] News of external events would have been slow to reach Kentchurch. Travel was almost impossible during the winter months, with journeys literally along 'ditches in narrow forest lanes or antiquated hollow ways, deeper than the head of horse and rider ... overhung by trees, the mire of January was hardly dry at Midsummer; in other places the bare rock, worn into inequalities by heavy rains, rose at ascents in ledges like stairs'. Another barrier to overcome was crossing the swift-flowing rivers and tributaries. There were only two bridges crossing the Wye in Herefordshire: one at Hereford and the other at Wilton, although numerous fords and ferries were in use. In Monmouthshire the Wye was bridged at Monmouth and the Monnow at Skenfrith and Monmouth, whilst there was the Corras ford at Kentchurch.[3]

In 1642, after two years of growing political tension between Charles I and the members of his Parliament, the two sides resorted to war, in what was to become one of the most turbulent events of British history. In Herefordshire the majority of influential landowners supported the Royalist cause, including Viscount Scudamore from Holme

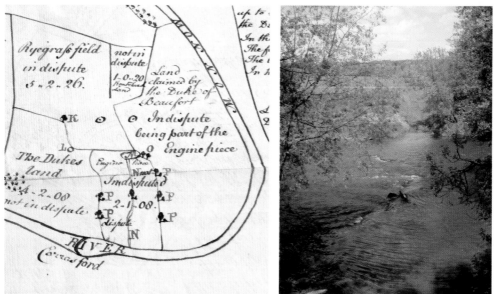

TOP: A holloway between Rowlestone and Llancillo (*Heather Hurley*)
BOTTOM LEFT: The Corras ford as shown on a plan of 1770 (*Herefordshire Archives*)
BOTTOM RIGHT: The Corras ford in 2017 (*Logaston Press*)

Lacy and Sir Walter Pye of the Mynde in Much Dewchurch. Some gentry who favoured Parliament kept their heads down, at least until 1645 when it became clear that the king was going to lose the war.[4] Others, such as Sir John Brydges at Wilton Castle and John Scudamore at Kentchurch Court, showed some reluctance to take sides.

The months between April and June 1642 saw the rise of the Royalist party in the county, with an increase in acrimony, threats and violence against those labelled as Puritans or Roundheads. Fervent clergy were threatened and certain people refused to pay traders branded as Roundheads.[5] During the civil troubles thousands were killed in battles, skirmishes and sieges, and widespread damage and plunder occurred in Herefordshire. According to Revd Webb in the *History of the Civil War in Herefordshire*, houses were

> riffled, doors, Chests and Trunks broken open, several families undone, most of all their Cattle, horses and goods taken from them, much money, plate, Jewels, and all kinds of rich household-stuffe, Rings, and other rich commodities, as wearing apparel, linen, books, the Plate and linen of divers Churches, neere all the horses, mares, & colts that ever they set their eyes upon, as wel from friends as others.[5]

Incidents and skirmishes were to occur throughout the war near to Kentchurch at Wilton, Sellack, Pengethley, Much Dewchurch, Aconbury and Ewyas Harold, culminating in the siege of Goodrich Castle, but no known incidents took place at Kentchurch itself. In 1647 those who had been more discreet now came out in support of Parliament. Amongst them were Sir John Brydges of Wilton, Robert Kyrle of Walford and father John and son William of Kentchurch.[7] In 1649, when the county was under the rule of the Parliamentarians, John Scudamore was instrumental in appointing the Sequestration Committee for the County, gaining the Scudamores of Kentchurch a return to county office.[8] Sequestration Committees were set up by Parliament to oversee the confiscation of property held by those who fought against the Parliamentarians.

Parliament's ordinance of sequestration was inoperative in Herefordshire while the county was controlled by the Royalists, but as soon as Hereford was captured by the Parliamentarians in 1645 a committee was able to put the new system into effect. A contemporary author wrote, 'for many years it placed the unfortunate sufferers under saw and harrows of iron, in the dismemberment of estates and ruin of families'.[9] After the execution of Charles I in 1649 and the start of the Commonwealth, John was involved in preparing a prenuptial settlement for his son, William, who was to marry Rachell, the daughter of William Herbert of Colebrook in Monmouthshire.[10]

In 1650 Miles Hill, a Hereford lawyer, published an account of all the losses and damage sustained by the inhabitants of Herefordshire. Kentchurch parish, listed under the hundred of Wormelow and the hundred of Webtree, appeared to have suffered very little compared to other parishes:

WORMELOW

Taken and plundered from the Inhabitants of Kentchurch to the value of £6. 14s. 6d
Taken and plundered from the Inhabitants of Rowlestone to the value of £59. 10s. 0d
Taken and plundered from the Inhabitants of Garway to the value of £401. 18s. 2d
In damage and loss to the Inhabitants of Kilpeck to the value of £104. 14s. 2d

WEBTREE

Taken and plundered from the Inhabitants of Kentchurch to the value of £54. 4s. 11d
Taken from the Inhabitants of Kentchurch & Howton to the value of £177. 18s. 10d
Taken and plundered from the Inhabitants of Abbeydore to the value of £1212. 3s. 0d
Taken from the Inhabitants of Much Dewchurch to the value of £689. 12s. 11d[11]

Between 1648 and 1654 John Scudamore, due to the lack of title deeds, was judged as to the ownership of his land and property in the manor of Kentchurch by William Herbert, his future in-law. It is not known how the judgement was effected as the old Court Rolls were burnt in the Clerk of the Peace's office in 1825. The manor of Kentchurch was resolved in 1650, and in 1654 John was named as a commissioner to eject scandalous and insufficient ministers and schoolmasters, as previously there had been no authority to deal with this. Although this ordinance was confirmed and continued for three years there was no evidence of proceedings taken under it.[12] John's son, William, had died by 1657, leaving John's second son, John the younger, as his heir, who married Mary Lloyd of Aston in Shropshire.[13]

The restoration of the monarchy with the crowning of Charles II in 1660 saw the start of a new era and a period of change. At Kentchurch, rural life continued, with a vacancy for a rector filled in 1662 by John Tyler. In 1663 the Militia Assessment in Herefordshire was established, this being a tax on property to maintain the local militia. The property of John Tyler, the rector, was valued at £2, which compares with John Scudamore's Kentchurch Court at £30, and John Scudamore junior's house in Kentchurch at £3 10s. Humphrey Baskerville, Sheriff and Justice of the Peace, had to pay £30 for his house at Pontrilas and a further £30 for his forge at Pontrilas.[14] The Hearth Tax returns of 1665 show that Kentchurch Court had 12 hearths, that John junior's house elsewhere in the parish had five hearths and that Humphrey Baskerville's house at Pontrilas was taxed on eight hearths. By comparison, most of the parishioners were paying for one or two hearths, and it appears that as the rector was not taxed he did not enjoy the comfort of a hearth.

Humphrey Baskerville and the Scudamores got into a dispute regarding an obstruction of the Worm brook leading to Baskerville's Pontrilas Forge, caused by a change to the water course that led to the Scudamores' Kentchurch Mill. The dispute was resolved and an undated plan of Pontrilas Forge probably dates from this time. It shows the forge and weirs on the Worm Brook which flows into the Monnow between Pontrilas and Kentchurch, together with the forge's finery and hammer ditches, forge pond, coal yard,

LEFT: Kentchurch Court as depicted c.1588 on documents relating to a dispute over mills on the River Monnow (*The National Archives*)

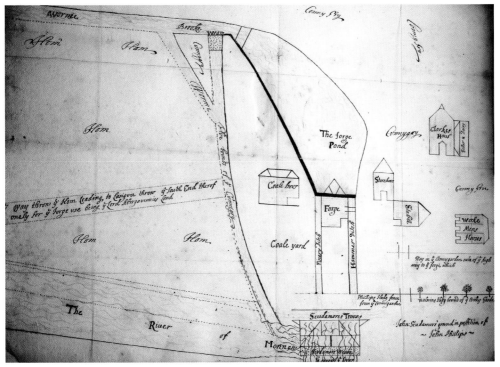

ABOVE: Plan of Pontrilas forge c.1665 (*Herefordshire Archives*)

RIGHT: The Monnow at Kentchurch (*Heather Hurley*)

clerk's house and workmen's houses. The last known record of Pontrilas Forge dates from when it was under Foley management in 1677, when 89 tons of bar iron was produced, although Old Forge Homestead and Old Forge Barn appear on later maps.[15]

Before John Scudamore the elder died in 1669 he was involved in sorting out the various bonds, mortgages and leases taken over by his successor John the younger. Amongst these were leases for a cottage and garden to a cooper, and a house, garden and orchard to a husbandman in Kentchurch. There was also a matter of trespass to be dealt with over land called Tanhouse Greene, the New Orchard and Corras Meadow in Kentchurch.[16]

In 1672 the forge and ironwork in Llancillo was leased by John junior and other members of his family to Henry and William Hall. The site alongside the Monnow comprised of outhouses, workmen's houses, storehouses and a messuage called Llancillo Farm with a meadow called Baylea. Scudamore was also involved with Hall in establishing a new furnace in the Forest of Dean at Gunn's Mill, which was eventually sold to the Foleys of Stoke Edith. Llancillo Forge was later reassigned to Paul Foley and under his management the forge produced 150 tons of bar iron in 1677 before Nathaniel Morgan of St Weonards took over the business. An inventory of materials and working tools carried out at the end of the seventeenth century provides an interesting example of a working forge of the time:

> 10 finery plates, 1 tun; 5 Chaffery plates, 15 cwts; 2 Loope plates 8 cwts; one hammer and one anvill, 12 cwts; one bridge plate, 1 cwt. One pair of Chaffery Bellowes and 2 pair of Finery Bellowes; 10 hoopes on ye Beame more than 13 to be left; one Bray and 2 collars; One Hurst, two Boyts and one set of Hurst wedges; 2 hoops on ye Anvil Block; 2 Merricks; 3 pair of Blooming Tongs; 3 pair of Shingling Tongs; 2 Costs, one hand hammer, 2 sledges and 2 furgan hammers; 4 furgans, one great Ringer, besides the Ringer to draw the floodgates; 1 hoope hammer, 3 clamps, 2 shovels, 3 Tuirons, one mandrell, 3 stoppers, 2 cold chisells, one Beame Scales, chaines and 4 half hundred.[17]

Known as an active prosecutor of Jesuits and other priests and Catholics during the unrest that followed the pretended revelations of the lying and unlikeable Titus Oates, (who, with William Bedloe and others, created the 'Popish Plot' with its allegations of a Jesuit conspiracy to murder King Charles II and restore Catholicism as the state religion),[18] John Scudamore was approached by Bishop Croft in 1678 to make enquiries and seek out Popish priests in his neighbourhood. The Catholics living in the Monnow valley in the seventeenth century were numerous and fairly well organised and supported by priests. They were strong in numbers, sheltered by a wild, inaccessible country and protected by prominent landowners. In this remote community Father Kemble, from Welsh Newton, ministered in the old faith to his scattered flock; however, in 1679 he was found and arrested by Captain Scudamore of Kentchurch.[19]

Amongst the various versions of the arrest and execution of John Kemble is the following, written by the Revd Seaton in his *History of Archenfield* published in 1903:

On December 7th 1678, the Bishop of Hereford was ordered to examine matters concerning the Combe [a college of the Jesuits]; upon the receipt of which notice he placed in the hands of Captain Scudamore of Kentchurch, who sacked The Combe, carried off the Books, Missals, and MSS, of which are now in the cathedral Library at Hereford, and proceeded to take Father Kemble to Pembridge Castle, and conducted him to Hereford Gaol, to be tried at the Lent Assizes, of which no account can be found. In April, 1679, he was ordered to be brought to London by the House of Lords, and was tried there, and sent back to Hereford Gaol, and executed at Widemarsh, August 22, 1679, aged 80.[20]

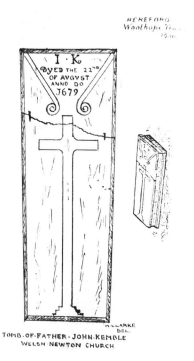

TOMB·OF·FATHER·JOHN·KEMBLE
WELSH·NEWTON·CHURCH

ABOVE LEFT: Kemble's tomb at Welsh Newton, as depicted in the *Transactions of the Woolhope Club* in 1900.

ABOVE: Father John Kemble, from the pen and ink sketch made by the governor of Hereford Gaol (*Herefordshire Archives*).

LEFT: Welsh Newton church c.1820, as illustrated by James Gregory Peene in *Churches and Mansions in South Herefordshire* (*Herefordshire Libraries*)

John Kemble met his death 'with resignation, and when the hour for his execution arrived he requested to be given time to finish his prayers and be allowed a pipe of tobacco, a cup of sack, in which the Under Sheriff joined him'. This is a well remembered saying at Kentchurch Court, of calling a parting pipe a Kemble Pipe and a parting glass a Kemble Cup.[21] It was reported after this tragic incident that 'Capt. Scudamore committed suicide', but as he was nominated to be a Deputy Lieutenant and is recorded signing documents at a later date, this statement must be incorrect.[22] Even so, in 1926 it was noted that there was a tablet at Kentchurch, presumably in the church, 'to the memory of John Scudamore gent. an active prosecutor of Jesuits 1679',[23] whilst Revd Webb suggests that Scudamore's 'wife, sister, or daughter, joined the Romish Church and were buried near Kemble'.[24]

According to R.R. Bromage, writing in 1902, 'A devout Catholic preserved the rope with which he was hung, and some time later Captain Scudamore's daughter was taken ill with a violent sore throat, which was considered dangerous, and at the suggestion of the said Catholic, she placed the cord to her neck, and was immediately cured. It may now be preserved in the same family'. At the time of writing, however, there is no knowledge of this relic at Kentchurch. Kemble's body was placed in a coffin and buried in the churchyard at Welsh Newton, except for one hand – 'a relic of the Holy Martyr' – preserved at St Francis Xavier church in Hereford.[25]

Thomas Webbe's almshouses in Ross (*Ross & District Civic Society*)

In 1686 John Scudamore of Kentchurch; Herbert Westfaling of Rudhall; John Kyrle of Ross; William Markey of Alton Court, Ross; and Richard Clarke of the Hill, Walford; together with William Merrick, John Baker, and John Furney all of Ross transferred the trusteeship of Webbe's Hospital, a freehold property in Copse Cross Street in Ross, to John Jones of Llantilio Crossenny in Monmouthshire.[26] Webbe's Almshouses were endowed by Thomas Webbe, a carpenter from Llanwarne, who left £100 to establish a hospital to house seven poor parishioners of the town. He also left a £700 endowment to fund the hospital and £200 to free Wilton Bridge of its tolls.[27]

During the reign of James II there was increasing fear of a Catholic succession and when James's wife produced a son and heir, this led to an appeal to William of Orange, the husband of King James' oldest daughter Mary, to claim the throne. In November 1688, William landed with an army in Brixham, Devon. James, deserted by the army and navy, fled abroad. In February 1689, parliament declared that James' flight constituted an abdication and William and Mary were crowned joint monarchs.[28] As a result of this coup the 'Commission of Deputy Lieutenancy' was granted to the ageing John Scudamore, who by then had fathered 14 or 15 children including Ambrose, his eldest son, Robert of Howton and Walter and

William of Orange (*Kentchurch Archives*)

Richard of Rowlestone.[29] Entries from the Kentchurch Parish Registers show that John Scudamore, his wife, son Ambrose and daughter-in-law were all resident at Kentchurch during the 1690s.[30] Ambrose had married Anne Fleet from Hallow in Worcestershire, and she produced an heir shortly before her husband's early death.

In 1691 John Scudamore leased a house in Kentchurch for 21 years to Phillip Kaswell, an innholder, the first known reference to an inn at Kentchurch. A few years later, during the Wars of the Spanish Succession, timber was needed for shipbuilding. At Kentchurch Joseph Batt, Purveyor, inspected Scudamore's timber, 'a large parcel still standing which appears to be sound and good' which he felled in 1695 and 'converted some of the trees and carried some plank to Monmouth' stating that 'more trees would have been cut if more workmen could be found'.[31] This timber would have been transported overland to Monmouth, conveyed on barges or floated down the Wye to Chepstow where sea-going vessels transported the navy timber to Plymouth Docks.[32]

Throughout 1699 and 1700 John Scudamore was signing leases, answering queries about a bill of complaint, producing a Schedule of Title Deeds, settling a bond addressed to him as Captain Scudamore and making his will. As his eldest son Ambrose had died, his heir apparent was William, Ambrose's eldest son. A prenuptial settlement was quickly arranged between William and Penelope Lechmere of Hanley Castle in Worcestershire, and the couple were married in 1701. In order to secure the property a long and complicated deed was made comprising £1,500 paid from the Lechmeres, and from the Scudamores the manors of Kentchurch with Kentchurch Court and other messuages in Herefordshire and Monmouthshire. This deed was probably designed to make sure that the right people got the right property, a convoluted way of eliminating an entail and ensuring the estate remained intact for the ultimate beneficiary, William.[33] After their marriage, William and Penelope appear to have settled at Kentchurch, as three of their children – Lucy, Mary and Penelope – were baptised at the parish church between 1702 and 1709. Their only son, John, died in infancy.[34]

John Scudamore died in 1704, his beautifully written will, made before Ambrose's death, leaving his properties to his large family – to his son and heir Ambrose, Mary, Ann, Margaret, Robert, Walter, Richard and his three younger sons. To his wife Mary he bequeathed 'all my goods, cattle and chattels'. He was buried at Kentchurch, and as Ambrose had died the successor was William, Ambrose's eldest son.[35]

Possibly influenced by Queen Anne's Bounty, introduced to supplement the incomes of the poorer clergy, the poor of Kentchurch parish benefited from two charities. In 1716, the Llangarron, Garway & Kentchurch Charity was established on the death of Frances Scudamore, the widow of the Revd Martin Scudamore, the last-born son of John and Amy. In her will, Frances, a Scudamore from the family branch at Llangarron, left rents to place two or more poor children, whose parents were not in the poor-book, as apprentices in a handicraft trade.[36] The money for this was to come from every third year's rent of Charity Farm, whilst the money gained from every third coppicing of a coppice on the same farm was to be distributed between six poor widows.

Then in 1729 John Beavan left a messuage in trust to Mrs Penelope Scudamore, the minister and churchwardens, in which to start a school in Kentchurch where children were to be instructed in reading, writing and the singing of Psalms. Beavan also left funds to provide ten poor day-labourers or their widows a 6d loaf to be delivered every Christmas Day and every Easter Day.[37]

By 1730 William's mother, the widowed Anne, had moved to Hereford and William was running the affairs of the estate, signing a transfer in 1730 for £965 Capital South Sea Stock and other specified sums of money, in trust for his three daughters. William's last official dealings were probably in 1733 when he leased a cottage, orchard, plock, and parcels of land including part of the Lower Wood in Kentchurch to the son of Revd Robert Watkins. It was three years later, under the Commissions and Inquisitions of Lunacy, that William was found unfit, due to his state of mind, to run the affairs at Kentchurch.[38]

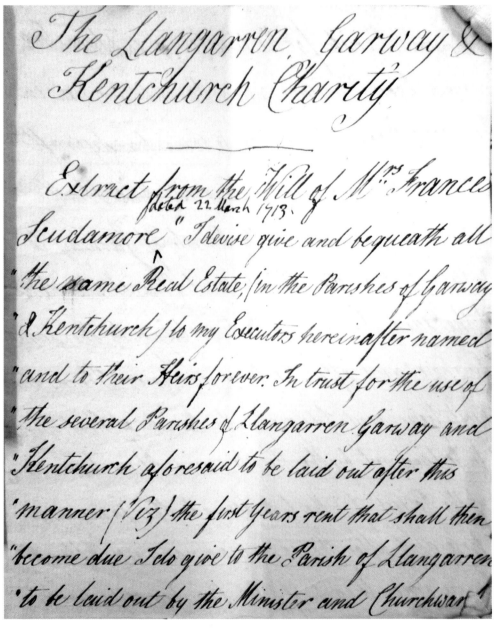

The Llangarren, Garway & Kentchurch Charity

Extract from the Will of Mrs. Frances
Scudamore "I devise give and bequeath all
"the same Real Estate, (in the Parishes of Garway
"& Kentchurch) to my Executors hereinafter named
"and to their Heirs for ever. In trust for the use of
"the several Parishes of Llangarren Garway and
"Kentchurch aforesaid to be laid out after this
"manner (Viz) the first Years rent that shall then
"become due I do give to the Parish of Llangarren
"to be laid out by the Minister and Churchwar"

dated 22 March 1713

The part of Frances Scudamore's will in 1713 that established a charity for the benefit of the parishes of Llangarren, Garway and Kentchurch by donating one year's rent for the purpose (*Herefordshire Archives*)

It was during the reign of George II that local road conditions began to improve with the setting up of Turnpike Trusts that maintained a network of roads, the work paid for from the tolls collected from road users. Under the terms of the required Acts, the trustees were empowered to erect gates, receive tolls, choose collectors, appoint surveyors, mortgage tolls, demand statute labour and elect trustees. The Hereford Turnpike Trust was established in 1729, turnpiking 13 routes, including a seven-mile road from the City 'to a Place called Pontrylas Bridge, in the Parish of Kentchurch'. The Scudamores would have benefited from these improvements, but had to wait almost 50 years before the road through the village was turnpiked.[39] Amongst the Kentchurch archives there is a mortgage of 1740 for £200 of the tolls and duties of gates erected or to be erected under the Act, subject to the mortgage already made of Widemarsh gate.[40]

In 1741 William died and was buried at Kentchurch.[41] His two surviving married daughters were not considered as his heirs so Kentchurch Court passed to his 14-year-old cousin, John, the eldest son of Richard Scudamore, deceased, of Rowlestone.[42] This caused a change of succession from the Scudamore family at Kentchurch to the Scudamore branch at Rowlestone, and due to John's young age led to the need to appoint suitable guardians for him. It appears that many people of note were vying for this guardianship as Mr J. Prichard, possibly a lawyer, implies a possible danger to John in a letter: 'Believe me twill not be safe to have the lad from the place where he is, at least not yet, for be assured there are people who will watch opportunities to catch him up or wheedle him away'. Prichard was also concerned about the arrangements made for John's younger brothers and sisters. Amongst the family letters of 1742 is one that names Herbert Westfaling, from Rudhall near Ross, and Thomas Gwillim of Whitchurch Court as guardians appointed by the High Court of Chancery. The Westfalings were a prominent family who had acquired the Rudhall estate near Ross from Mary Rudhall,

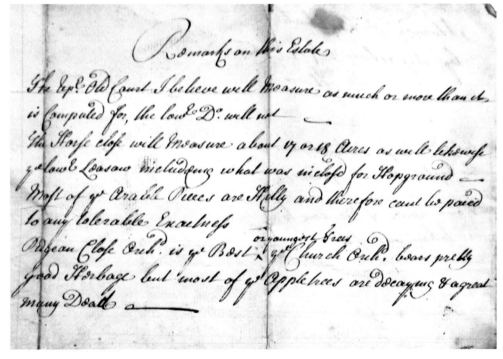

Remarks made in 1742 after a survey of the Kentchurch estate (*Herefordshire Archives*)

whilst Thomas Gwillim was from an ancient family whose restored monuments stand in the churchyard at Whitchurch. Mr Westfaling placed Mr George Smyth at Kentchurch Court to look after the house, garden, park and woods, to assist in Master Scudamore's affairs and to help supervise the younger children, with the eldest of them going to Mr Westfaling and the youngest to be cared for in a house in London.[43]

The change of ownership at Kentchurch and difficulties caused by the age of the young successor led to the land agent making an abstract of title of parcels of land called Mill Meadow and Corras Meadow, followed in quick succession by a rental and survey of the Kentchurch lands. This shows the extent of the estate, which included lands in Kentchurch, Howton, Grosmont, Llangua, Llancillo, Rowlestone, Cloddock, Kilpeck and Orcop. The Rental of 1742 lists the names of the tenants paying rent for various properties including Corras, a tenement in Kentchurch, Boulstone Court, the Old House, the blacksmith's house, Kentchurch Mill, Court Farm, a cottage at Howton for the parishioners, a Grist Mill and Forge at Llancillo, and the Court and Park at Rowlestone. The document shows a division of rents and land between John Winde representing the estate of the late William Scudamore and his replacement Mr William Fortune, attorney-at-law, representing the young John Scudamore. The land use is listed on the survey by George Smyth, who remarks that 'the Old Court I believe will measure as much or more than computed', that the Lower Leasow was 'inclosed for Hopground' and 'Most of the Arable pieces are Hilly and can't be paled', and added that the 'Church Orchard was pretty good Herbage but most of ye apple trees are decaying and a great many Dead'.[44]

View of Kentchurch in 1795 by James Wathen (*detail*)

4

Colonel John Scudamore and Keck's Remodelling of Kentchurch Court

> The Mansion stands about twelve miles south-west from the City
> of Hereford. Its erection was commenced by the late Colonel
> Scudamore, father of the present possessor, by whom the building
> was completed, after the death of the founder, partly from a
> design by John Nash, Esq., with the addition of a porch designed
> by Mr. Tudor of Monmouth, Mr. Scudamore's receiver, who,
> although not a professional man, is considered to be well versed in
> the style of architecture here adopted. The House stands exactly
> on the site of the original mansion of the Scudamores, and the
> tower is actually part of the ancient structure.
>
> *Samuel Meyrick K.H., 1835*[1]

DURING the 1740s Kentchurch Court would have been a silent house since the succession of the estate had passed to John, the 14-year-old son of Richard Scudamore of Rowlestone. In 1744 John was sent to be educated by the Revd Philips at Bisley in Gloucestershire, and his brothers Richard and Walter were sent to school in Hereford with their books, shirts, shoes, stockings and hats forwarded by George Smyth from Kentchurch.[2] George Smyth had been placed at Kentchurch by Mr Westfaling, one of John's guardians, to look after the house, garden, park and woods, and to assist in his affairs. Smyth's letters indicate some neglect of the estate, describing the court as quaint and irregular, with its five-storey tower and two high gabled buildings and a deer park covered with woodland. The rents were paid to William Fortune, surely the same agent employed by the Governors of Guy's Hospital who, in 1731, had acquired the Herefordshire estates of James Brydges, Duke of Chandos.[3]

In his late teens John Scudamore was admitted to Lincoln's Inn, where students at that time were taught very little law, only reciting lines from a prepared card and not expected to sit any exams. A contemporary student confessed he never opened a law book during the first month; more importantly he was expected to give the appearance of a

45

Portraits dated 1766 of John Scudamore, his mother and sisters (*Kentchurch Archives*)

gentleman.[4] By 1750 John, as a lawyer and now in his twenties, returned to Kentchurch to take over the management of the estate. It appears that there was a shortage of funds from which to finance his lifestyle as an eighteenth-century young gentleman. He there-fore immediately prepared titles to his estates and mortgaged the manors of Kentchurch with Llanithog and Corras, Kentchurch Court, Howton Court, the manors of Llancillo, Rowlestone and Gwerngenny, together with the water corn-mill at Kentchurch and the forge at Llancillo for an amount of £1,000. John then purchased the Bennarth estate in Kenderchurch for a net price of £592 19s 4d from Mr Richard Watkins.[5]

John, although a young man, had been encouraged to make out his will to ensure that provisions were made for his younger brothers and sisters.[6] He received further loans from William Fortune who collected the rents, and the previous mortgage of £1,000 was increased to £6,000. Between 1752 and 1754 the rents were carefully detailed by George Smyth noting the amount of £384 9s from the Manor of Kentchurch, £115 5s from the Manor of Howton, together with rents from Grosmont, Llangua, Rowlestone, Cloddock, Kilpeck, Orcop and Llancillo. The whole estate now ran to just over 2,164 acres.[7] In 1754 George was replaced by Edward Smyth, who prepared a statement of accounts showing a profit of £952 16s from rents and paying John Scudamore £574 5s in cash. Other outgoings included £32 5s 11d for repairing Llancillo Forge and over £26 for repairs to Howton and Rowlestone Courts. A payment of £8 18s 6d was also made for stripping and hauling bark. Once dried in large ricks, the bark was cut into small pieces and sold to tanyards at Monmouth, Ross and Hereford as an ingredient for converting raw hide into leather which was then used for making shoes, boots, gloves, saddles and harnesses.[8]

Stacked bark at Kentchurch (*Herefordshire Archives*)

In 1755 John Scudamore assigned a mortgage for coppice woods in the parish of Yazor in the north of the county. This was the same year that his eldest sister Catherine's pre-nuptial settlement was agreed with Philip Westfaling of Rudhall near Ross, and the year in which his sister Mary married Samuel Torriano, a banker, at St George's in Hanover Square, London.[9] It might have been at this wedding that the eligible John Scudamore met his future wife, Sarah, the sole heiress of London merchant Daniel Westcombe from whom she inherited a fortune of at least £3,000 and his properties in Lincolnshire, Essex, Norfolk and Middlesex. It appears that Sarah's grandfather, Ambrose Page, a wealthy man, had been involved in the South Sea Company and a large brewery at Bow in London which was sold when the 'bubble' burst.[10] When Sarah's mother remarried, an inventory was made of her valuable diamond, gold and silver which may have been inherited by Sarah as the only heir.[11]

In 1756 the ambitious John married Sarah, who, apart from being wealthy, was an educated young lady who had corresponded, since 1746, with the novelist Samuel Richardson (who gave her away at her wedding). Richardson was trained as a printer and, although self-educated, became known as one of the first English novelists. He wrote his popular books, *Pamela*, *Clarissa* and *Sir Charles Grandison* in letter form, and he corresponded with several female acquaintances regarding his writing projects. The correspondence with Sarah continued until after her marriage, when the newly-weds resided at her house in Enfield, Middlesex. After Sarah became pregnant, John and Sarah moved to Kentchurch Court, where she became absorbed with its history and enjoyed mixing with the local gentry. Her son John, known as Jacky, was born in 1757 and Sarah, as mistress of Kentchurch Court, lost interest in making the long and difficult journey to London to see her friend Samuel, who died four years later.[12]

Appointment of John as Deputy Lieutenant in Herefordshire in 1757 (*Herefordshire Archives*)

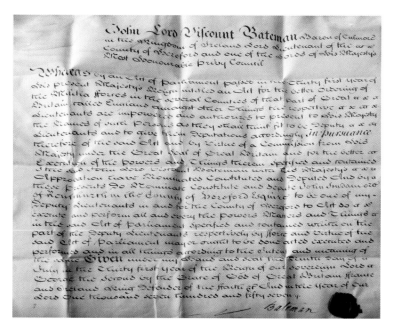

Now settled at Kentchurch Court with his wife and a growing family, in 1757 John was invited by Lord Viscount Bateman to serve as one of his Deputy Lieutenants in Herefordshire. This was the first of many official positions sought by and offered to John.[13] In the mid eighteenth century he was appointed as a turnpike trustee under the Brecon Road Act, 'for repairing the Roads from the Town of Brecon to the Parish of Brobury, and to Whitney-Passage in the county of Hereford, and for building a Bridge over the River Wye at Bredwardine-Passage'. He continued his involvement in improving communications through the turnpike system and supported the 1756 Act for 'the Preservation of the Publick Highways and Turnpike Roads of the Kingdom'.[14]

During the last years of the 1750s John's bills were paid by James Woodhouse, successor to William Fortune as agent to the Guy's Hospital estate and a relative of the Woodhouse family at Aramstone, Kings Caple. Bills paid by James included household payments for butter and cheese, for 40 dozen bottles from a hogshead of cider, corks and washing bottles, butcher's meat, coal, his expenses in travelling to Lincolnshire, various repairs and repaying drafts.[15]

In 1760 George III ascended the throne when the country was still at war with the French during the Seven Years War. But this was also a time when there was a huge leap forward in science, cultural life, the arts, architecture and agriculture. Roads were improved by the turnpike trusts, canals were constructed and river navigation developed. Cottage and rural workers were gradually drawn towards the growing industrial towns with the importance of Hereford diminishing in comparison with other cities.[16] Along the borders of Herefordshire and Monmouthshire the farms were in a poor state owing to the landowners leaving repairs to the tenants. Few farms had enclosed yards, and many barns were roofless due to lack of thatching materials and the high cost of timber which was then in demand for shipbuilding. Another reason for neglected farms was the current fashion for short leases being granted to farmers instead of longer leases of 21 years, which would have encouraged improvements to be made.[17]

In 1760 John Scudamore was commissioned by Viscount Bateman, Lord Lieutenant of Herefordshire, with the rank of major in the militia and command of the county company – a commission that required him to train and discipline those who were chosen by parish ballot to serve for three years. The militia had been introduced under the Militia Act of 1757 when there was a growing fear of a French invasion.[18] In some counties there was a lack of enthusiasm and opposition to these measures as it was widely thought that the new force would favour landowners at the expense of the poorer classes.[19]

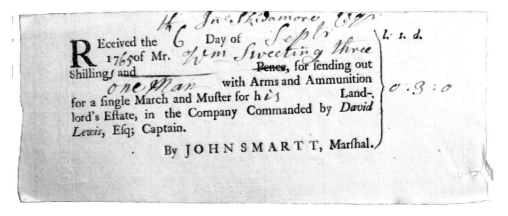

A militia receipt of 1765, showing 3s received of William Sweeting, Scudamore's London agent, for sending an armed man to a muster (*Herefordshire Archives*)

LEFT: Llangua mill as depicted on what has become known as 'The Grosmont Map' of 1588 (*The National Archives*)

BELOW: A receipt for the annual 'licence' fee for a four-wheeled carriage, paid by John Scudamore in 1766 (*Herefordshire Archives*)

From the 1760s some records have survived of the yearly amounts paid by the Kentchurch tenants for chief, reserved and copyhold (customary) rents, with a separate entry for Llangua, a small Monmouthshire parish adjoining Rowlestone in Herefordshire.[20] In 1762 William Griffiths leased Llangua Mill from John Scudamore. This was a corn grist mill with barns, stables, yards, gardens, orchards, houses, outhouses adjoining meadows and pasture land in the parishes of Llangua and Rowlestone, together with weirs, dams, sluices, cogs and watercourses. The lease reserved rights to all timber and trees, which John Scudamore's servants and workmen could cut down and carry away with horse teams and carriages at any seasonable time throughout the term of 21 years.[21] Llangua Mill dates from the thirteenth century when it provided one of the highest incomes from a Monmouthshire mill, but its site remained a mystery until recently. It had been suggested that it lay on a tributary of the Monnow at Pentwyn where there is a field named Mill Meadow, but the site has now been identified near Llangua Church, adjoining a Mill Meadow in Rowlestone.[22]

Bills during the 1760s show that the family paid for 'three couple of chicken'; 'two couple of duck', '13 stone of beef'; 'masons' work'; 'flooring a barn measuring 222 feet'; 'hops and bullocks'; 'squaring timber' and 'making doors' at Kentchurch. John paid £7 7s 12d for his militia expenses; £5 8s 6d for hiring four horses from Hereford to London for seven days; £2 1s 0d for a hogshead of cider; £3 11s 7d for herrings and oysters and £1 12s 1d to the gardener and his son.

Wages would also have been paid to the servants at Kentchurch Court, at a time when domestic servants were in demand and their numbers on the increase to carry out duties ranging from a lady's maid, a cook, groom, gardener and scullery maid. Assuming the wages were the same as at Tyberton in Herefordshire, where the Brydges resided, they would have varied between £3 and £8 a year for females, and between £5 and £20 a year for men.[23] (Tyberton is in the Golden Valley and the Brydges became distant relatives of the Scudamores, which explains why a document covering wages paid at Tyberton has become part of the Kentchurch archive.)

In 1764 John Scudamore was successful in winning the contest to become Hereford's Member of Parliament, a seat he held unopposed for a number of years. Although Whigs and Tories were names in use, the Members of Parliament were independent country gentlemen who owed their seats to themselves and not to a political party and could vote as their consciences guided them. The electors chose their Members of Parliament who fought their seats on local and personal matters rather than national policies. Scudamore's land crossed the Monnow into Monmouthshire, and so he would have shown interest in a by-election held in the county in 1762 following the death of Thomas Morgan. The

MEMBER	YEAR	PARLIAMENTARY SEAT
John Scudamore Esq.	1764	Hereford City
John Scudamore Esq.	1768	Hereford City
John Scudamore Esq.	1774	Hereford City
John Scudamore Esq.	1780	Hereford City
John Scudamore Esq.	1784	Hereford City
John Scudamore Esq.	1790	Hereford City
John Scudamore Esq.	1796	Hereford County

Table of John Scudamore as Member of Parliament during the reign of George III, and the seats he held

by-election saw a fierce contest between John Morgan and the Duke of Beaufort's candidate, Valentine Morris from Piercefield near Chepstow, leading him to give one of his only two speeches in Parliament. In 1764 he voted with the opposition against the issuing of general warrants which allowed custom and other officials to search anyone, and he supported Jenkinson's plan for a stamp tax on paper in the colonies.[24]

It was around this period that an interesting story exists relating to John Scudamore and George White of New Weir at Symonds Yat. The latter 'lay ill of a disorder, which hourly threatened him of his life; but by the skill and care of a surgeon, he was restored to life'. The surgeon required no other payment except the bones of a gigantic skeleton found in a cavity on the Doward in Whitchurch. The skull was given to John Scudamore, a friend of White's to whom he had sold some woods near Kentchurch. The surgeon set sail for Jamaica with the bones but 'the ship was cast away, and himself, with the bones, were buried in the sea'.[25] The skull has not yet been discovered.

A sheaf of domestic bills for Kentchurch in 1765 (*Herefordshire Archives*)

Before 1770, accounts and valuations of John's estate were prepared with the intention of 'settling the affairs of John Scudamore Esq.' These suggested that he was thinking of assigning all his freehold and copyhold estates to his son, also John, who would pay his father an annuity of £400 a year until a trust was formed and debts paid, but the proposal is unsigned. Nevertheless John junior was given the power to fell and sell timber and coppice wood for raising funds, though the house, park and Rowlestone remained in father John's possession.[26] At this time the paled deer park was used for timber production or grazing and the deer herd had been reduced in size. In the park a small stone building known as the deer larder was built in the early eighteenth century as a cold bath, with a changing room below a pavilion, and sited near the cold plunge pool.[27]

The 1770s saw the start of several unpleasant legal cases against John Scudamore senior, which continued up to his death. The first, in 1772, was a complicated dispute over ownership of a property at Campston Hall in Grosmont, which led to a writ served on John Scudamore and James Woodhouse to appear before the Court of Chancery regarding their unscrupulous dealings with Anne Pritchard, a widow in poor health. Other similar cases were recorded of John taking advantage over people's title and inheritance of properties in Herefordshire, Monmouthshire and his wife's estates in the London area and East Anglia.[28] John was described as being 'extremely disagreeable' and comments were made that 'if Mr Scudamore has several Chancery

Suits it is not to be wondered at'. He was troublesome over business matters and was later hauled up by the King's Bench for his misdemeanours committed as a Justice of Peace, 'without just cause and with malicious motive'.[29] Despite his disagreeable character, a few worthy deeds were attributed to him. He made a gift of £5 5s to the Charity Schools in Hereford (the Blue Coat established by the Jones Charity at the end of the seventeenth century),[30] sent congratulations to his 'dear friend' and attorney, William Bird, on being made Mayor of Hereford and offering his coach for the occasion with 'no box nor any horses or driver fit to appear!' He possibly instigated his son 'to pay the gaoler subsistence of three deserters during their confinement', voted for parliamentary reform, and, according to Richardson, the early years of his marriage to Sarah were harmonious. Perhaps to please her, John started to refurbish Kentchurch Court.[31]

When Sarah first arrived at Kentchurch Court she had found the house old and irregular with few rooms fitted and furnished in modern taste. After her arrival some work was carried out by Francis Thomas, a builder and carpenter from Hereford.[32] During the later part of the eighteenth century many neighbouring gentrified families were rebuilding, refurbishing or intending to remodel their antiquated country houses, as for example the Hoskyns at Harewood, the Woodhouses at Aramstone, the Herefords at Sufton, the Harleys at Berrington, the Prices at Foxley and Richard Payne Knight at Downton. At Moccas Court, Longworth Hall and Canon Frome the Cornewalls, Walwyns and Hoptons had employed Anthony Keck, an architect based in the West Midlands and South Wales.[33]

In 1773 Francis Thomas produced detailed plans to unite and partly gentrify Kentchurch Court, as proposed by Anthony Keck and according to John Scudamore's requirements. The present dining room and drawing room with bed-chambers above were reconstructed from the remains of a medieval hall, and a fine marble fireplace was inserted into the drawing room. A vestibule (hall), back stairs, servant's hall, butler's pantry and a new passage with gallery above were to be constructed. The gallery and stairs were proposed to be lit by a large ecclesiastical style window inserted in the area known as the Chapel Room. The east wall of the old laundry was demolished and the outside walls and chimneys were to be finished in a workmanlike manner by Thomas under the direction of Keck. Thomas signed and agreed on 7 April 1773 'to the foregoing proposals and to cover it in by the first of December next for the sum of 445 pounds including all the Drains under the new Building'.[34] Keck moved on to other commissions including the remarkable Orangery at Margam Park in Glamorganshire.[35]

Apart from the work at Kentchurch, John was also overseeing repairs to his London properties in Cannon Street and Petticoat Lane, and insuring them with the Amicable Society.[36] Amongst all the disturbance of the builder's bricklaying, plastering, carpentry and masonry work, John Scudamore was carrying out his parliamentary duties as a Whig supporting Fox but opposing Pitt during the years of the American War of Independence; years which led to demands for parliamentary and administrative

TOP: The top of the Amicable Insurance document for London properties in 1774 (*Herefordshire Archives*). ABOVE LEFT: Assignment of tolls in proportion to £100 advance by John Scudamore in 1773 (*Herefordshire Archives*). ABOVE RIGHT: Richard's oath as Freeman of the City of Gloucester in 1789 (*Herefordshire Archives*)

reform.[37] At home in Herefordshire he was involved in the Crickhowell Turnpike Trust; in the navigation of the Rivers Wye and Lugg, and campaigning for the 1774 election in Hereford (where he breakfasted with his supporters, as he assumed most people thought Kentchurch was too much out of the way). On the morning of the election, however, he entertained many at Kentchurch, which concerned his opponent who strove to encourage the voters to breakfast at Eywood, a home of the Harley family who supported Thomas Foley as candidate, 'least Mr Scudamore should turn a great many, when he has got them shut up at Kentchurch'. Some freeholders 'were entertained at the Three Horse Shoes, going to and returning from the Election over the three days',[38] this inn being a 'well accustomed house with good stabling and cellaring', situated in Hereford near Eign Gate, 'the entrance to this city from the principal parts of South Wales'.[39]

Although a son and daughter had died in infancy, John and Sarah's two surviving sons were ready to enter upon their careers.[40] In 1776 the eldest son, John sought a commission in Sir George Howard's regiment, which cost 1,000 guineas paid by his father with financial help from James Woodhouse, to be repaid by whatever means Woodhouse could devise. Two years later the 21-year-old became a lieutenant, and a note remains of his expenses amounting to £169 12s 6d.[41] A year later his younger brother Richard, then aged 17, was admitted to the Inner Temple where he was articled as a clerk for five years with John Harwood, attorney of the Court of King's Bench.[42] Richard kept an account book of his payments for washing, clothing, shoe cleaning and hairdressing, and was in need of financial help from his mother who had borrowed £400 in order to pay his debt to Mr Harwood (and his father in London had already asked her for £100 to get him home!) Sarah obviously paid the £100 to her husband but Richard denied receiving the money and Mr Harwood's bill was probably settled by Bird.[43] Richard continued in law as a Freeman of the City of Gloucester and became Deputy Lieutenant of Herefordshire.[44]

For the Scudamores and other landowning families in the late eighteenth century, the cities and towns of Gloucester, Hereford, Monmouth and Ross were important administrative and trading centres with livestock markets, river trade and a network of turnpike roads. When John Byng visited Monmouth in 1781 he found the road from Gloucester very beautiful astride his 'clever horse distaining to trip on any stone'. The market was busy but there was a lack of young men due to the regular and militia troops training in local camps in readiness for the American Revolutionary War.[45] The town had plenty of venison obtained from gentlemen's parks, which may have been poached, as in an incident at Kentchurch when John Scudamore hunted down the miscreants. As a magistrate he bound over the culprits but 'Lewis the principal of his Gang' had escaped and Scudamore in his characteristic way was determined to pursue the 'scoundrels'. On another occasion he convicted a labourer for using a gun, greyhound and spaniels for the destruction of game without a licence, and in 1787 a Mr

Parry and others were convicted for having venison, skinned and cut for sale, in their possession.[46] Following another incident that year, John Scudamore placed a notice in the *Hereford Journal* of 14 March offering a reward of five guineas for information concerning the 'evil-minded person or persons' who 'wickedly and maliciously unlocked the door of the kennels in Kentchurch Park and loosed out a number of young hounds which killed upwards of twenty sheep .. [and who] ... broke into and entered the garden at Kentchurch and loosed the water out of the fish-pond, with intent to kill and destroy the fish'.[47]

With growing debts, including a long overdue amount of £1,024 16s 8d owed to James Woodhouse and further expenses accrued during the 1780s, the Scudamores managed with incoming rents amounting to £1457 10s 0d. Their land in Kentchurch, Llanithog, Kenderchurch, Howton, Rowlestone and Llancillo now contained 35 messuages, 2 water corn grist mills, 90 gardens, 1020 acres of land used as meadow, pasture and woodland with 300 acres of heath and common pasture. Attempts were made to value and sell timber and bark during the following years, with over 5 tons of bark produced one summer.[48] In 1793 Oak Timber 'fit for the Navy' and Ash 'for making of white hoops' from Rowlestone and Llangua were auctioned at the Swan and Falcon in Hereford. From the Kentchurch quarries limestone was cut and fired in a lime kiln to produce lime in demand for agricultural improvement, building and tanning. This may also have been offered for sale.[49]

A collection of family letters written during 1785 and 1789 reveals the uneasy relationship between Sarah and John Scudamore and their two sons John and Richard. Sarah estimated that their debts were at least £31,000, whereas their property was only worth £20,000. She despaired about the public knowledge of their family debts that were described as a 'scandalous affair', and which was not helped by John's court cases escalating with one taken to Chancery at a 'frightening great expense'.[50] In preference to Kentchurch Court she often resided at 3 North Parade, Bath, and did not like the thought of moving back to Kentchurch Court. It was 'so large an establishment' without 'comfort, convenience and propriety', and she understood, incorrectly, that due to the financial situation it was to be sold. Sarah's Essex estates were already up for sale, but the title deeds could not be found despite a thorough search by her solicitor Mr Harwood, John's solicitor James Woodhouse and their lawyer son Richard.[51] There was also concern over the debts of the two brothers. Sarah refers to the 'insurmountable indolence and inattention that prevails in our family' and urges the necessity of fit trustees, but John in a letter to Bird explained that Sarah had no 'understanding of business'.

By 1788 when John and Sarah were at Kentchurch, they had their own apartments at opposite ends of the house. John was not always well enough, due to gout, to move to his own quarters and at times Sarah was indisposed and thought to be 'in some danger'. Large quantities of wine and port were purchased by John including £38 0s 6d paid for claret, equivalent to over 250 bottles.[52] His gout kept him from attending 'sessions' and the attacks became 'more violent' and developed in his hands. He was unable to join his sons at Arundel where great sport was expected shooting grouse with the Duke of Norfolk.[53] Letters mention the sons participation in racing, bowling, hunting and beagling at home and away.[54]

In 1793 there existed a threat of invasion at the start of the Napoleonic Wars. John Scudamore junior, now a major, was commanded by the Duke of Norfolk to London to stay with his regiment, which was then sent to the barracks at Plymouth Dock. The following year his father, as Lt Col of the Herefordshire Militia, was marching to Winchester whilst John junior was on leave enjoying himself hunting for three weeks, attending a 'very splendid Masque Ball' and receiving the honour of being a 'Steward

SALE OF TIMBER.

TO BE SOLD BY AUCTION,

At the Swan-and-Falcon, in Hereford, on Saturday, the second day of March next, between the hours of three and five in the evening, subject to such conditions of sale as shall be then and there produced,

The several Lots of TIMBER following;

Lot 1.

CONSISTS of 126 OAK TIMBER TREES, marked and numbered with a scribe, now growing on certain estates called the Goytree Old House Lands and Rowlstone Park, situate in the parishes of Rowlstone and Lancillo, in the county of Hereford ; together with a quantity of ASH growing on an adjoining farm, called Penyworlocd.

Lot 2. Consists of 191 OAK TIMBER TREES, marked and numbered with a scribe, growing on certain lands, called Prior's Wood and Pontowin Farm ; together with a quantity of ASH, growing on a piece of land, called the Old House Rough, in the parish of Langua, in the county of Monmouth.

The greatest part of the above Timber lies near the turnpike-road leading to Monmouth and Abergavenny.

Great part of the Oak Timber is fit for the Navy, and the Ash for making of white hoops, and other useful purposes.

John Williams, of Kentchurch-Court, will shew the Timber ; and for other particulars apply to Mr. Bird, Attorney, or Mr. Benjamin Watkins, Auctioneer, in Hereford.

Hereford, Feb. 12, 1793.

TOP: An advert in the *Hereford Journal* of 12 February 1793 regarding the sale of oak (suitable for the navy) and ash growing on parts of the Kentchurch estate. BOTTOM: Lime kilns in Kentchurch Park (*David Whitehead*)

ABOVE: Colonel John Scudamore (*Kentchurch Archives*). BELOW: Detail of the above portrait, showing John holding Nash's plan for Kentchurch Court (*Kentchurch Archives*)

A 1799 copy by James Wathen of a drawing of Kentchurch 'as it appeared in 1774' (*Kentchurch Archives*)

of the Herefordshire Society',[55] possibly the forerunner of the Hereford Agricultural Society formed a few years later.[56] After a few quiet years at Kentchurch with some debts paid by the sale of properties in London, Lincolnshire and Essex, John Scudamore was determined to complete the remodelling of Kentchurch Court according to the plans allegedly designed by John Nash in 1795. Nash's drawing is shown in a portrait of John Scudamore holding the design, which depicts the crenellations on the tower, the proposed circular tower and an oriole window above the present terrace room.[57]

During the late eighteenth century, the prominent architect, John Nash, was in Herefordshire accepting commissions from the gentry to remodel their country houses. He was involved in designing several Welsh houses and in 1795 was paid £720 for work on the new Hereford Gaol.[58] As Scudamore was on the Hereford Gaol committee with George Cornwall of Moccas and Richard Payne Knight of Downton Castle, it is likely that Scudamore met Nash who was employed later by these two gentlemen on their estates. So there is a possibility that Nash did produce plans for Kentchurch Court, although 'no papers survive that could throw light on the history of the commission'.[59] As it was, John Scudamore, Colonel of the Militia and Member of Parliament, died soon after his re-election in July 1796, as recorded by the *Hereford Journal*:

> On Monday died, at his seat at Kentchurch, in this county, in the 68th year of his age, John Scudamore; Esq., recently elected to represent this city in the ensuing Parliament. Mr. Scudamore was first choice, one of the Members for

Hereford in the year 1768, had represented the city in five successive Parliaments, and was a sixth time returned but a few weeks previous to his death, which was precipitated by incautiously suffering the perspiration to be suddenly checked after returning from hunting on Thursday last. He was universally beloved; and has died sincerely regretted.

Another account of John's death records that he died from a chill after a strenuous day's hunt in the park (although hunting does not usually take place during July).[60] John was buried at Kentchurch and his monument was placed behind the altar at Hereford Cathedral. The tablet of white marble was inscribed:

> John Scudamore, Esq., late of Kentchurch, in the County,
> died greatly regretted July 1796, in the 69th year of his age.
> A gentleman in whose life and conduct were happily exemplified,
> elegance of manners, liberality of sentiment, and elevation of mind.
> by the free suffrages of generous and discerning citizens, he was repeatedly
> chosen to represent the City of Hereford in Parliament, and discharged the
> important duties of the situation during a series of 34 years, to the satisfaction
> of his constituents, and with honour to himself, uniformly supporting those measures which
> he considered best calculated to maintain the rights of
> Englishmen, and to promote the general interest of mankind.
> This humble stone is erected to preserve the memory of exalted worth, and to gratify the
> feelings of warm and respectful friendship'.[61]

These public and traditionally worded eulogies of John Scudamore of the late eighteenth century do contrast with the life he led, but he is well remembered at Kentchurch Court as an important member of the family who married an heiress and remodelled the Court attributed to John Nash. Known as Colonel Scudamore, his portrait depicts a genial man holding his intended future plans for the Court.[62]

Sarah, John's wife, died a year later and was also buried at Kentchurch, leaving a will with a codicil changing the executor from her son Richard the lawyer to her eldest son John. He inherited the remains of her estate except for a bequest made to Sarah's daughter Mary, who married James Hereford of Sufton.[63] This unexpected death thrust the military-trained son, John, into becoming successor to the unfinished refurbishment of Kentchurch Court. This upheaval led to a series of detailed accounts, surveys and inventories of the house and the estate, which form the start to the next chapter.

5

John Lucy Scudamore, John Nash's Legacy and Thomas Tudor

> This ancient building is a spacious building constructed at
> different periods, its architecture shewing work of the 15th
> and following centuries. It was largely rebuilt in 1824. The
> oldest portion comprises a corner tower, square, massive and
> battlemented, with square perpendicular windows and bold
> hood-mouldings. This is known as the Glyndwr Tower. Next to
> it is the domestic chapel, its large pointed window containing
> Perpendicular tracery inserted in an early period of the Gothic
> revival. The chapel roof is pinnacled, and surmounted by a cross.
> *J.H. Matthews, 1912*[1]

BEFORE Colonel John Scudamore died in July 1796 his son, John junior, had married Lucy, the daughter of James Walwyn of Longworth Court, Lugwardine, in May of that year. A prenuptial settlement was agreed between John Scudamore and James Walwyn settling the manors and capital messuages of John's estates in consideration of Walwyn paying £6,000. There were legal claims on the estates but a substantial sum was due to John for sale of timber.[2] As heir to Kentchurch Court, John junior took over the 'estate matters' from his father and seriously scrutinised the accounts and rents, made inventories of the house and surveys of the estate. It was probably due to lack of funds that Colonel John's previous plans for remodelling the court were put aside until a future date.

An inventory of household furniture at Kentchurch Court was compiled in 1797. It listed the contents under each named room and provides a clue to the start of remodelling, with the 'New Building Green Room' already furnished with a bedstead and dressing table. Other rooms included a yellow and blue room, a green room, an old parlour, a garret over the old parlour, a dining room, a study, the Beaufort room, upper and middle rooms in the tower and a 'large room'. The working part of the house consisted of a hop closet, dairy, flour room, bacon room, laundry, brew house, a servant's hall and rooms for the gardener, footman, coachman and groom.[3] Having compiled this account of the household contents, John Scudamore updated the list of property rentals in Herefordshire, Monmouthshire and the remaining properties in Norfolk, Essex and Middlesex which he had inherited from his mother, Sarah.[4] About the same date he commissioned Joseph Powell to survey the Kentchurch estate and produce a volume of the *Maps of the Kentchurch Property in the Counties of Monmouth and Hereford*. The court, gardens and park were excluded, but the Scudamore properties in Kentchurch, Llancillo, Rowlestone, Garway, Kenderchurch, Grosmont and Kilpeck were shown together with field names, land use and acreages.[5]

By 1798 John had succeeded unopposed to his father's seat as MP for Hereford, and had joined Brooks's, an exclusive gentleman's club in St James's, London. In parliament he was a devotee of the Duke of Norfolk, a staunch Whig supporting Fox, but was prevented from voting for reform in 1797 due to being on active service as Lieutenant Colonel in the Essex Light Dragoons.[6] He was with his regiment at Ayr Camp when six recruit horses were purchased for 17s each and new uniforms were bought and introduced by Colonel Burgoyne. This led to a dispute over the costs and behaviour of the Colonel who was charged with misconduct at a General Court Martial held in Dublin. Lt Col Scudamore was called as a witness at the trial where the Colonel was found not guilty and only reprimanded. While in Ayr, Scudamore was admitted as Burgess and Gild Brother of the Burgh of Ayr.[7]

In February 1798 John and Lucy's only son was born, and was named John Lucy Scudamore. Tragically, Lucy died from the effects of childbirth a few days later. Her short life was commemorated on a marble tablet to the 'Sacred Memory of Lucy Walwyn, wife of John Scudamore Esq.' erected in St Mary's church at Kentchurch.[8]

The following year John returned with his regiment to Ireland and kept in touch by letter with his attorney concerning the estate, Rowlestone Mill, disputes and the payment of tithes. During his absence and after his return financial accounts were kept from 1799 to 1801 of wages paid and hours worked by labourers on the estate, and also on work carried out by the builder, Francis Thomas. Payments were shown for bottling beer and wine, burning lime, mowing, making and hauling hay, hedging, constructing a pool in the park and cutting barley, wheat and peas. Other outgoings included the purchase of mutton and coal, and payments for turnpike tolls, land tax, hop rates and donations to the poor. A small income was shown from the sale of lambs' wool, timber and tack for cattle grazing in the park.[9] The Land Tax paid for Kentchurch Court in 1799 was £6 12s 4d, which compares with the £2 19s 4d paid by the rector James Roberts and the 12s 6d paid by the miller for the Mill.[10]

In 1803 Thomas Bird prepared a list of the rentals, showing a total of £406 2s 1d per year in income from receipts of the estates in Herefordshire and Monmouthshire, which included Llanithog, Llancillo Forge, Llangua Mill, Kentchurch Mill, the Blacksmith's Shop, Greenway farm, a cottage at Kentchurch, Court Grove, Crab's Castle, Corras,

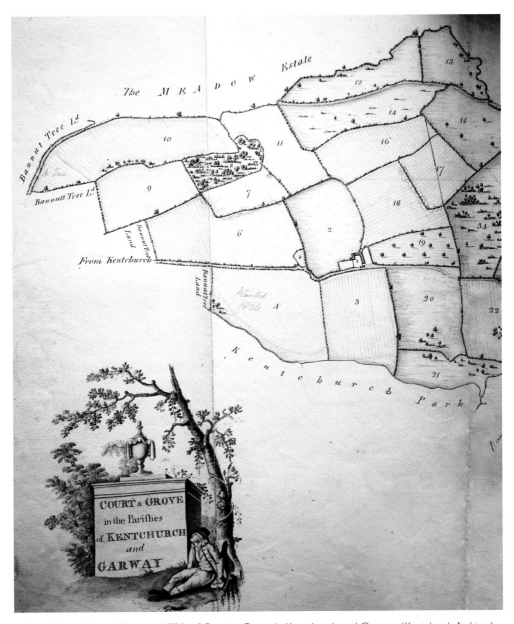

Part of Joseph Powell's map, c.1790, of Court a Grove in Kentchurch and Garway (*Kentchurch Archives*)

Kentchurch Hill, Elms and Old Forge, Pistle Brook, Houghton and Bennarth. A few months later John commissioned John Harris, land surveyor, to produce a Survey and Valuation of his farms in Hereford and Monmouth. Only Kentchurch Farm, Barton Hill, Cabins and Rowlestone Park were listed in Herefordshire, together with a few in Monmouthshire including Monmouth Cap in Llangua which were shown on a map which was not in the deposit. The quality, values and areas of the named fields are

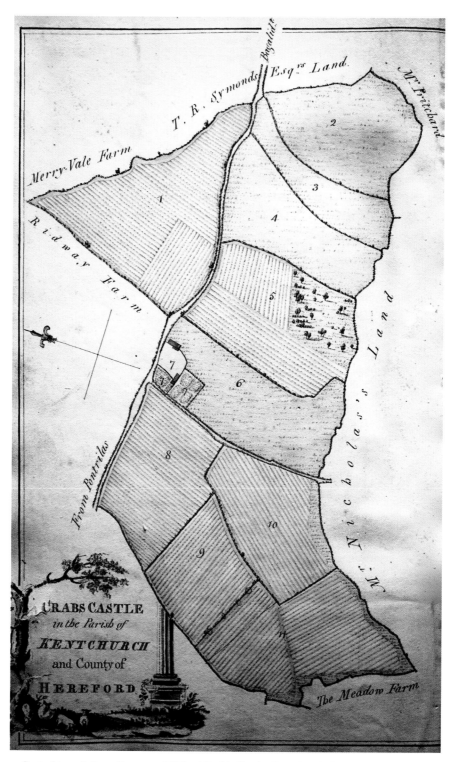

Part of Joseph Powell's map, c.1790, of Crab's Castle, Kentchurch (*Kentchurch Archives*)

listed together with additional comments on the buildings and soil. For example, at Kentchurch Farm, Well Meadow was sound but in need of improvement, House Close Orchard was to be taken in hand, Lower Close Orchard had decayed apple trees, Forge Meadow was swampy near the forge, and the Great Meadow was a good meadow that needed to be watered.[11] A contemporary memo in the archives describes the turning of clover, the cleaning of barley, the cutting of thistles, the moving of wheat and laying traps for moles.[12]

When King George III became unfit to rule due to his recurrent fits of insanity, a Regency Bill was passed to enable his son to eventually become Prince Regent. This was not a popular choice as the Prince was a heavy drinker, a compulsive gambler and a great spender who enjoyed the high life.[13] This life-style is associated with the Regency period when the wealthy took pleasure in hunting, shooting, racing, fishing, gambling, drinking and having a good time. Private clubs, such as the one on the Kymin near Monmouth, were established by a group of gentlemen, 'for the purpose of dining together, and spending the day in a social and friendly manner'. When the Naval Temple on the Kymin opened in 1802 with 'great festivities' consisting of a public breakfast and dancing on the hill, it was followed by a 'sumptuous dinner' at the Beaufort Arms Inn attended by 'John Scudamore MP for the city of Hereford'. In fine form, his companionable talent of singing 'pleasant memories' was much admired before the partying continued at a ball held in Monmouth Town Hall.[14]

With a growing population in Hereford needing coal, ambitious plans were made to achieve a regular supply to the city. Suggestions included the cutting of a canal linking the Wye to the Severn collieries, constructing a horse-drawn tram road from the Forest of Dean coal mines, and improving the navigation of the Wye by providing a horse towing path. After a meeting held in 1802 at Hereford in support of a horse towing path, John Scudamore, chair of the committee, wrote to the mayor expressing his views that the creation of such a path would deliver a 'Cheaper and more certain supply of Coal to the City of Hereford'. These moves eventually led to the Rivers Wye and Lugg Horse Towing Path Act.[15] The same year John was successfully re-elected as MP for Hereford and continued to support parliamentary reform until 1805 when he was taken ill in the House of Commons and died a few days later. His obituary in the *Gentleman's Magazine* noted that 'in private life he conciliated the esteem and respect of every party. His education was classical, correct, and elegant, his opinions were liberal and free from prejudice, his manners polished and highly insinuating'.[16]

The death of John Scudamore at the relatively early age of 48 caused unsettlement at Kentchurch Court as his only son, John Lucy, was just seven years old. The family's attorney, Thomas Bird, represented the 'infant', whilst his uncle Richard Philip Scudamore defended what he saw as his own entitlement which eventually led to a Chancery case with the title of the Kentchurch Court estates being investigated until young John Lucy became of age. As a politician, Richard followed the family's tradition in parliament in being as 'silent as they had been in the House', supporting Catholic relief and parliamentary reform, and voting against the repressive measures proposed following Peterloo.[17] In Herefordshire, Richard was commissioned as a Captain in the Wormelow and Greytree Volunteers in 1803, and a Deputy Lieutenant in 1807, and was a shareholder of the Wye and Lugg Horse Towing Path Company in 1810.[18] The Chancery case lingered on with Richard serving as a trustee of the Kentchurch estates until John Lucy, his nephew, reached the age of 21 in 1819. By this time Richard's finances were in disarray, so perhaps this was the unnamed Scudamore who, by family tradition, sold the contents of the court to pay for gambling debts in London. When Richard was not residing at Kentchurch, he was living with Mary Webb at Caroline Place in Regent's Park, London, where he remained unmarried and childless, leaving unpaid debts of £3,600.[19]

The young John Lucy Scudamore was educated at Eton College and continued his studies from 1815 at Brasenose College, Oxford. He left university without gaining a degree, and soon after attaining his 'coming of age' was busy at Kentchurch Court reviewing accounts, mortgages and titles to properties, dealing with Richard's debts and arranging for the timber and under-wood to be viewed and sold, including 457 maiden oaks standing and growing in coppice woods on the Kentchurch estate that were fit for naval purposes.[20] In

TOP: Certificate confirming John Scudamore's membership of the Royal Jennerian Society in 1820 (*Herefordshire Archives*). BOTTOM: Portrait of Sir Harford Jones-Brydges (*Kentchurch Archives*)

1820 he was awarded an Honorary Diploma, or a certificate for membership, of the Royal Jennerian Society, which had been formed in 1803 to promote the eradication of smallpox through vaccination.[21] Sometime before 1821 John Lucy had been introduced to his wife to be. Sarah Laura Jones-Brydges was the eldest daughter of Sir Harford Jones-Brydges

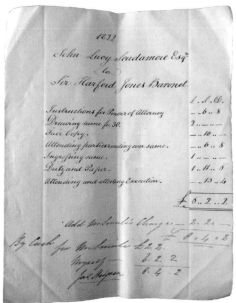

TOP: Boultibrook near Presteigne (*Kentchurch Archives*). BELOW LEFT: Lady Sarah Harford Jones-Brydges with daughter Sarah Laura (*Kentchurch Archives*). BELOW RIGHT: Document relating to the granting of Power of Attorney by John Scudamore to Sir Harford Jones-Brydges in 1822 (*Herefordshire Archives*)

of Boultibrook near Presteigne in Radnorshire, a prominent diplomat who served in the East India Company, represented Britain as its first ambassador in Persia and succeeded to a baronetcy.[22] Marrying in October 1822, the young couple decided to take a long honeymoon in Europe, journeying to Florence and other places. Before leaving, John Lucy signed a power of attorney to Sir Harford who, since 1821, had kept accounts of workman's wages and managed the cultivation of the Kentchurch estate.[23] It was clear that

TOP: Hauling timber in Kentchurch Park (*Herefordshire Archives*). BOTTOM: Bills relating to Sir Harford Jones-Brydges of weekly returns of expenditure for 1823 (*Herefordshire Archives*)

Sir Harford's intention was to transform Kentchurch Court into a fashionable and comfortable house, possibly influenced by Nash's plans, for his eldest daughter to live with her new husband. Harford set about extensive remodelling of the house, landscaping the park and improving the estate.[24]

In 1823 George Gould, from Golfa in Welshpool, valued 378 oak timber trees growing in Kentchurch Park and described the trees 'as fine naval timber as ever was sent out of the county' and valued them at £3,895. At auction the timber was divided into four lots but only three lots were purchased, with no bidder for the fourth. A few days later an offer was received for £3,600 for all four lots. Gould also made a detailed report on the woods and coppices of the estate and gave a further valuation for 723 trees that he recommended to be sold. In 1824 Hezekiah Swift, a timber merchant from Monmouth associated with Swift & Co. barge owners based at Chepstow, purchased 155 oaks, even though the timber trade in the town was on the decline due to foreign imports of deal.[25] At Little Corras, oak, elm, ash, beech and 12 acres of coppice were valued for sale at £176 4s 6d. From 1824 the accounts show a yearly routine of sowing, reaping, threshing, thatching, hedging, ditching, felling and hauling trees, and raising and breaking stones from the estate quarries at Corras and the Elms. Carpenters, blacksmiths and masons were paid for repair work, and coal, seeds, ironmongery and animal feed were purchased. There were awkward interactions too. In a letter John Powell disputed the grazing of John Lucy's sheep on Garway Common and threatened to impound them and charge one shilling per head 'according to custom'. Harford Jones used his diplomatic skills on behalf of John Lucy who was still abroad, and in communication with Powell got the latter to confirm that he 'did not deny' that John Lucy had the right to graze sheep and lambs bearing his mark of JLS.[26]

Whilst John Lucy and Sarah Laura were away on their extended honeymoon, a letter from Bird in 1823 from Drybridge in Hereford announced the good news he had heard from Florence of the birth of a son, though unfortunately he died as an infant.[27] During their period of 'absence' the Kentchurch estate was run and maintained by Harford Jones in close association with Thomas Bird, the attorney, and Thomas Tudor, the land agent. Tudor came from Monmouth, was the son of a bookseller and had trained at the Royal Academy and exhibited his paintings there, but his main business was as a land agent, surveyor and amateur architect.[28] From the numerous vouchers

Kentchurch Court in the 1820s, as depicted by James Gregory Peene in *Churches and Mansions in South Herefordshire* (*Herefordshire Libraries*)

and accounts between 1822 and 1826 it appears that Tudor, under the supervision of Harford Jones, carried out the major rebuilding of Kentchurch Court. Tudor's letters and accounts contain information on the paint and lead delivered by wagons, the timber from a supplier in Bristol and a good supply of deal delivered to Kentchurch. He noted that Llewellyn the carpenter had a narrow escape when he fell from the top of the house into the paved court. Although much bruised, he was able to return to work. Masons were working on the front of the house and replacement windows were cut with new sills and cornices, and the battlements were sealed. Glaziers and painters were busy and a kiln was repaired where lime was burnt for building purposes. A large amount was also spent on repairing the buildings and farms on the estate including work at the Bridge Inn

TOP: The Bridge Inn in 2016 (*Heather Hurley*). BOTTOM: A note of items acquired to effect repair work on the Bridge Inn in 1822 (*Herefordshire Archives*)

and the Cottage by the Road. One year's cost of repairs to Kentchurch Park in 1822 amounted to £1,561 4s 4d for labour and materials.[29] The deer park was estimated to be three or four miles in circumference and contained some fine timber in its 251 acres. After a period of neglect with trees felled and cattle grazed Sir Harford and Tudor set about repairing the park's boundaries and constructed a ha-ha to keep the deer from the garden grounds.[30]

In 1825, in the midst of the major refurbishment of the court, Tudor wrote to Sir Harford at Boultibrook hoping that his improvements at Kentchurch were found to be satisfactory and reported that the work was proceeding well although the house was in a state of 'great confusion'. He explained that the new kitchen was to be roofed and the entrance passage to be reduced in height and made much lighter. He continued that the frontage would be covered with Roman cement and the old porch would be replaced in a different position and built in stone with the 'intermediate space' between the porch and the 'handsome chimney' to have a stone front despite the additional cost. In his letter Tudor showed concern

TOP: The carriage drive at Kentchurch in 2017
(*Heather Hurley*). BOTTOM: The gatehouse in 2017
(*Heather Hurley*)

over the labourers' wages, which due to demand at the Cheltenham ironworks had been raised from 2s to 3s a week. He added that the barn doors had been made and that Mr John Lucy Scudamore wished to get rid of the thatched buildings.[31] This was not the end of the remodelling and refurbishment of Kentchurch Court, as further repairs to the house were paid for, including for interior paintwork in the tower, pantry, back kitchen and girl's room, and for developing the picturesque landscaping of the park, planting shrubs and flowers in the gardens and improving the farm between 1828 and 1830.[32]

It appears that during part of the remodelling period, John Lucy resided either at Boultibrook with his father-in-law, or in London, and also spent some time in Tunbridge, Eastbourne and abroad in Paris. In 1828 John Lucy directed the release of the Kentchurch Court estate from earlier mortgage deeds and marriage settlements.[33] His uncle, Richard, was still making claims on the estate, demanding funds of £500 to pay his debts and requesting £2,000 – or at least £1,500 – and explaining that his ill health made it impossible for him to travel from London.[34] Letters and documents from 1828 do suggest that John Lucy had by now matured and was taking a genuine interest in the estate and the neighbourhood. A new carriage drive was constructed from Kentchurch village near Grosmont Bridge, and at a later date an impressive gothic-style gatehouse was added where the drive left the turnpike road. This drive gave visitors a pleasing drive through an avenue of elm trees to St Mary's church, before proceeding along the present drive to the stable yard. It replaced a longer drive that had offered picturesque views as it wound its way behind the house and buildings before arriving at the front door.[36] After the completion of the new drive the Revd W. Bowen, who resided at the Rectory next to the church, wrote to John Lucy requesting permission to also use it and to have 'a little gravel out of the brook'.[37]

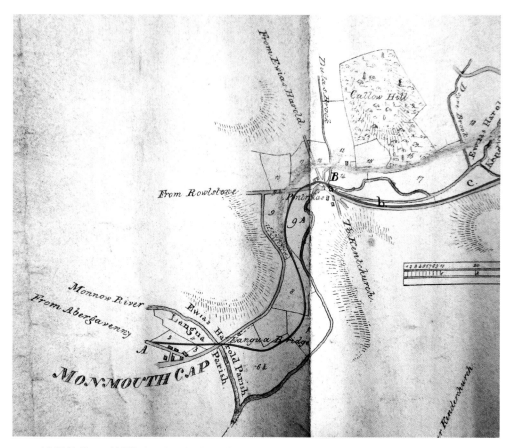

ABOVE: Plan of 1825 showing the line of the tramway (in dark brown) through Pontrilas and Monmouth Cap (*Herefordshire Archives*). BELOW: The line of the tramway appears on Bryant's map of 1835 (*Landscape Origins of the Wye project*)

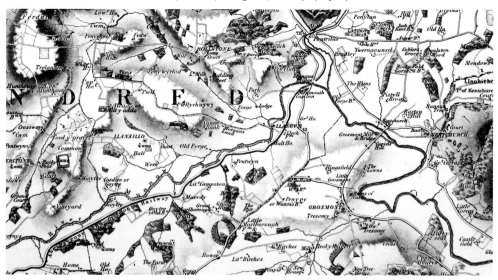

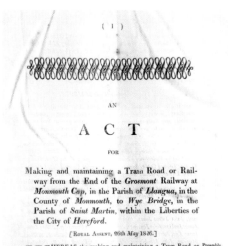

(1)

AN

A C T

FOR

Making and maintaining a Tram Road or Rail-
way from the End of the *Grosmont* Railway at
Monmouth Cap, in the Parish of *Llangua*, in the
County of *Monmouth*, to *Wye Bridge*, in the
Parish of *Saint Martin*, within the Liberties of
the City of *Hereford*.

[Royal Assent, 26th May 1826.]

WHEREAS the making and maintaining a Tram Road or Preamble.
Railway for the Passage of Waggons and other Carriages
properly constructed from the End or Termination of a
certain Tram Road or Railway called the *Grosmont* Railway at
Monmouth Cap in the Parish of *Llangua* in the County of *Monmouth*,
to extend to and terminate at or near *Wye Bridge* in the Parish of
Saint Martin within the Liberties of the City of *Hereford*, will be of
great Public utility, will open a Communication between the County
of *Monmouth* and City of *Hereford*, will facilitate the Carriage and
Conveyance of and render cheaper the various Products and Commo-
dities of the said Counties of *Hereford* and *Monmouth*, and will
materially assist the Agricultural Interest as well as the general Traffic
of the Country, and tend to the Improvement and Value of Land and
Estates in the Vicinity of the said Tram Road or Railway :
[2.]   A   And

TOP: The first page of the 1826 Act of
Parliament for 'making and maintaining a Tram
Road or Railway' from Monmouth Cap to
Hereford (*Herefordshire Archives*)
BOTTOM: A note totalling the cost of additions
to the Cap Inn (*Herefordshire Archives*)

At 30 years of age, John Lucy assisted by Thomas Tudor, his land agent, kept himself involved with local and Kentchurch affairs. They dealt with sporting rights, trespassers, boundaries, a proposition to place stakes in the Monnow to prevent the rapid changing course of the river, concern over female poachers who 'disturb and destroy' the game and nineteenth-century improvements in travel and communications.[38] In 1827 John Lucy received his endorsed survey of his land proposed to be used for the construction of the Hereford Railway, a horse-drawn tramway connecting Abergavenny to Hereford via Pontrilas, which opened in 1829.[39] As a turnpike trustee John Lucy was active in improving and re-routing the roads around Garway, Kentchurch and Pontrilas, including a long-distance turnpike route from Ross to Crickhowell, developed from a maze of lanes by the Ross, Monmouth, Crickhowell, Abergavenny and Grosmont Trusts. The committee recorded that in all great probability a coach starting from Ross to Abergavenny by their new road could be offered a toll-free journey for one year, but this was found to be unacceptable.[40] Thomas Wakeman, road surveyor, reported to the Grosmont Trust on the condition of the turnpike road from Pontrilas, and the superior work undertaken by Mr Scudamore on the roads through Kentchurch parish.[41]

At Llangua a Scudamore property that was known as the Monmouth Cap Inn suddenly became of importance due to its situation on both the turnpiked road leading from Abergavenny to Hereford and the horse-drawn tramway which delivered coal and lime to Monmouth Cap and Hereford at a reduced price. From Monmouth Cap John Lucy benefited from the reduced cost of coal and lime transported on the tramway with amounts of £26 13s 6d and £38 2s 0d paid for coal and lime delivered to Kentchurch Court and Bannut Tree Farm in 1833.

Under the supervision of Thomas Tudor the old coaching inn at Monmouth Cap was extended at a cost of £522 18s 4d in readiness for the expected increase in trade. The toll road also passed the Great House, another Scudamore property standing in a prominent position at Llangua. In the adjoining parish of Grosmont there was a problem

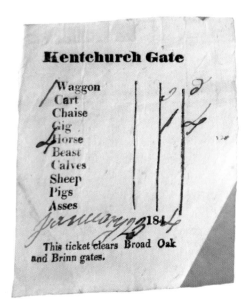
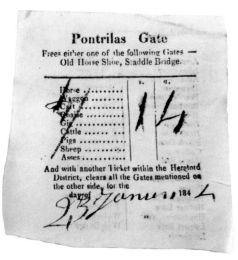

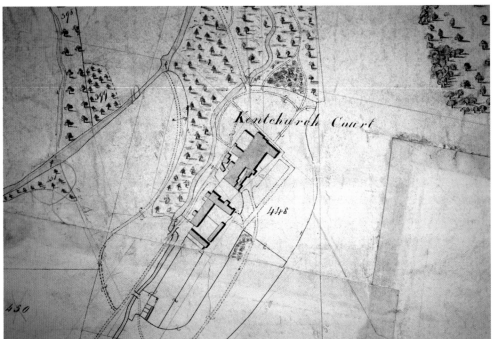

TOP: Tickets for the toll gates at Kentchurch and Pontrilas in 1844 (*Herefordshire Archives*). BOTTOM: Kentchurch Court as shown on the Tithe Map of 1839 (*Herefordshire Archives; photo: David Lovelace*)

with the watermill and mill house which were in a state of dereliction. The buildings were surveyed by the tenant, Mr Foster Williams, who was granted permission to fell elm trees for the repair of the water wheel, but there was a query over the costs and he failed to carry out the work. It was a few years later that John Lucy applied to Messrs Powell & Stevens from Hereford to propose new work and repairs at the mill.[42] As a trustee of the Grosmont and Monmouth Trust, and Surveyor of the Highways of Kentchurch, John Lucy dealt with proposed new lines of roads which included a new road to be constructed from Grosmont Bridge almost following the line of the carriage drive to join the road to Corras and a new line from Pontrilas to Grosmont.[43] He was also involved with subscriptions towards the turnpike costs, collecting tolls, estimates for repairs and the 'stopping up' of a certain road from the Blacksmith's Shop in Kentchurch village to Bowlstone Wood.[44]

At Christmas in 1833 John Lucy and his wife Sarah held a family party at Kentchurch with their guests Sir Harford Jones, his daughter Miss Harford Jones, George Bentham (a respected botanist), his sister and Mr Clive of Whitfield. The time was spent very pleasantly, and on New Year's Day George Bentham proposed to Miss Harford Jones and arranged a quiet wedding to be held at Kentchurch in April. Although George enjoyed the Scudamores' hospitality he was not impressed with the Welsh parson who 'could just mumble through two or three services on a Sunday, without ever troubling himself about his parishioners on other days; if he was asked to dinner at the Court, as soon as dinner was over, he liked to adjourn, not to the drawing-room, but to the

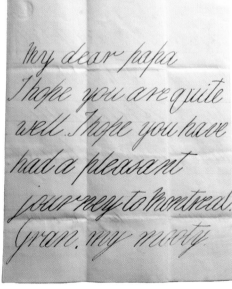

LEFT: Portrait of Laura Adelaide, daughter of John Lucy and Sarah Scudamore, born in 1831 (*Kentchurch Archives*). RIGHT: Laura Adelaide's letter to her father expressing the hope that he had had a good journey to Montreal (*Kentchurch Archives*)

housekeeper's room'. At that time the ageing James Roberts was the parson living at Kentchurch Rectory. George and his sister remained at Kentchurch for a further ten days, visiting the Clives at Whitfield, attending the Hereford County Ball and sleeping at Cheltenham before returning to Lincoln's Inn. The young couple spent their honeymoon at Boultibrook, exploring the beautiful countryside and visiting Downton Castle where they found Andrew Knight 'in good health and spirits – absorbed in pears and potatoes' in his garden that did not 'do much credit to the President of the Horticultural Society'.[45] Letters from Harford Jones to John Lucy during the 1830s reflect a warm affection between the two men, with Harford advising John Lucy on property and financial matters. Harford writes with sentimentality and fondness about his daughter Laura and his granddaughter Laura Adelaide, known as 'Buzzy'. In one letter he wrote 'Pray tell Buzzy I have a most amicable black kitten that plays all sorts of monkey tricks with the rope at my bed-head which rings the bell to the great annoyance of the servants'. Laura Adelaide's beautifully-written letters show great affection for her father, and when staying at Boultibrook she wrote to her father in Montreal, 'I breakfast every morning at nine o'clock with Mooty [her cat], gran and uncle' and concluded with 'good night dear Papa, I remain your affectionate Laura Adelaide Scu'.[46]

Life continued amiably for the Scudamore family during the 1840s, with John Lucy becoming Lieutenant Colonel in the local militia and serving as a magistrate, but not standing for his uncle's seat in parliament when Richard retired as MP for Herefordshire. The Scudamores' faithful attorney, Thomas Bird, had been replaced by John Cleave from Hereford with assistance from William, of the Bird family, a Justices Clerk. As the proud parents of their only child Laura Adelaide, John Lucy and Sarah Laura had her portrait painted at Kentchurch Court by Joshua Cristall, a watercolour artist who lived for nearly 20 years at Goodrich. Cristall founded the Water Colour Society and served three times as its President. He is known for his sketches, oils and watercolours of classical and rural scenes, and from the late 1830s painted portraits and landscapes of the Herefordshire gentry.[47] When Laura Adelaide's parents were away she was left with a married couple who may have been relatives of the family, with the wife working as Laura's governess. The Court was kept running with a large staff of eight female and two male servants, with a young 'keeper' living at Copse Cottage on the estate.[48]

In 1840 the Pontrilas estate with lands in Kentchurch, Ewyas Harold, Kenderchurch and Rowlestone had been acquired by John Lucy who leased the seventeenth-century gabled stone mansion to Charles Everett and the Revd George Everett for one year.[49] In 1846 the mortgage of the Kentchurch estate for £10,000 was assigned from the Hotham family in Suffolk to the Earl of Buckinghamshire. Between 1842 and 1848 many bundles of vouchers confirm that John Lucy paid for further improvements at Kentchurch in the house and garden. Bulbs and flower roots were purchased from Lockhart & Duncan in London, box trees and holly from Saunders of Abergavenny, dozens of garden pots, timber and slate from Nicholas & Co. at Newport, timber from

Swift of Monmouth, whilst a hot water system for Kentchurch Court and other goods were purchased from Bristol. Many items were bought for the Home farm – agricultural implements, wire fencing equipment, seeds, vetches, bran, barley, wheat and, for the household, flour (this being supplied by W. & E. Preece, millers and mealmen at Pontrilas Mills). Half-yearly rents were paid to the Duke of Beaufort and Lord Southwall for lands at Grosmont and Garway. As a turnpike trustee John Lucy was responsible for 'keeping' the Grosmont Bridge Toll Gate at Kentchurch and the gate at Pontrilas near the mills. He kept bundles of toll tickets reflecting the usage of the roads by coaches, carriages and droves of livestock etc., and was asked for a subscription 'to instate a Mail Coach on the Abergavenny Road'.[50]

A list of minor expenses for repairs, leading, glazing and painting show the existence of the following rooms at Kentchurch Court in 1843: butler's bedroom, lady's maid room, servant's bedroom, study, billiard room, boot hall, house-maid's closet, dining room,

Mrs Scudamore's sitting room, boy's bedroom and a school room. The latter two suggest that another son was perhaps expected and that Laura Adelaide, at 12 years old, was being educated at home by a governess. Other repairs and rebuilding were carried out, converting old barns and stables into the upper lodge, the coach house, the best stable, the two-stall stable and the three-stall stable for the cost of £63 6s 7d which included work on Pontrilas Court and Pontrilas Mill. Another snapshot of life is seen from a bill for Lt Col John Lucy Scudamore's travels from Monmouth Cap: 'horses to Hereford and back £1 11s 6d; fly and one horse to Hereford and back £1 1s od; together with horses to and from the Clive family at Whitfield and to balls held there in December and January when the roads were in a treacherous state.'[51] In August 1850 John Lucy and Laura were in France staying at a hotel in Boulogne when one evening, while he was strolling along the pier, he fell into one-and-a-half feet of water from a height of 26 feet and fractured his right leg and left kneecap. Fortunately, a woman came to his rescue and had him carried to the hotel and thence to the Sisters of Charity where he was attended by a surgeon.[52]

The coach house at Kentchurch Court
(*Heather Hurley*)

The census of 1851 records that Kentchurch had a population of 261, showing the curate, Revd J. Scullen, was living in the Rectory, Richard Kennett the blacksmith and wheelwright living near the Bridge Inn where Daniel Powell was the victualler and postmaster. John Nicholas was a beer retailer at Llanithog, John Hodges a miller at Grosmont Mill, J. Preece a corn miller at Pontrilas Mill and George Bentham, a magistrate and relative of the Scudamores was living at Pontrilas House (later Court).[53] John Lucy his wife Laura and their unmarried daughter, Laura Adelaide, were residing at Kentchurch Court with household duties carried out by five female and four male servants, and John Lucy employed ten men to farm his 250 acres.[54]

ACCIDENT TO COLONEL SCUDAMORE.—It is with much regret we have to confirm a report of a serious accident which was said to have happened to Col. Scudamore, of Kentchurch, in this county, who has latterly been residing with part of his family at Boulogne, for the benefit of his health. It appears that Col. Scudamore was walking on the cliffs, when his feet unfortunately slipping, he was precipitated about forty feet down the rocks, by which, we are sorry to state, both his legs were broken, and he was otherwise seriously injured; he was immediately conveyed to his residence and received the best surgical attendance. It is satisfactory to add that we have just seen a letter which states that the Colonel is progressing as much as possible under the distressing circumstanses of the case, and that with the skilful medical treatment he is receiving it is hoped he may soon be restored to health :—a hope in which we most sincerely and cordially join.

Le 15 du courant, entre dix et onze heures du soir, M. Sendamore, colonel anglais, âgé d'environ 60 ans, débarqué la veille, venant de Folkstone et descendu à l'hôtel du Pavillon, s'est, en se promenant, laissé tomber sur l'escalier en pierres de la jetée, près de la batterie, et s'est fracturé les deux jambes ; il a été de suite transporté à son hôtel où il a reçu les soins éclairés de MM. les Docteurs Duuand et Perrochaud.

Les jetées de Boulogne, construites pour le service de la navigation et non pour la promenade, peuvent quelquefois causer des accidents ; il serait donc à désirer que les étrangers qui n'en connaissent pas parfaitement les détours, ne s'y promenassent qu'avec la plus grande précaution, surtout pendant la nuit.

John Lucy's accident as reported in English and French newspapers in August 1850
(*Kentchurch Archives*)

6

Laura Adelaide, the Lucas Family and the Colourful Twentieth Century

> The situation of Kentchurch, approached by a long avenue of elm-trees, and backed by a noble park, which stretches up the steep slopes of Garway Hill, is extremely picturesque, and in spite of the proximity of the railway, the scene retains the same air of wildness and seclusion which must have characterised it when it formed the refuge of Glyndwr.
>
> *Charles Robinson*, **Mansions of Herefordshire**, *1872*[1]

LAURA Adelaide Scudamore, the only surviving child of John Lucy and Laura, spent her childhood at Kentchurch after her birth in 1831 at Gloucester Place, London. Known as 'Buzzy', she was educated at Kentchurch Court in the schoolroom by a governess and grew up as a young lady, rather gauche with her best feature being her 'pretty hair'. In 1850 at the age of 19 she was expected to marry Mr Wallis of 'Castle Dismal' (Drishane Castle), County Cork. Clearly Buzzy was not attracted to this Irishman, for within two years she had married the dashing 29-year-old Fitzherbert Dacre Lucas of Castle Shane, Co. Monaghan. The marriage at Pau in France was apparently an elopement of which Laura Adelaide's father did not approve and with which he found hard to reconcile. Fitzherbert, who was the third son of the Rt Hon. Edward Lucas, was a prominent citizen serving as a JP, MP and High Sheriff in Co. Monaghan and as Under-Secretary of State for Ireland.[2]

Fitzherbert was born in 1823 at Geneva during his parents' long tour of the Continent, travelling great distances by post coach and packet steamer to France, Switzerland, Italy and Germany, visiting cathedrals and churches and enjoying the theatre, concerts, opera and ballet.[3] Fitzherbert is portrayed as a handsome young man and described as an Irish gentleman, traveller and speculator. Upon his marriage, he resigned as a captain in the South Tipperary Militia and spent a period in France with Laura, where their son, mirroring his own birth on the Continent years before, was born in 1853. Christened Edward Scudamore Lucas he was always known as Eddie. Although

Portrait of Fitzherbert Dacre Lucas in 1852 (*Kentchurch Archives*)

planning to reside in Northern Ireland, the footloose Fitzherbert travelled to India where he speculated on a deal worth £2,737 and found himself caught up in the Indian Mutiny at Lucknow in 1857.[4] In this dangerous situation, and without a chance to escape by road or river, Fitzherbert volunteered his services as a soldier to General Sir Henry Lawrence. Fitzherbert survived the defence of 'Gubbins's Battery', but on 29 September 'he received a fatal gun-shot wound' and passed away the following day. He is remembered on a tomb at Lucknow, in a *Times* obituary and on a memorial wall tablet erected in St Patrick's church, Monaghan (*right and below*):[5]

(*Kentchurch Archives*)

In memory of
Francis, eldest son of the Rt Hon. E. Lucas, and formerly Lieut in H.M. 46th Regt,
Born at Castle Shane 8 May 1813. Died at Hamburgh 21 April 1846
and of his brother
Fitzherbert Dacre, formerly Capt in the S. Tipperary Militia
Born at Geneva 31 August 1823. Died at Lucknow 30 September 1857.
Repairing to Lucknow on the 30 May to offer his services and accepted by Genl. Sir Hy Lawrence at noon,
he was that evening (when the mutiny broke out) and thenceforward, engaged in action and dangerous duty.
Of six officers appointed with him to the defence of 'Gubbins's Battery'
three were shortly killed and three severely wounded.
He survived unhurt until September 29th,
when, at the close of a successful sortie, he received a fatal gun-shot wound.
His end was that of a soldier and a Christian.

As a speculator Fitzherbert had invested money acquired from his father and father-in-law with an agent in Calcutta, but a few weeks before his death a letter from the agent suggested some concerns about some mismanagement of the funds.[6]

Laura Adelaide Lucas was left a young widow with an infant child, a situation that caused concern for the two families of grandparents. The Rt Hon. Edward Lucas wrote to John Lucy expressing his wish that their grandson's birth be registered in London (if this had not already been done) in order to prove parentage in England or Ireland. Laura Adelaide's mother refers to the 'dear, dear child' and offered 'to keep baby' until Laura Adelaide was settled. In fact, within two years she had married John Donegan, another Irishman, at Rathdrum in Wicklow. He was described by the family as a 'low coarse man', who in his Irish accent said he was 'never aisy unless breaking his neck to get back to his Pussy'. Her mother, Mrs Scudamore was disgusted and shocked by him and his graphic language.[7] Adelaide returned to Ireland, leaving baby Eddie with his English maternal grandparents who kept in contact with Edward Lucas in Ireland. He reported in 1860 that, after some concerns, Fitzherbert's 'Indian speculation' had produced a satisfactory result in leaving £1,600 to be invested in Railway Debentures, and suggested that 'careful management of the interest should by the time the young gentleman comes of age' be worth £2,000.[8]

Daily life for the Scudamores at Kentchurch was ably overseen by a host of servants, a butler, coachman, page, two house maids, three kitchen maids and a scullery maid who looked after the household duties even when the family were away. On one occasion in 1861 there was a family gathering at Boultibrook hosted by Sir Harford

The Rt Hon. Edward Lucas of Castle Shane
(*Kentchurch Archives*)

Jones junior and his wife Lady Jane, and attended by John Lucy, his wife Sarah, their eight-year-old grandson Eddie, and various friends and relatives born as far afield as Canada, Russia and Barbados. Sir Harford's staff was even more impressive, consisting of a butler, coachman, three house maids, laundry maid, ladies maid, kitchen maid, scullery maid and a footman. A young governess accompanied Eddie who shared his time between Kentchurch and Boultibrook throughout his childhood.[9] Towards the end of her life Eddie's maternal grandmother, Laura, became known as a melancholic and narcotic character who disliked living at Kentchurch and had an increasingly poor relationship with her husband John Lucy. Previously, the Scudamores had been living abroad for a number of years on the Continent and in Ireland, and Sarah commented on their return that 'all our misfortunes have come upon us', referring to her daughter marrying Donegan; to John Lucy's accident in France; the death of her father; her orphaned grandson Eddie, and the state of their financial affairs which included a loan of £20,000 from the Land Improvement Company.[10] She returned to the family home at Boultibrook and died there in her sixties in 1863.[11]

In 1867 Kentchurch parish had expanded to a population of 325 inhabitants. The church had been rebuilt in 1859 at a cost of £1,200. The school for boys and girls was under the supervision of Mrs Mary Ann Hall and the rector, Revd Sellon, had rebuilt the parsonage to a design by the architect J.P. Seddon. The horse-drawn tramway

TOP LEFT: Kentchurch church before rebuilding, as depicted by James Gregory Peene in *Churches and Mansions in South Herefordshire* (*Herefordshire Libraries*). TOP RIGHT: Kentchurch church in 2015 (*Logaston Press*). BOTTOM LEFT: Pontrilas Court (*Kentchurch Archives*). BOTTOM RIGHT: Kentchurch Rectory (*Herefordshire Archives*).

had been replaced by a section of the Great Western Railway, with steam trains to Newport, Abergavenny and Hereford from a station at Pontrilas. Railway communication had attracted the development of timber mills, chemical works and coal, lime, and slate merchants in Pontrilas. William Jones had opened the Scudamore Arms, a 'Family Hotel and Boarding Establishment' in the former 'baronial mansion' (Pontrilas Court) fitted out for 'gentlemen and families of position, with extensive right of fishing on the river Monnow'. Mr George, meanwhile, ran the Pontrilas Inn as a typical railway inn near to the station where a proposed 'Golden Valley Railway' was to commence from a junction on the Hereford to Abergavenny line. John Lucy was residing at Kentchurch Court, his steward at Monmouth Cap House and his bailiff at Bannuttree.[12]

Young Eddie Scudamore Lucas was educated at Eton and, when approaching his late teens, his Irish grandfather, Edward Lucas, wrote to John Lucy saying that although John had entered Eddie for Christ Church College, Oxford, where 'he would always find ... a large society of old Etonians', he could alternatively consider encouraging him to enter the army.[13] His aging grandfather was visiting Boultibrook in 1871 at the time that Eddie, as a 'scholar', was finishing his schooling in Devon before starting at university. He was boarding at Torquay with nine other scholars ranging in

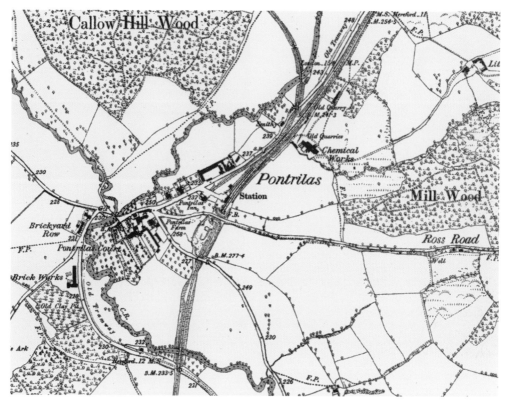

Pontrilas and its locality as shown on the Ordnance Survey map of 1888

age from 11 to 18, with Revd Thomas Stebbing a 'Clergyman Without Cure of Souls' (without a parish) and his wife Mary as a tutor.[14] Eddie then attended Christ Church and New Inn Hall at Oxford University and then left the country to join his Irish grandfather at Castle Shane.

In 1875 John Lucy died at Kentchurch and was to be buried in the family vault, but since the rebuilding of the church 'the entrance to the Vault was unknown' – until an old woman living at Little Corras Cottage remembered it and, upon payment of a pound, pointed it out.[15] From this date Kentchurch Court was unoccupied by the Scudamores except for a skeleton staff of two maids and a gardener. An Inventory and Valuation of Furniture and Effects was made by Edwin Stooke, detailing the contents of two libraries with its collection of books, two studies, two drawing rooms, billiard room, smoking room, school room, dining room, butler's pantry, two closets, one dressing room and several bedrooms called Green Room, Boudoir, Brown Room, White Room, Saxon Room, Upper Saxon Room and the Bear's Paw Room in the fourteenth-century tower.[16] (The Bear's Paw issuing from a ducal coronet is the Scudamore family crest denoting a second son, which features as a frieze in the same room today.)[17] Also recorded were six men's and six servants' rooms all furnished with bedsteads, making a total of at least 18 beds in the house.

LEFT: Edward (Eddie) Lucas c.1870 (*Kentchurch Archives*). RIGHT: Edward Lucas, 1888 (*Kentchurch Archives*)

Within a year of John Lucy's death Kentchurch Court was tenanted, as the next of kin, his daughter Laura Adelaide Donegan, was living in Ireland. The court was, however, still described as the 'seat' of her son, Eddie, whom she had deserted, and who had succeeded his English grandfather as JP for the counties of Hereford, Monmouth and Radnor and as Deputy Lieutenant for Herefordshire.

In 1876 Revd William Sellon continued as the Rector of Kentchurch and Llangua. A sum of £50 had been spent on repairing the old school where 24 children were taught by Mrs Nobbs. In previous years the school master was Mr Harris, a good scholar who had a reputation for being strict and punishing the boys very harshly.[18] At Pontrilas another school, blacksmith and post office had been established, and Pontrilas Court had reverted from an inn to a private mansion. In Kentchurch village, Richard Harris ran the Bridge Inn and James Kennard was the blacksmith and post-master. Between Pontrilas and Kentchurch a beer house called the Royal Oak had opened to serve customers on the road to Orcop and Ross.[19]

In Ireland, Eddie had succeeded his uncle, Edward W. Lucas, at Castle Shane and to the positions of JP and Deputy Lieutenant for County Monaghan, and High Sheriff in 1879. As the relatively young Eddie Lucas was regularly attending the courts as a JP in England, Ireland and Wales, he was always on the move, travelling by train, coach and boat with little time to attend his club in London (called the new University Club and established for Oxbridge graduates), or to fulfil his role as Major and Hon. Lt Col of the 4th Battalion Shropshire Light Infantry.[20] It appears that by this time Eddie's mother, Laura, had left her second husband in Ireland, as she had taken up residence at a property on the Abergavenny Road at Llangua. At the time of the 1881 census her household consisted of two female servants and a male visitor from Ireland.[21]

After the tenant had vacated Kentchurch Court in 1881, J.F. Symonds, a solicitor based in Hereford, advertised the property to let at £500 per year, describing it as

> a handsome castellated Mansion, with a substantial Tower, situated in a lovely Valley on the Western Slope of Garway Hill, and the seat of the ancient family of Scudamore. It is approached by a fine avenue of Elm Trees, and fronts an extensive Deer Park, magnificently timbered, and abounding with picturesque undulations and wild scenery.

The mansion was described as being well furnished 'not in modern style, but very comfortably so', with a handsome suite of large and lofty rooms consisting of a drawing room, dining room and library opening into each other, a billiard room and gun room with a further library and long gallery above leading to the best bedrooms warmed in winter with hot water pipes. Altogether there were 25 bed and dressing rooms and good servants' quarters. New tenants would be pleased to learn that Kentchurch Court had an abundant supply of spring water, about 30 acres of pasture ground and garden with glass and forcing houses, stabling for 12 horses and a coach house, good shooting over 4,700 acres for the sportsman, hunting with the Herefordshire and Monmouthshire packs of hounds and trout fishing in the river Monnow.[22]

Whilst the house was left empty for viewing by prospective tenants, a minimal staff of two maids and a gardener kept the property in good order. Nearby houses on the estate included the gardener's lodge, the avenue lodge, the gamekeeper's house and two cottages, one of which was the former Waterloo Cottage where a retired farmer lived with his son. The cottage was built on waste land and named after the 'loo' in a shelter by the water; the name probably deriving from an iron toilet cistern bearing the name Waterloo. This cottage and garden stood between the road and the river, and was purchased by the Scudamores to be demolished during the twentieth century.[23] As an absentee landlord in 1890, Eddie became concerned with the condition of his land in the parishes of Kentchurch, Kenderchurch and Kilpeck, and applied to the Board of Agriculture under the Acts of Improvement of Land and Settled Land Acts for a loan of £2,184 with yearly payments of £147 14s 6d. The money was spent on improving drainage until 1900 when the loan was repaid.[24]

During the 1890s George Lee Morris, a retired medical officer in the civil service, and his wife were the tenants at Kentchurch Court. The head gardener was living at the Laundry, while at Lower Lodge lived a widow who looked after her niece, an adopted daughter and a lodger, and the Upper Lodge was inhabited by a general labourer. The rector, Revd Morgan George Watkins, who penned a history of Kentchurch in 1891,

Clog makers at Kentchurch (*Herefordshire Archives*)

and photographed the clog, timber and bark industries, was resident at the Rectory with his wife and expanding family of scholars, consisting of four sons, a nephew and a cousin whose domestic needs were looked after by a cook and housemaid.[25]

Despite travelling between Herefordshire and Monaghan in the 1890s, Eddie, an eligible bachelor now in his thirties, spent time in his London house at Chelsea, at Boultibrook and at the Cap House in Llangua. His mother's second husband died at Cavan in Ireland,[26] which may have prompted Laura Adelaide, living at Part-y-Seal in Grosmont, to release her life interest in part of the Kentchurch estate to her estranged son Eddie in 1893 for a consideration of an annuity and a payment of £25. The agreement was duly signed, sealed and delivered by Laura Adelaide, and by so doing she severed her awkward, unfortunate and unhappy association with her family and Kentchurch Court. Eddie immediately mortgaged Adelaide's portion for £40,000 from the Scottish Provident Institution.[27] With money now to hand, the 40-year-old Eddie of Castle Shane, Honourable Colonel in the 4th Shropshire Light Infantry, changed his name by royal license to Lucas-Scudamore, and during 1900 courted the attractive 22-year-old Sybil Frances Webber. Whilst serving with the Shropshire Light Infantry in Waterford and Mitchelstown in Ireland, he wrote very affectionate letters to Sybil, which detail his travels to Dublin, to the Cap House in Llangua and

Part-y-Seal, Grosmont (*Heather Hurley*)

to Hyde Gate, London before their wedding held at St Georges, Hanover Square.[28] Sybil was the third daughter of Col George Webber and had been born in Jamaica, brought up in Ireland and educated in Northampton at the home of Anne K. King, an author and artist from Ireland. At the wedding the best man was the Hon. Harry Scudamore-Stanhope who later became 11th Lord Chesterfield and whose family were

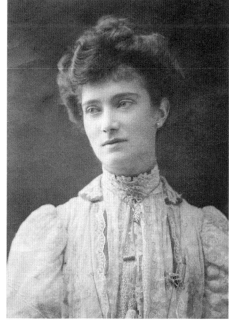

LEFT: Edward Lucas-Scudamore in 1908. RIGHT: Sybil in 1900 when she married Eddie
(*Kentchurch Archives*)

formerly at Holme Lacy. Sybil was given away by her uncle Major Webber, and her sister was one of the bridesmaids. The couple then left for Paris en route to Cairo where they spent their honeymoon.[29]

The rector, Morgan Watkins, recorded that, 'owing to Col Scudamore's wedding and the repairs of the Court', more trees than usual, especially in the park, were cut down and sold in the spring of 1901. These included 471 oaks (137 of which came from the park) and 981 other trees – elm, ash, larch, spruce fir, alder, beech, aspen, birch and Spanish chestnut. After their honeymoon, Eddie and Sybil settled at the Cap House, Llangua although their son John, known as Jack, was born at Boultibrook in 1902.[30] Morgan Watkins baptised him as John Harford Stanhope Lucas-Scudamore, the christening being attended by Lady Brydges, Mr Stanhope, friends and relatives. To celebrate the occasion the church bells were rung and the font was decorated with white flowers, whilst the rector planted a small oak, grown from an acorn at Llangua, on the right of the churchyard entrance and another on the left side to commemorate the coronation of King Edward VII who succeeded Queen Victoria.[31]

In 1905 the Revd Watkins was still at the Rectory, and the tenant at Kentchurch Court was Francis Somerville Head. Between a change of tenant and rector a special parish meeting was held at Kentchurch School to consider the demolition of the old and disused parish pound. After much discussion it was decided to let the new rector raise sufficient funds to carry the work through and improve the entrance to the church-yard. This was obviously of interest to the Scudamores as the work would enhance the entrance to Kentchurch Court.[32] Eddie and Sybil now divided their life between Castle Shane and the Cap House – and now with two children, as Jack had been joined by Geraldine (Gill). The two were proudly photographed in a Panhard motor car purchased by Eddie from Charles Rolls in 1905.[33] At about this time Eddie pur-chased Pontrilas Court and its estate, which extended to over 1,500 acres.[34] Although Eddie and Sybil's main residence was Castle Shane, Monaghan, where Edward served as MP, JP and Deputy Lieutenant, he must have spent time at the Cap House near his 'seat' at Kentchurch Court, enabling him to serve as JP and Deputy Lieutenant in Herefordshire, JP for Radnorshire and stand as a liberal candidate in the 1906 election after retiring from his post as Colonel in the Shropshire Light Infantry.[35]

From 1907 Eddie and Sybil were on the move again, visiting Dinard in France with their two young children and attending Kentchurch Court for socialising and parties, where they were captured on film playing the roles of the Scudamores at the time of Owain Glyndwr. Then over the sea to Castle Shane where Jack and Gill enjoyed riding their ponies, leaving Kentchurch unoccupied between tenants and in the care of a butler, a kitchen maid and two housemaids.[36] Whilst the house was vacant during 1912 Eddie took the opportunity to modify the building. Plans show how extensive the build-ing was, with its former servants' and domestic quarters, and with a slightly different arrangement of rooms to include a gymnasium/ billiard room in the present Terrace

TOP: Jack and Gill at Monmouth Cap. MIDDLE: Castle Shane in 1917. ABOVE LEFT: Sybil's Red Cross class of 1917. ABOVE RIGHT: Sybil at Castle Shane in 1919 (*all from Kentchurch Archives*)

Room.[37] Kentchurch Court was then let to Joseph Shaw, KC, a major industrialist in the South Wales coalfields and a benefactor of Wolfson College, Cambridge. As Shaw wanted to rent the Court unfurnished, Sybil had to sell the contents.[38]

The rather forgotten Laura Adelaide, who had been responsible, through her first marriage, for uniting the Scudamores with the Lucas family, died in obscurity in 1912 at the age of 81 and left death duties to be paid. She had been involved with the Skenfrith United District School but after a carriage accident in which she broke her arm and sustained other injuries she moved to Raglan in 1906. No record has been found of her burial, although her name was inscribed on the family cross in the Kentchurch church graveyard.

In January 1913, Eddie and Sybil, and their daughter and governess, travelled by passenger ship to Madeira from Liverpool, returning on 31 March on board the *Hilary*. They arrived back safely in time for their third child, Oriel, to be born in Dublin just before the outbreak of the Great War.[39] With Jack

CARRIAGE ACCIDENT AT GROSMONT

Mrs. Laura Adelaide Donegan, of Pant-y-Seal, was thrown out of her carriage on Monday at Lower Tresenny, and sustained a broken arm and other injuries. The horse bolting caused the carriage to collide with a bridge over a brook, and Mrs. Donegan was thrown over the parapet of the bridge into the water. The horse had to be shot.

TOP: Laura Adelaide's accident of 1901 as reported in the *Evening Express*.
BELOW: Oriel riding at Castle Shane in 1917
(*Kentchurch Archives*)

at Eton the remaining family returned to Castle Shane with a reduced staff due to men being enlisted into the war effort. The energetic Sybil ran a hospital supply unit in Monaghan and organised parcels to be sent to Paris from London. She also learnt first aid and trained nurses and VAD (Voluntary Aid Detachment) members of the Red Cross throughout the war years, and was involved with the Women's National Health Association of Ireland. For her dedicated work she was awarded a Red Cross medal and an MBE. Eddie helped Sybil with her voluntary work until 1917 when he died suddenly shortly after he had recovered from a gallstone operation in Dublin.[40]

Eddie's body was transported to Kentchurch where he was buried and remembered on a white cross in the churchyard:

> In Loving Memory of Edward Scudamore Lucas Scudamore
> Son of Fitzherbert Lucas of Castle Shane, Monaghan
> and Adelaide daughter of John Lucy Scudamore of Kentchurch Court
> aged 64 deeply loved and missed.
> This cross is erected by his wife and children

Eddie's will was complicated with many debts to pay and 'awful death duties'. Jack was left Castle Shane with its mortgages amounting to £10,000 and Sybil was left the English estates for her life. Under the terms of a later agreement she altered the arrangements which the trustees considered to be very liberal in favour of her son.[41] Although Joseph Shaw was still the tenant at Kentchurch Court, Pontrilas Court was uninhabited and in a dreadful state. The strong-minded and widowed Sybil, living at Castle Shane, had two estates to maintain, children to educate, and debts to settle – all on an income from the trustees of £100 a month.[42] Presumably to ease financial matters the land, farms and sporting rights of the Pontrilas Court estate were sold for £16,500 at auction in November 1919, and the following year four farms including Llancillo Court and Rowlestone were sold for over £19,000.[43] This was the least of her troubles for on a February night while she and her daughter Oriel were at

Eddie's grave in Kentchurch churchyard (*Heather Hurley*)

Castle Shane, a disastrous fire spread through the building and destroyed it. The local newspaper reported that, 'later in the day a large number of the townspeople drove or walked out to the scene of the outbreak. By the forenoon, the interior of the Castle was entirely burnt out, and only the bare walls remained. Throughout the progress of the fire the roof gradually fell in and crashed down to the basement, becoming a smouldering heap of broken masonry and twisted metal-work'. Mr Morgan, the estate steward, and the workers were quickly on the scene making strenuous efforts to cope with the spreading flames. Fortunately no lives were lost and Sybil and her daughter were taken by the high sheriff to his home where they could recover from the unexpected shock, before travelling 'to one of their English properties, the principal of which is Kentchurch Court'. Jack was away at the time, serving as a midshipman on the battleship HMS *Revenge* in the Mediterranean as part of attending the Royal Naval College at Greenwich.

Although Castle Shane was covered by insurance it was not enough to compensate the loss of its contents. The family lost silver, jewellery, family portraits, prints and heirlooms including rare old furniture, a Georgian suite and an old fashioned wine-table. From the treasured library a rare copy of the *Nuremburg Chronicles*, a seventeenth-century prayer book and first editions of the works of Sir Walter Scott were never recovered.[44] It was later reported that the prayer book, known as the Charles 1 Prayer Book, was beautifully bound with two gold clasps and bore the Royal Coat of Arms, and that the *Nuremburg Chronicle* of 1493 by Hartmann Schedel was one of the most important incunabulum (early printed books) of the fifteenth century.[45] Castle Shane

MONAGHAN CASTLE DESTROYED BY FIRE.

Castle Shane, the home of Midshipman J. Lucas-Scudamore, Royal Navy, H.M.S. *Revenge*, was burnt to the ground on Sunday, the 15th inst. The outbreak was discovered in the dining-room at about 7.30 a.m., but the flames had obtained such a hold, that all efforts towards extinguishing them were unavailing. **Mrs. Lucas-Scudamore**, and her little girl, governess, and maid escaped in their night attire. No one was injured. The connection between the Castle and the servants' quarters was cut off, and that part of the buildings and stables were saved. A large quantity of china and silver, some engravings, and furniture were saved, but the library, containing many valuable first editions, &c., was completely destroyed. Among the books were heirlooms like the Prayer Book used by Charles II. while he was at Exeter, 1645, Charles I.'s letter appointing Lord Scudamore Ambassador at the Court of Louis XIV., "The Nuremberg Chronicle," 1495, &c. All the family pictures, miniatures, and records were destroyed. Midshipman J. Lucas-Scudamore is at present with the Atlantic Fleet in the Mediterranean.

TOP: Castle Shane after the fire of 1920 (*Kentchurch Archives*)

LEFT: A newspaper report of the fire at Castle Shane (*Kentchurch Archives*)

ABOVE: Castle Shane in 2017 (*Jocelyn Lucas-Scudamore*)

was a huge building, originally built during the mid seventeenth century, which had been rebuilt and extended on three occasions. The servants' quarters and stables (called the Riding School) were saved as they were not connected to the main building.[46]

Following the fire, many letters of sympathy were sent to Sybil from her friends in London and her Irish neighbours. The latter included the Leslie family from nearby Glaslough where Sybil's great friend Leonie lived (Leonie came from a distinguished Irish family, and her favourite nephew was Winston Churchill.)[47] An extremely sad letter was sent from Sybil's daughter, Gill, who was away at the time of the fire. She expressed her sorrow, writing 'everything we love goes', 'the link which Castle Shane had with Daddy is broken', 'I can't believe it, I did so love Castle Shane', 'I suppose all my things were burnt' and 'I am longing to know what was saved.

TOP: Sybil at Glaslough, Ireland, in 1915 (*Kentchurch Archives*). BOTTOM: Charlie Noble in 1920 (*Kentchurch Archives*)

It's so awful being so beastly far away'. Sybil left George Morgan, the steward, in charge of the estate and the remaining building which was broken into and fired again almost immediately after the disaster. Morgan reported on a monthly basis to Sybil, keeping her in touch with the livestock, crops, tenants and workmen, and sent her regular parcels of produce. A carpenter named Charlie Noble applied to Morgan for work but in order to keep the 'labour account' down he was sent to Pontrilas as Sybil knew him as a good worker. He subsequently moved to Kentchurch Court as house carpenter. Morgan's letters in 1922 refer to the Irish 'happenings' that started in May when the rebels gave him 72 hours to clear out, but he did not leave, although there was a boycott against working for and supplying Castle Shane. Despite the problems in Cork and Tipperary, Morgan's children coped; however his wife became nervous

TOP LEFT: Jack's car, a Ballot, in 1920. Jack was a keen participant at Oxford University in the Inter Varsity Speed Trials held at Aston Clinton. TOP RIGHT: In this photograph he is shown racing his Ballot motorcar at Brooklands in 1922. ABOVE: Jack's 2-litre Ballot at Pontrilas in 1923. It came complete with a touring body and was capable of 100mph (*all from Kentchurch Archives*)

and could not sleep. One letter from Morgan to Sybil finishes with, 'trusting yourself, Master John, Miss Geraldine and Miss Oriel are all well and happy away from all the troubles of this country',[48] referring to the outbreak of the Irish Civil War which tore many families apart.

As Kentchurch Court was still let to Mr Shaw, Sybil settled at Pontrilas Court which she claimed 'swallowed up' her money in repairs and restoration. Finances were eased when Lady Brydges died and bequeathed some furnishings from Boultibrook, which were sold at auction and raised funds which allowed Sybil to take Gill (Geraldine) to study in Florence and Oriel to France in order to learn the language. Unknown to her, Jack was then in France and suddenly and unexpectedly became engaged to a beautiful older woman whom he married in 1926, a marriage which turned out to be a disaster and was later dissolved by divorce.[49] Since attending the Royal Naval College Jack had gone to Oxford University, during which time he began to race cars.

The 1920s were a colourful period for Sybil and her family with trips abroad, entertaining notables such as George Bernard Shaw the playwright, her friend Robert Baden-Powell who camped at Kentchurch and the Hon. Lady Bailey, a pioneer aviator who gave an exhibition of flying at a Kentchurch pageant. As a performer Sybil acted and sung on stage at the Kemble Theatre in Hereford to raise funds for the Irish Loyalists.[50]

At this time Sybil was anxious to move into Kentchurch Court but the tenant, Joseph Shaw, was reluctant to leave and caused problems. He left the shoot in a neglected state with no birds, fences down, no cover in the woods, a deer fence that had to be removed and a depleted fish stock. During Shaw's tenancy a total of 14,675 pheasants were killed whereas 13,858 were reared leaving a deficiency of 817, and whilst the First World War was raging, the sport at Kentchurch had continued with 19,597 partridge, pheasant, rabbit, woodcock and wild duck shot. A certain amount of dilapidation to the property had accrued, which Shaw had to settle with the agent, and as he left before the lease expired, due to ill health, rents were due. Eventually, Kentchurch Court was reoccupied by the Scudamore family in 1927, and refurnished with Sybil's choice of furniture from Pontrilas and Boultibrook together with new purchases, as Shaw had left the Court 'very sparsely furnished', albeit with electricity installed.[51]

The uneasy relationship between Sybil as 'lady of the manor' and her son Jack did not improve as she battled on throughout the 1930s with travelling abroad, Geraldine's wedding, Oriel's schooling and Jack's divorce from his first wife Elsie Scott and marriage to Constance Primrose Carpenter. With her many commitments to the Girl Guides, Rural District Council, Women's Institute, Health Associations and the Unionist Association she was honoured in the *Who's Who* in Herefordshire, published in 1933.[52] In 1937 Sybil opened the house and gardens of Kentchurch Court to the public for the first time, in aid of the Queen's Institute of District Nursing.

When war broke out in 1939 the fun-loving Jack, with his naval background, found his forte and 'did very well' after signing up on 1 December and becoming a Lt Cmdr in

Court Circular

FORTHCOMING MARRIAGES
Mr. J. H. S. Lucas-Scudamore and Lady Patricia McDonald

The engagement is announced, and the marriage will take place shortly, between John Harford Stanhope, only son of the late Col. Edward Scudamore Lucas-Scudamore and of Mrs. Lucas-Scudamore, M.B.E., of Kentchurch Court, Hereford, and Evelyn Patricia Mary, only daughter of the Earl of Chesterfield and of Mrs. R. M. Doughty, of Wellington, New Zealand.

TOP: The Hon. Lady Bailey gave a flying display at Kentchurch air pageant in 1922. The photo in the newspaper report shows, from left to right: Lt Richardson (who also took part), Lord Treowen, the Hon. Lady Bailey, Mrs Lucas-Scudamore, Miss Lucas-Scudamore, Mrs Greene and Capt. Arkwright. ABOVE LEFT: A greeting card received from Robert Baden Powell in 1933. MIDDLE RIGHT: The announcement of Jack's marriage to Lady Patricia McDonald in 1947. BOTTOM RIGHT: George Bernard Shaw with Sybil at Kentchurch in 1923 (*all from Kentchurch Archives*)

the Royal Naval Volunteer Reserve. His wife Constance (Connie) worked in Cairo for ENSA (Entertainments National Service Association) which had been formed to provide entertainment for the British Military.[53] In 1941 it was planned to use Kentchurch Court as an auxiliary hospital but the plan appears not to have been implemented. During the war Sybil provided knitted jerseys and socks for the Merchant Navy Comfort Service, kept busy writing numerous letters and sent a collection of several thousand Kentchurch Court documents and papers to the National Library of Wales.[54] Once the war was over Sybil went to visit her married daughter in Egypt and on her return found that

TOP LEFT: Stone bears being taken in 1952, by Roy Lane, originally from Holme Lacy House to Kentchurch Court where they were erected at the entrance (*Kentchurch Archives*). TOP RIGHT: The stone bears standing at the entrance to Kentchurch Court in 2017 (*Rosie Watts*). BOTTOM: The Lucas-Scudamore family in 1955 (*Kentchurch Archives*)

TOP: Photographs showing the damage caused by the flood in 1959 (*top left and middle left Kentchurch Archives; top right Herefordshire Archives*). BOTTOM: Kentchurch Court in 1959 (*Kentchurch Archives*)

Jack, renowned for his wit and style, had dissolved his second marriage and had become engaged to Lady Patricia, the only child of the 12th Earl of Chesterfield, a Scudamore-Stanhope whose family were once at Holme Lacy. Sybil invited Jack and Patricia to live at Kentchurch Court where their daughter Charlotte and son John were born in 1949 and 1953, and looked after by their nanny Daisy Rees. During this quiet post-war period Lady Patricia acquired many family portraits, the Grinling Gibbons carvings from Beningbrough, near York, that had formerly hung at Holme Lacy House, and the gate piers topped by the Scudamore stone bears that had originally stood at Holme Lacy House. Just as Sybil, at 81 years of age, was sitting back thinking that her 'life's work was really finished' another disaster happened.[55]

On a stormy night in May 1959 torrential rain and strong gales caused a nearby stream 'to burst its banks becoming a fast swirling river which brought down trees and poured into the historic mansion'. Sybil, sitting in the library, was suddenly aware of water coming in under the door and within minutes she was waist deep in water. The indefatigable Sybil climbed onto the furniture to avoid being drowned and was rescued by her servants. The flood damaged thousands of pounds worth of furniture, carpets, books and china, which led to a nightmarish clean-up operation as 'massive antique furniture had been overturned, damaged and swept through the house to lie in mud stained heaps, inches deep mud covered the lawns and carpets, windows were smashed and doors were broken. A heavy Aga cooker was carried yards across the kitchen and a tarmac drive was ripped up.' The water reached a depth of 5' 4" in the front rooms and 9' 7" in the kitchen, and as a result of this freak flood part of the house had to be demolished. With Sybil so 'very weak and unhappy' with all her 'treasures gone again' Jack and Lady Patricia thought she wouldn't survive this terrible disaster, but she did and continued to live a few more years.[56]

Sybil received many letters of sympathy and although she compiled a list of her own personal effects that had been damaged in the flood, it was Jack who took over claiming for insurance, purchasing replacements and undertaking the mammoth task of restoring and conserving the antique furnishings. The library was badly damaged, with many old and rare books never recovered, and only a few suitable for repair, including Scudamore's *Cyder*, Coxe's *Monmouth* and Shirley's *Monaghan*.[57] It took two years for the house to dry sufficiently, before the floorboards and furniture could be reinstated and Jack and his third wife Lady Patricia could return to the family home.[58]

7

The de Lacys and the Early Scudamores at Holme Lacy

Holme Lacy occupies some of those favoured tracts of country
of which the beauty of the scenery and richness of the soil
have from the earliest records attracted those in power. Walter
de Lacy, that great Lieutenant of the Norman Duke, settled
here soon after the Conquest, and so vast were his possessions,
that his son Roger, in the reign of the Conqueror's successor,
William Rufus, boasted of no less than sixty-five lordships in
the county, the principle being this Hamme, the old Saxon
equivalent for the modern Holme or Home.

Holme Lacy Sale particulars, 1909[1]

Holme Lacy lies on the banks of the river Wye, four miles south of Hereford and eight miles north of Ross. Its early history is complex but at Domesday it was recorded as 'hamm' (land in a river bend), an estate of the Bishop of Hereford and held by Roger de Lacy, the son of Walter who died in 1085 after falling from St Peter's church in Hereford during the construction of the church. Walter de Lacy was known as 'a valiant Norman, who acquired great possessions in the county of Hereford soon after the Norman Conquest' and his son Roger held 65 lordships with the principal one at 'Homme' in exchange for the service of two knights.[2] The connection with the powerful de Lacys led to the addition of Lacy to its place-name. The population in 1086 included 16 villeins (un-free tenants), 4 bordars (lowest rank of worker), 1 reeve, 1 male slave and 2 female slaves, 1 priest and 1 Frenchman, who between them had 20 and a half ploughs.[3]

In 1108 Hugh de Lacy, grandson of Roger, founded an Augustinian Priory at Llanthony in Monmouthshire, which became 'deserted' after attacks during a Welsh rising. It was refounded in 1136 as New Llanthony at Hempsted, one mile to the south-west of Gloucester on the river Severn.[4] Hugh was followed by Walter II, when knight service degenerated into a system of money paid to the king and the de Lacys began to divide the estate into smaller portions. Walter granted 30 acres of woodland at Holme

Dore Abbey as depicted in M. Gibson's *Churches of Dore, Home-Lacy and Hempsted* (1727)

Lacy to his wife's foundation of a nunnery at Aconbury, and in 1225 a further income from his 204 acres of land and his house at Holme Lacy to the Grandmontine brethren at Craswall in the Black Mountains. Other lands were bought by William Fitzwarine who gave them to the White Canons of Lavendon in Buckinghamshire so that they might build and sustain an abbey at Holme Lacy. However, due to the intervention of two bishops, Ralph de Maidstone and Peter de Aquablanca, the abbey was never built.[5] Walter II's son, Gilbert de Lacy, confirmed a grant of land at Mascoit (Maes-coed) near Longtown, a previous gift which the monastery held from Ralph de Scudamore to the monastery of Dore in 1225.[6] A further grant of rent in exchange of land in the manor of Hamme (Holme Lacy) mentions free men and customary tenants both Welsh and English and a grant of the demesne to Craswall Priory.[7]

Walter II, 'worn out by suffering and blind from old age', died in 1241, breaking the family's succession and leaving his 'wasted' inheritance to his granddaughters.[8] The Devereux family were to inherit some land from the de Lacys, giving their name to Devereux Court in Holme Lacy.[9] This later became part of Bower Farm which lies to the north of Holme Lacy parish near Bury Court and adjacent to the church with Wood Court in the Upper Bogmarsh area.[10]

Around 1253 the Bishop of Hereford was able to recover land from the de Lacys and gifted that which included the Holme Lacy manors of Bury Court and Wood Court to

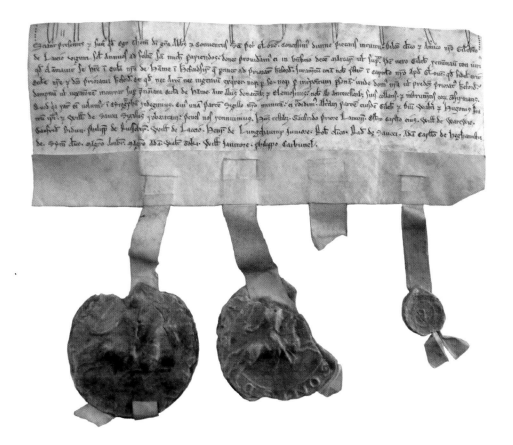

Seals of Walter de Lacy and another member of the family together with a small counterseal on an agreement dated 1285, whereby the Abbot of St Peter's, Gloucester, granted Gilbert de Lacy 20 shillings annually in return for the latter giving up his claim to the church of *Hamme* (the early name of Holme Lacy) (*Hereford Cathedral Archives*)

the Dean and Chapter, who farmed the estate with 24 oxen, 2 draught animals, 1 cart, 4 wagons, 4 ploughs and 4 harrows.[11] During a period of great disturbance caused by the rebellion of Simon de Montfort during the reign of Henry III, the Bishop of Hereford, Peter de Aquablanca, a flamboyant 'foreigner with never a word of English', handed over Holme Lacy manor to the Dean and Chapter, on condition they made a gift of corn every year to the poor at the Bishop's Palace. The manor was then leased from the Dean and Chapter by the abbot of Dore on the same condition. However, due to the disturbed state of the country, managing the land was not easy to carry out. The situation was not helped when the barons, headed by Roger de Clifford, sent a body of armed men to raid Holme Lacy, whereupon the abbot of Dore took fright and sought protection in Hereford, only to find that the bishop, the dean and some of the canons were imprisoned in Eardisley Castle. The abbot rode to the castle, but as there was no help from the cathedral he 'brought off' Roger de Clifford for £42. After this incident the abbot gave up his tenancy, and the bishop, once released from prison, returned to his native Savoy in France.[12]

TOP: Holme Lacy church, as painted by Charles F. Walker in 1860 (*Herefordshire Libraries*)
BOTTOM: Fourteenth-century stalls in Holme Lacy church (*Heather Hurley*)

In 1266 the mill and fishery at Holme Lacy were rented for 240 loads of wheat and rye, and in the late thirteenth century the prior of Grandmontine was requested to repair 'the pond of their mill of Hamme'.[13] During the reign of Edward III a weir at Holme Lacy manor was held by John de Homme when Gilbert de Homme established a chantry to St Mary in the church dedicated to St Cuthbert, with a row of eight

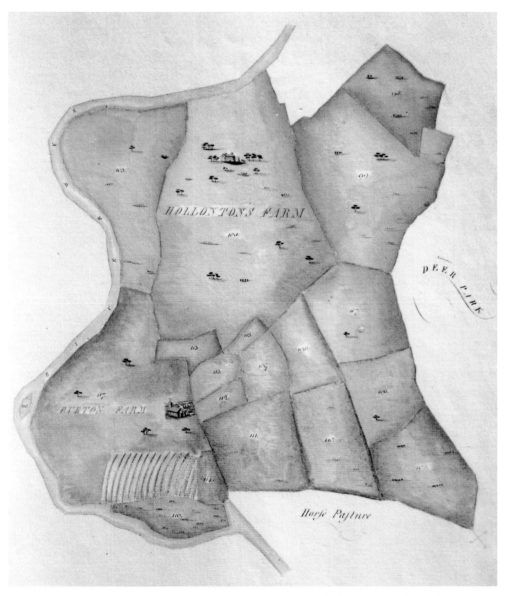

Burton Farm and Hollington as depicted on a map of 1780 (*Kentchurch Archives*)

old stalls for the chantry priests in the Lady Chapel.[14] Only five of the fourteenth-century stalls have survived, with misericords featuring a grotesque head, a dog, a bird, a demon and a man in a tunic.[15] From the end of the thirteenth century, endowing a chantry chapel became a popular way of directing people's piety in place of founding religious houses. (A chantry was a mass recited at the altar for the well-being of the founder during his lifetime, and for the repose of his soul after death. Part of an aisle was commonly used as a chantry – or alternatively, as at Holme Lacy, the South Chapel, enclosed with timber screens, was utilised.)[16]

Remains of the medieval village have been identified around the church and include fish ponds, a pattern of roads and evidence of ridge-and-furrow on land prone to flooding. The remains of this former settlement may represent the site of Bury Court where a later house was known as Burton House. Other remnants from the medieval period are the churchyard cross and various coffin lids in the church.[17] A number of different factors appear to have caused the desertion of medieval villages – land clearance for sheep pasture, change of ownership and economic depression were some, but the Black Death was the most common. The latter ravaged England in

Churchyard cross at Holme Lacy church
(*LOWV 2008*)

1348 and 1349 and is estimated to have swept away at least one third of the population. Another reason for the desertion of the village site at Holme Lacy could simply be due to flooding. Whatever the reason, the Black Death would have affected Holme Lacy through a reduction in the population, including a decrease amongst the clergy.[18] The Registers of John de Trilleck, Bishop of Hereford, record that he was ordered by the Bishop of London to hold special services to avert the threatened pestilence in 1348, and in 1349 he offered thankfulness for the removal of the great plague. Once the plague had ceased the bishop ordered priests without cures to fill the vacancies in churches left vacant by reason of the plague.[19] At Holme Lacy church a vacancy was taken by David de Homme in 1349, who exchanged parishes with Richard Banerton in 1350.[20]

In 1352 there was a writ from officials of the Exchequer to search the records and inform the king whether the manor of Holme Lacy was held by military service and how many knights' service of each lord. The findings recorded numerous entries relating to its tenure from the time of King Henry and naming Hugo, Gilbert and Walter de Lacy until the 26th year of the reign of Edward III.[21] By 1364 the manors of Holme Lacy, Bury Court and Wood Court were leased to Thomas Hakkeluyit from the Dean and Chapter, which granted him the corn crop, the cattle, sheep, implements and utensils, in return for which Thomas had to keep the mill, millpond and weir in good repair and restore the land to good cultivation before the end of the term.[22]

It was through the marriage of Thomas, the son of John Scudamore the third of Rowlestone and Abergavenny, that the manor of Hollanton (Hollington), in the southeast corner of the parish adjoining Bolstone, descended to Thomas's son Philip, the first Scudamore who 'planted himself at Homme' in 1382. At Hollington, on rising ground overlooking the river Wye, Philip founded a 'family of minor gentry', which flourished

ABOVE: 1409 Lease of land in Holme Lacy by the Dean and Chapter to Gilbert Goderyche (*Hereford Cathedral Archives*)

LEFT: Transcription of 1406 gift of Richard Scudamore (*Herefordshire Archives*)

into a powerful and prominent family.[23] Philip and his unnamed first wife produced a son, John, and by his second wife, the widowed Agnes, a younger son named George. In 1406 land at Kilforge in the adjoining parish of Ballingham was granted as a gift by Richard Scudamore, citizen of Hereford, to Philip and others, and in 1409 Philip, George and John Scudamore with a large party of Welshmen raided the house of William Hamme in Holme Lacy in order to right some unspecified wrong. William Hamme was so incensed that he requested King Henry IV to issue a writ summoning them.[24] Names of other Holme Lacy inhabitants during this period have emerged including Gilbert Tyler, Walter Payge, Thomas Gorway, John Walsse, George Gylle, Thomas Philippu, William Abolston, Maud Mason, Walter Jackson, John Granger, Margaret and Gilbert Goderyche, Robert Walyshe, Richard Whittard, John Hommes Lord of Devereaux, Richard Scudamore a steward, Thomas Skydmor and vicars Edward Ion, John Chamberlain and William Andrews.[25]

John, the older son of Philip Scudamore of Hollington, also held the manor of Strangford (ford with the strong current) now in Sellack, and was appointed by Bishop

LEFT: Aconbury church in 2014 (*Heather Hurley*). RIGHT: Aconbury church as painted by Charles F. Walker in 1867 (*Herefordshire Libraries*)

Edmund Lacy to serve as constable of Bishop's Castle. It was his younger brother George who followed his father and held Hollington. He married Elizabeth Burghill (of Burghill in Herefordshire) and expanded the Scudamore lands into Ballingham and Hentland. George's son Philip continued to hold the manor of Hollington which consisted of 140 acres of arable and meadow land, the manor of Bury Court from the Dean and Chapter, Devereux Court, and other lands in Herefordshire, Buckinghamshire and Essex;[26] however, Philip granted his lands at Ballingham and Treaddow in Hentland to his younger brother William who became the first of the Ballingham branch of Scudamores.[27] Around 1442 Philip married Wenllyan Osborne of London and their eldest son Thomas inherited land and tenements from his grandmother Elizabeth, but he died within his father's lifetime. His younger brother William became the heir. His brother Edward, settled in Gloucestershire, and his sister Anne married John Scudamore, a distant cousin from Rowlestone.[28]

William Scudamore of Hollington was born in 1464 and at the age of 24 married Alice Mynors of Treago, situated on the west of the Wye in Herefordshire. William and Alice became the parents of five children named John, Richard, Roger, Mary and Joan. Richard became a Benedictine monk but exchanged his monkish habit for the garb of a secular priest, whilst Roger served as a captain and fought in France. The eldest daughter married and the younger one is presumed to have been the Prioress of Aconbury which formerly stood a few miles from Holme Lacy.[29] The eldest son and heir, John, was born in 1486 at the end of the Wars of the Roses, and just after the crowning of Henry VII. This John Scudamore ultimately became the 'true founder of the fortunes of the Scudamores of Holme Lacy' and forerunner of the 'branch of the ancient stock that had taken firm root in the new soil and begun to assume the proportions of a stately tree'.[30] In 1511, before

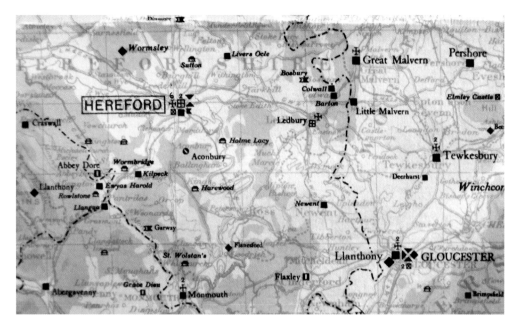

Detail from a Map of Monastic Britain made by the Ordnance Survey in 1950, simplified to remove differences between religious houses closed or abandoned before 1500 and those that survived to the Dissolution. The Hereford place-name is shown within a frame as it was the centre of a see in 1500; Gloucester only became the centre of a see in 1541

KEY

Monks:
Benedictine (including Orders of Grandmont & Tiron)   ■

Cistercian   ▯

Canons:
Augustinian   ◆

Nuns:
Augustinian   ◒

Friars:
Franciscan   ▼
Dominican   ▲
Carmelite   ►

Knights Templar then Hospitaller   ⅀Ⅱ

Monasteries of uncertain Order or foundation, larger cells etc.   ⌂

Hermitages, large chantries etc.   ⏠

Secular Colleges of canons or priests   ⊠

Hospitals and Hospices:
Greater, under religious rule   ⟐

Lesser (net income under £50)   ⳾

Diocesan boundary   — · —

his father, William, died, the young John married Sybil Vaughan of Hergest near Kington after a licence had been granted by Bishop Richard Mayhew for the couple to be married at St Weonard's church.[31] This church features the Mynors' Chapel and was probably chosen because of being in his mother's parish.

Being an ambitious young gentleman, John gradually expanded his properties and lands, and took on many local offices including becoming a Member of Parliament for Herefordshire, High Sheriff of Herefordshire, Steward to the Duchy of Lancaster and Justice of Peace in the counties of Herefordshire and Worcestershire. Presumably due to his reputation he was appointed one of the four Gentlemen Ushers at the court of Henry VIII, an honoured position as a servant to the royal household which led to many later offices both locally and nationally, including 'one of the Esquires for His Highness' as inscribed on his tomb in Holme Lacy church.[32] His local standing and influence as a result of such appointments is almost impossible to investigate.[33]

Being in parliament and with his ear at the royal court it is not surprising that John Scudamore became involved in the early stages of the Reformation and, unlike his distant relatives at Kentchurch, embraced the forthcoming Dissolution. In 1534 Scudamore and his fellow justices were asked by the mayor of Hereford to examine Richard Stopes, a pewterer, who had been reported to Thomas Cromwell for his treasonable words. Scudamore had already found favour with Cromwell over a letter regarding a fight which had taken place between 'a lewd boy of mine' and a servant of Cromwell's, 'a good master of mine', in which he had promised to put the offender in prison for a year if he caught him. It is not known whether the scoundrel was ever caught. After the death of Bishop Booth in 1535, Cromwell appointed Scudamore to prepare leases of the bishop's lands, and ignored a statement from the president of the Council in the Marches who sought to prevent his promotion, 'as he is a gentleman dwelling nigh the welshry and kinned and allied in the same'. In fact Scudamore asked Cromwell whether he should not treat those parts of the Marches annexed to the county as shire ground, adding that 'the people are not well furnished but seem willing to serve the King if need be'.

The next year Scudamore brought a case against Sir Edward Croft, a former sheriff of Herefordshire. He claimed that in April 1534, three days after parliament had finished its sitting, he had obtained a writ for expenses, which he had delivered to Croft at Hereford in June and which the sheriff had executed at Ross in October, but since then Croft had refused to pay him. This had caused him financial loss that he estimated amounted to £20, which represented the amount of his wages for the 154 days that he had spent in attending parliament. Scudamore evidently meant something to Cromwell, for he had placed a circle against his name on a list of nominees for parliamentary vacancies, and also included his name on a list written on the back of a letter of December 1534 understood to be of members having a connection with the Treason Act. Scudamore served on a committee for an Act concerning farms and sheep, and may have sat in the Short Parliament of 1536, in accordance with the king's general request for the return of previous Members, but it is unlikely that he did. As the result of his suit against Croft is unknown, it is impossible to know whether financial considerations deterred him from seeking to prolong his parliamentary career, which was short and probably due to the shire's preference for regular change in its representation.[34]

Many Acts were passed during the 1530s including that for the Dissolution of the Lesser Monasteries in 1536, which enabled small monasteries to be closed if a survey had found them full of corrupt and immoral practices. This started the process of closing hundreds of monasteries, nunneries and friaries. Scudamore, already familiar with the administration of ecclesiastical property and making leases for the bishop in Hereford, was appointed Augmentation Receiver in 1536 for the counties of Herefordshire, Staffordshire, Shropshire and Worcestershire, which led to great rewards from the sale of church lands and the suppression of Dore Abbey.[35] In Herefordshire there was no evidence to indicate that the Church was in a degenerate condition but there were

Hempsted church in 2017
(*Heather Hurley*)

Gift of Hollington in 1538
by Thomas Bodenham of
Rotherwas to Anthony
Hungerford and others
(*Herefordshire Archives*)

signs that it had become tired and listless and had lost its vitality. Life at Hereford Cathedral had hardly changed after the introduction of the Reformation Acts, but the Dissolution of the monasteries and religious houses was not a popular move and did not meet with the approval of the public.[36]

In Gloucestershire the manor of Hempsted continued to be held by Llanthony Priory until it became the first monastery to be suppressed in the county. The Manor of Hempsted with a fishery in the Severn was then granted to Thomas Atkyns. Other lands, tithes and a fishery in the Severn lying in Hempsted, previously belonging to Llanthony Priory, were granted to Arthur Porter for the sum of £723 16s 8d, and later through marriage passed to John Scudamore of Holme Lacy.[37]

Part of Saxton's map of Herefordshire of 1577, showing Kentchurch (*Kynechurch*) near the bottom
(*Birmingham University*)

In 1537 Scudamore reported to Thomas Cromwell that two well-learned lads had
arrived in Ross from Exeter where they had been schoolmasters. One intended to teach
at a school in Ross, which may have led to the re-establishment of the Churchyard
School as a Latin Grammar School.[38]

During the early years of the sixteenth century the largish population at Holme Lacy
was served by a succession of vicars including Henry Warren, whose vicarage was valued
at £8 when John Scudamore was an absentee landowner. He was then living at Wilton
in Bridstow, sometimes referred to as Wylton in Peterstow, except for a short period in
1536 when he was appointed to attend upon the king with 40 men to help counter the
northern rebellion against Henry VIII's religious and fiscal policies.[39] After a lease for
the term of 29 years was made between the Dean and Chapter and John Scudamore for
the manors of Holme Lacy, Bury Court and Wood Court, he was offered the office of
steward to Ballingham manor in 1538.[40] The same year the manor of Hollington with
lands where the Scudamores had been subtenants was gifted from Thomas Bodenham
of Rotherwas to several gentlemen of Holme Lacy. This coincided with John selecting a
suitable site to build Holme Lacy House near Devereux Court (Bower Farm).[41]

8

John Scudamore, Sir James and Sir John Living at Holme Lacy House

Long after their settling at Holme Lacy, the members of this family were in great esteem in the country, court and camp. John Scudamore of Holme Lacy, was High Sheriff of the county in the 16, 21, and 35 of Henry VIII; he married Sybell, daughter of Watkin Vaughan, of Hergist; he lived to a great age and was buried in the Church at Holme Lacy.

Burke's **Visitation of Country Seats and Arms,** *1862*[1]

JOHN Scudamore was appointed by the Crown as an Augmentation Receiver in 1536, so placing him in charge of monastic lands across a number of counties. With this authority John bought nearly all the valuable goods from Dore Abbey and other religious houses. His list of purchases from Dore included building materials such as lead from the roof, household goods, corn wains, livestock and the abbey's gold plate. He also acquired the site of the abbey with certain demesne lands, Gilbert's Hill Wood in Abbeydore and at a later date bought the rectory and tithes. He also received a pension of 50s a year awarded by the Crown, which was used to pay a priest-in-charge at the ruinous Dore Abbey. John's activities at Dore led to many disputes and enquiries, for unlike his namesake at Kentchurch, who remained with the old faith, he welcomed the new Protestantism and profited from the Dissolution.[2] He also purchased lands from the Crown in the adjoining parish of Bolstone where he had served as steward of the manor for the Knights Hospitallers, their property being described as a 'capital messuage or mansion' with meadows, pastures, feeding grounds and two mills on the Wye.[3]

With his growing wealth it is not surprising that John needed a home at Holme Lacy in keeping with his status, but until his new house was built, he remained at Wilton with Sybil his wife and their children. Holme Lacy House – initially called Holm Court, Home Court or Hom House – was built in the newly fashionable brick, traditionally upon the site occupied by the dwelling of the de Lacy family.[4] Scudamore's tall building, built around two courtyards, featured picturesque gables and stone mullions, and from

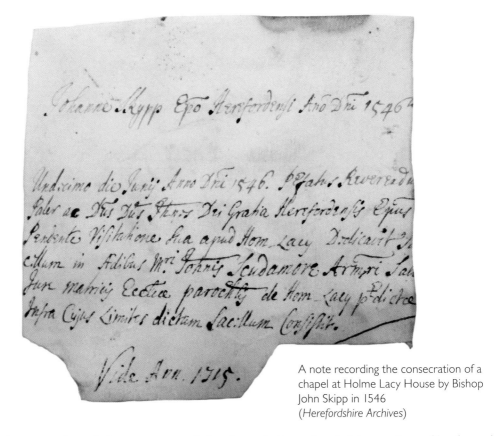

A note recording the consecration of a chapel at Holme Lacy House by Bishop John Skipp in 1546
(*Herefordshire Archives*)

its east and south fronts commanded a view of a 'most bewitching variety of landscape' from its elevated situation overlooking the river Wye. By 1546 the large building was completed when an interior chapel was consecrated by John Skipp, Bishop of Hereford, a keen supporter of the Reformation during the reign of Edward vi,[5] with former painted glass in the house featuring the badges of Edward vi when Prince of Wales.[6] A great gate with a porter's lodge led into the outer court which contained a kitchen, barns and stables, and off which another gate led to the inner court and the main house which comprised a great and little hall, two parlours, a great and little gallery, bed chambers, a study and a press chamber.[7] John also created a paled deer park around his new house.[8]

There are no known dates of the births of John and Sybil's nine children, but it is thought that they were all born before Holme Lacy House was built. The eldest son William finished his education at Oriel College, Oxford and at Lincoln's Inn, and became his father's chief deputy in surveying and disposing of the dissolved monastic properties. The second son Richard followed his elder brother at Oriel College before beginning a colourful and exciting life. Appointed by the Crown as 'Yeoman of the Toils', he was responsible for trapping and snaring wild animals, and in 1541 caught and conveyed 500 deer from Windsor Great Park to Hampton Court Palace. Two years later he super-vised the capture and transportation of 700 fallow deer to Epping Forest. Two younger

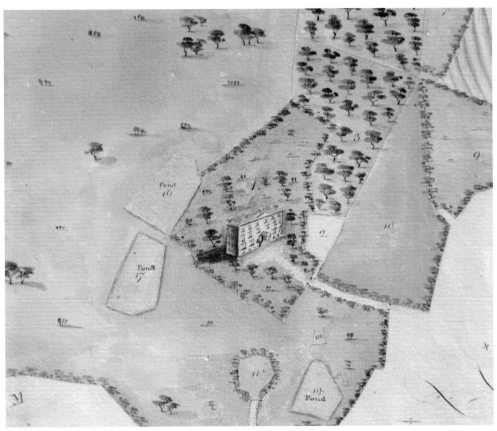

TOP: Holme Lacy House as depicted on a map of 1780 (*Kentchurch Archives*)
BOTTOM: The old part of Holme Lacy House as depicted in Revd Charles Robinson's
A History of the Mansions and Manors of Herefordshire (1872)

ABOVE: Portrait, said to be of Ursula, daughter of the Pakingtons.
TOP RIGHT: Portrait of Sir John Pakington.
BOTTOM RIGHT: Portrait of Lady Pakington
(*Kentchurch Archives*)

brothers were named John and Philip. Their five sisters all married into notable families. Joan, sometimes referred to as Johan, married Thomas Scudamore, son and heir of John Scudamore of Kentchurch, thus forming one connection between the two branches of the Scudamore family. Joan bore no children and died early in life, leaving her widowed husband to remarry (*see Chapter 2*). It is understood that despite the family's involvement with the Reformation, some members remained quietly true to the Catholic faith.[9]

During the first year of Queen Mary's reign in 1553/4, John Scudamore was a member of the Council in the Marches of Wales, an appointment which he owed to his past Catholicism, which had led him to be honoured by the Catholic Queen Mary and her Privy Council, which apparently sought help from him in 'Matters of Speedy Execution'.[10]

Portrait of Sir John in 1569
(*Kentchurch Archives*)

In 1553 John Harford and John Farley granted John Scudamore and his son William the living and advowson of the rectory and church at Fownhope, together with a portion of Strangford tithes (then in Fownhope) and, 'all messuages, tofts etc for a consideration of £101 6s 8d.'[11] William was to marry Ursula, the daughter and coheir of Sir John Pakington of Westwood Park, Worcestershire and after the births of his five children he died in 1560, a few years before his ageing father married Joan Reade, a widow and daughter of William Rudhall of Rudhall near Ross.[12]

During the 1560s John Scudamore was still making transactions with the Dean and Chapter, purchasing woods and selling his 'tithe wool due to him in Strangford, except his tithe lambs' for 46s 8d per year.[13] He remained active in county affairs but unlike his

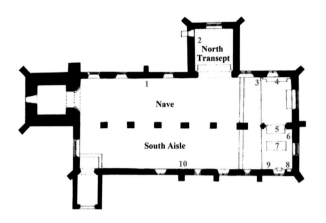

Key for plan:

1 Two hatchments, one with motto *in coelo quies* for Frances, Lady Scudamore, d.1750; and one with motto *Scuto amoris divini* for Frances, Lady Scudamore, d.1716

2 Wall monument to Charles Scudamore-Stanhope, Captain of HMS *Caledonia*, who died on active service in 1871

3 Marble monument to Jane Scudamore, d.1699

4 Large marble monument to James, son of 1st Viscount Scudamore, d.1668, and husband of Jane (no.3)

5 Tomb chest to John, d.1571, and his wife Sybil in alabaster

6 Wall monument to Dorothea, Countess of Chesterfield, d.1923

7 Two tomb chests, one to Frances Fitzroy-Scudamore, d.1749, and her daughter Frances, Duchess of Norfolk, d.1820. The other is to Captain Evelyn Scudamore-Stanhope, d.1925.

8 White marble wall monument to Mary Scudamore-Stanhope, d.1859

9 Elaborate monument to John Scudamore, 1st Viscount Sligo and Baron of Dromore, d.1716.

10 Two hatchments, both with motto *Sola virtus invicta*, for Charles, 11th Duke of Norfolk, d.1815, and his wife Frances, d.1820

TOP: Plan of Holme Lacy church
BOTTOM: The alabaster effigies of John and Sybil Scudamore in Holme Lacy church (*Logaston Press*)

Kentchurch kinsmen he took the Oath of Supremacy in 1569 despite his sympathetic attitude to Catholicism.

Before his death in 1571, he had his own altar tomb erected.[14] There is evidence suggesting that the tomb once stood over his grave in the 4th and 5th vault under Holme Lacy church, but the elaborate tomb now stands in the chancel. It features alabaster effigies of John in sixteenth-century armour, and his wife Sybil in a plain gown, on a base depicting the arms of the Scudamore and Vaughan families. The inscription, now indecypherable, was copied in 1822 and reads 'Here lyeth John Scudamore esquire sometyme one of the four gentlemen ushers unto our late sovereign Lord King Henry the eight, afterwards admitted one of the Esquires for his highness body & Sybil his wife. John deceased [...] in the year of our Lord God one thousand five hundred [...] praying them that passeth hereby of their charity to say for their soules a paternoster and an ave'.[15]

As John Scudamore's eldest son William had predeceased him, Holme Lacy passed to William's eldest son, John. One of his uncles, Richard, William's brother, attended his father's funeral but died a few years later. Another uncle, George, became the ancestor of the Treworgan branch in Llangarron and uncle Rowland was appointed to the office of Gaoler and Keeper of Prisoners in several counties in England and Wales, and purchased Caradoc in Sellack.[16] Grandson John had been educated at the Inner Temple and married Eleanor, the daughter of the powerful and influential Sir James Croft of Croft Castle in Herefordshire. As his father had died, the wardship of the young Scudamore had been given to Sir James in order to further this marriage between the Scudamores and Crofts, which developed into a life-long relationship of patronage, friendship and an introduction to the Court of Queen Elizabeth.[17] During a period of political and religious intrigue John Scudamore's life blossomed at Court under Sir James Croft, the controller of the royal household, as well as at Holme Lacy.

John and Eleanor's five children comprised the eldest son Henry, educated at the Middle Temple and arrested with other friends on the order of the Privy Council for causing a riot in Ross; the second son John who was ordained as a priest; James, who died before his father; Ursula who married into the Walwyn family, and the unruly Alice who died as a child. The three sons received their initial education at Holme Lacy from Thomas Holford, who became a Catholic priest. After Eleanor's death in 1569 it was rumoured that John Scudamore, aided by Sir James Croft, entered into a secret marriage with Mary Shelton the queen's second cousin and a 'gentlewoman of the Queen's private chambers'. This marriage angered the queen because she disliked her ladies of the bedchamber to be married. Scudamore's attendance and influence at Court grew and led him to become an Usher to the queen, a Gentleman Pensioner, a Standard Bearer of the Pensioners and finally to be knighted.[18] Sir John Scudamore managed to keep his religious beliefs unclear, so weaving through the various factions whilst remaining loyal enough for the Privy Council to seek his advice over controversial cases.[19] As a friend of John Bodley, Sir John made a donation to the Bodleian Library for purchasing a manuscript and books for the scholars at Oxford University.[20] His marriage to Mary Shelton was childless, but she got on well with her stepchildren and 'interceded with her husband on behalf of his wayward eldest son and, known as a 'barbarous brazen-faced woman', continued to serve the queen until Elizabeth died.[21]

Although Sir John's demands at Court were great, in Herefordshire he served as a Member of Parliament, a Justice of the Peace, Deputy Lieutenant, Sheriff, *Custos Rotulorum* (keeper of records) and a steward (the official agent for the lord of the manor who usually presided over the manorial courts) for many places including Hereford, Ross and Ledbury. At Ledbury he also served on the committee of a hospital, presumably that of St Katherine's Hospital. At Ross, the town with its market and quarterly fairs had developed into an important thoroughfare that relied on access over a dangerous ford and ferry crossing over the Wye to Wilton in Bridstow. Sir John

Scudamore was instrumental in replacing the crossing with a bridge and for compensating Charles Brydges of Wilton Castle for the loss of the ferry tolls. The necessary Wilton Bridge Act, passed in 1597, established an amount of £840 that was to be collected from the Herefordshire Hundreds by some of the county's leading men, including Thomas Coningsby, William Rudhall, Herbert Croft, John Kyrle and John Scudamore.[22]

Towards the end of the sixteenth century Sir John's uncle Rowland purchased Cary Craddock from John Abrahall. This estate in Sellack, often known simply as Caradoc, consisted of a messuage, tofts, 2 gardens, 40 acres of land, 50 acres of meadow, 600 acres of pasture and 120 acres of woodland.

The house was in a bad state of repair, which Rowland remodelled to contain a hall, great parlour, a little parlour, dairy, bed chambers, servants' quarters, kitchen, a cider mill and a remaining kitchen, hall, chamber and barn from the original building, which must have been in better repair. From the Dean and Chapter of Hereford Cathedral he leased the Canon Barn, a barn that once stood near Sellack church and was used to store grain for the Canon's Bakehouse in Hereford. A clause in the lease stated that the 'barn and chancel of the parish church were to be kept in good repair'.[23]

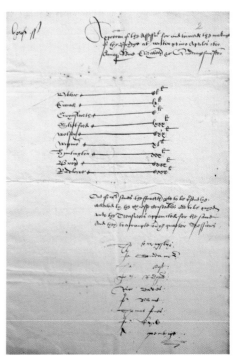

As the seventeenth century approached, Sir John appears to have led a quieter and more retired life at Holme Lacy, where he was joined by his third son, James. James had made his name as a soldier in 1596 under the Earl of Essex at Cadiz in Spain, where he was knighted. As a talented horseman he gained such a reputation on the field and in tournaments that it is said that Edmund Spenser used his name for a knightly character in his epic poem *The Faerie Queen*, published in parts between 1590 and 1596. Sir James appeared at Court as a Gentleman Pensioner and performed at many tilts before the queen at Whitehall between 1596 and 1600.[24] From this date James returned to Holme Lacy where he joined his father in

TOP: A record of the money collected for Wilton Bridge in 1600 (*British Library*)
BOTTOM: A drawing of Caradoc c.1820s, as depicted by James Gregory Peene in *Churches and Mansions in South Herefordshire* (*Herefordshire Libraries*)

running a stud and a riding academy where horses were bred for military use and riders trained to be 'brave cavaliers'. Due to his renowned horsemanship he became Captain of Militia Horse, a local position supplying horses, tack and men for the cavalry from horse-owners of a high social standing. Sir James was elected in 1604 as Member of Parliament for Herefordshire, served as a Justice of the Peace and was appointed as the deputy *Custos Rotulorum* for the county of Hereford during the reign of James I.[25]

The first marriage of Sir James was to Mary Houghton, who lost her life in childbirth in 1598. In the following year James married another Mary, the daughter of Sir Thomas Throckmorton of Tortworth, Gloucestershire. It was not a happy union although it produced nine children, including the eldest son John, who, due to his father predeceasing him, became the heir to Holme Lacy. The second son James was a captain in the cavalry and whilst serving in the army in the Low

Portrait of Sir James Scudamore
(*Kentchurch Archives*)

Countries was involved in a duel fought on horseback and died soon after. The third son Barnabas became infamous during the Civil War (*see Chapter 9*), and the eldest daughter Mary married Sir Giles Brydges of Wilton Castle. The troubled relationship between Sir James and his wife did not improve. She complained that her father-in-law had driven her from Holme Lacy, but that after being persuaded to return, he would not have her back so she went to live with a kinsman. Here she was cruelly treated by her son from her first marriage, who clapped her in irons and starved her into submission. She managed to escape with help from her mother whom Sir James then prosecuted for her 'evil offices' between him and his wife, a woman known to have a 'badly confused' mind.[26]

One event which involved Sir James was an unpleasant incident that took place in 1605 during the Whitsun Riots in the Welsh Borders. It all started when a Recusant died and was refused a burial by the Anglican Vicar of Allensmore. The Catholic community was furious and held a burial by torchlight with all due Catholic ceremony, news of which reached the Bishop's Palace. The bishop issued a warrant and the High Constable of Hereford set off and arrested three men. A struggle then arose when 40 or 50 armed men appeared and outnumbered the constable and his party, who immediately returned to Hereford and informed the bishop of the details, who in turn sent news of the incident to the Privy Council. King James I declared in a speech that there was 'no longer any need to spare the blood of Recusants' and that Herefordshire men could set an example, but there was a reluctance to use force for fear of provoking a more serious uprising. However the bishop, accompanied by Sir James Scudamore and Sir Roger Bodenham, set out for Treville near Allensmore where almost 100 armed Catholic sympathisers assembled to ambush them; but as the magistrates were summoned to arrest the rioters they scattered in fear and hid in the Monnow valley until the Sunday when they attended Mass at the Darren in Garway, expecting more trouble. It was not until mid-week that the Justices, Sir James Scudamore and other prominent men with a strong force searched the Darren and adjoining villages, making a 35-mile sweep along the borders. Many altars, images, books and relics were discovered in the deserted villages from where the population had fled across the border into Wales. Scudamore acted with discretion but gained a reputation of being the 'most ready and faithful' of the county magistrates in the suppression of Popery.[27]

In Bolstone parish a place called Gannah (a name derived from 'gamen' meaning game) was probably the site of a hunting lodge established by the Scudamores. It adjoined a deer park, a large fish-pond and an eyrie for hawks, so providing all the facilities required for hunting within the wider Holme Lacy Park. The seventeenth-century Bolstone Court and its ancient church also formed part of the expanding Scudamore estate.[28] In the adjoining parish of Ballingham, William Scudamore, a close relative of the Scudamores of Holme Lacy, had built a fine stone house of two storeys bearing a datestone of 1602 over the porch. William married Sarah, the daughter of Anthony Kyrle of Walford, and their daughter Penelope married a kinsman of the Scudamores. When Penelope became pregnant for the fourth time after losing two infants and having a third sickly child, distraught and weak she pleaded with the curate of Ballingham to forgo the Lenten diet that forbade any kind of 'meat'. Her request was granted for her and her sickly son on medical grounds:

> To all to whom this writing shall come and apportion. I Richard Charles Clark Curate of the Parish Church of Ballingham do send greetings in our Lord God and ... whereas Penelope Scudamore, the wife of John Scudamore of Ballingham, Esq. being now with child, and having borne three children before this time with great sickness and danger that two of ye said three children were borne dead and ye third a very weak & sickly child, and that ye said Penelope is at this present sick and cannot eat fish & such other things as one appointed to be eaten on fish days without much danger to herself and the child she now breedeth, now know ye that I the said Richard Charles tending ye safety and health of ye said Penelope and of her son John Scudamore now living who is at this present a very weak child and sick have given and granted, and by those presents do give and grant licence and liberty generally and respectively to ye said Penelope & John her said son as ... by the laws and statutes of this realm of England I beg to eat all sorts of flesh, Beef & Veale excepted, during the continuance of the general sickness of the said Penelope and John.[29]

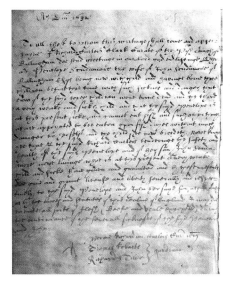

LEFT: The text granting Penelope Scudamore the right to eat meat during Lent on medical grounds (*Herefordshire Archives*). ABOVE: Bolstone church in 1837 (*Herefordshire Libraries*). BELOW: Ballingham Hall, built in 1602, in a photo of 1909 (*Kentchurch Archives*)

By 1612 Sir James was so concerned about his health that he travelled to Bath to seek advice and take the waters, and as his health improved he was able to stand for election again in 1614 at the age of 46. The government appointed him to eight committees and named him as one to consider a bill 'repealing the Crown's power to legislate for Wales by ordnance'. But he became disillusioned with parliament and reported to his father that 'I can write you no comfort of the hope of any good in this Parliament', claiming that there was a fear and danger to the king and kingdom. Three years later Sir James was appointed onto the Council in the Marches, which he had previously

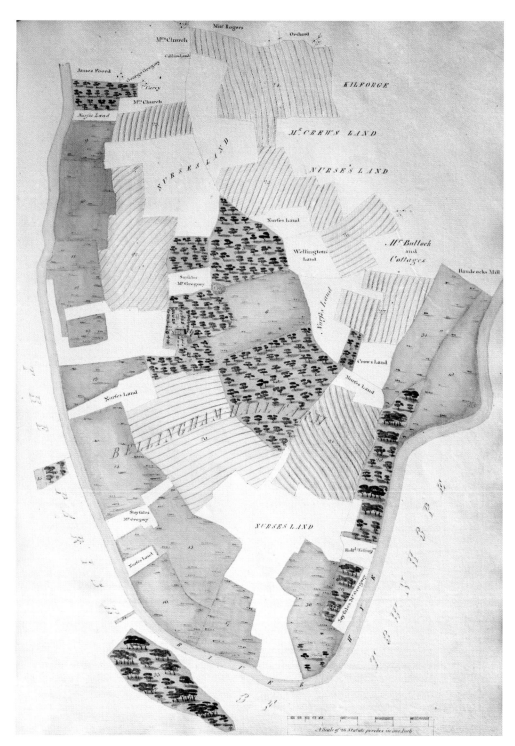

Scudamore lands in Ballingham as depicted on a map of 1780 (*Kentchurch Archives*)

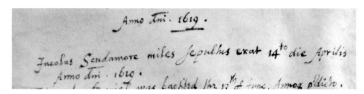

TOP: The burial record of
Sir James in 1619, in the
Parish Register
(*Herefordshire Archives*)

MIDDLE: The opening text
of Sir James' will of 1619
(*The National Archives*)

BOTTOM: The burial
record of Sir John in 1623,
in the Parish Register
(*Herefordshire Archives*)

been against. After all this political activity, and with his health deteriorating once
again, in 1618 he made another visit to his doctors in Bath. After purging, bleeding and
bathing the doctors declared they had lessened the pain in his legs, but he nevertheless died the following year. Sir James left a personal estate of £21,000, a gold chain to
his father, a ring valued at £5 to his wife, and his interest in an 'iron-mill and furnace
built at Piddork (?) a mill at Linton' to his eldest daughter Mary. His armour, sword
and pistols were inherited by his eldest son and a horse from his stud was bequeathed
to the family lawyer.[30]

Similar to the Scudamores of Kentchurch Sir James had invested in iron-making, an
industrial activity generally sponsored by local landowners during the sixteenth and seventeenth centuries. The Linton forge is somewhat obscure and understood to have been
based either at Steelworks Farm in Gorsley where a quantity of slag has been identified,
or at a field called the Furnace where blast furnace slag and top slag has been found.
The Steelworks site lies near Linton Wood on the Eli Brook and continued to be in use
throughout the seventeenth century.[31] John Kyrle and the Foleys also had an interest in
this site where steel was made from iron by the cementation process, by which bars of
iron were heated in a sealed vessel with charcoal all in a solid state. Furnace field is situated near Lynders Wood which was once associated with the Scudamores.[32]

Mary, the wife of Sir James, survived him, and his father Sir John lived a few more
years and died at the age of 81 and was buried at Holme Lacy. Monuments of these three
Scudamores are not displayed in Holme Lacy church, but the frail parish registers reveal

Lord Scudamore's bed of carved oak and covered in red damask. The bed is now in the National Trust's Beningbrough Hall in Yorkshire (*Kentchurch Archives*)

their burials – Sir James on 14 April 1619 and Sir John on 14 April 1623. When the vaults were checked in 1822 the scribe recorded that there was no appearance of any vault for Sir James and his first wife. Ground covered by a flagstone was therefore opened up near the north wall at the west end of the 8th vault, but as there was no sign of a further vault it was immediately closed.[33]

Sir John's eldest son, Henry, had predeceased him in 1591, as had his third son James. The rather elusive second son (another John) had, for a while, been employed as a confidential secretary to Sir Francis Walsingham, Queen Elizabeth's 'spymaster' (perhaps best known for his part in the trial and execution of Mary, Queen of Scots). Walsingham sent John to watch and keep an eye on a young nobleman from Derbyshire called Anthony Babington who was intent on assassinating Queen Elizabeth, John helping to uncover the plot.[34] He had, however, subsequently gone abroad, joined the Catholic faith and became ordained as a priest, leading a strange and unconventional life before returning to England. He apparently distributed devotional articles said to have been blessed by the Pope, and was himself arrested on charges of involvement in a Popish plot, but was released. He is one of the few Scudamores whose presence and features in his younger days were described: 'a tall man aged 30, long-visaged, his nose long and thick, his beard stubbed, round cut and somewhat long, of a dark colour. He holdeth his head a little down, his cloak and breeches were near a peach colour, his stocking orange tawny'. After the deaths of his brother and father he disappeared into obscurity without a mention in either of their wills.[35]

Whilst this John should have succeeded to Holme Lacy, instead it passed to Sir John's grandson through the legal channels of Chancery, and is recorded at Holme Lacy in 1624 in a document headed 'Release and Confirmation of the manor of Holme Lacy ... and all other manors of Sir John Scudamore decd., and Sir James Scudamore' to the grandson.[36]

Portrait of Viscount John Scudamore (*Kentchurch Archives*)

9

Sir John 1st Viscount – Civil War, Holme Lacy, Dore Abbey and Hempsted

> The remarkable studious, and sober, and pious, and hospitable
> Life he led, made him respected and esteemed by all good Men;
> and especially by Bishop Laud, who generally visited him in his
> going to, and returning from his Diocese of St. David's; and
> found his Entertainment as kind and full of Respect, as ever
> he did from any Friend... Mr Scudamore's Interest in his native
> Country was so eminent, that he was unanimously chosen one
> of the members of Parliament for the County of Hereford, in his
> one and twentieth year. The same year he was created Baronet.
> *Matthew Gibson, 1727*[1]

A T Holme Lacy, Sir John Scudamore was succeeded by his grandson John, the son of Sir James who predeceased his father. John, born in 1600, became a most respected and well-educated gentleman known for his charm and grace of manner, who became the first Scudamore to be created a baronet. Apart from being born into what was then seen as the 'most prominent' family in Herefordshire, he inherited a taste for scholarship from his father and grandfather, and from his earliest years held deep religious feelings which strengthened throughout his life.[2] As a young man he swiftly completed his early education: first under a 'domestic tutor', then at Magdalen College, Oxford in 1616, and finally at the Middle Temple in 1617 (when aged just 17) before he obtained a licence 'to travel in Foreign Parts for his better Experience and Knowledge of the Languages'. He wrote an account of his travels in three manuscript volumes which were published and sold in the nineteenth century.[3] The illness and death of his father, Sir James, brought him home in 1619, and the following year he was created a baronet by a patent dated 1 June. The reason for this is unclear, though it may have been due to his association, whilst at Oxford, with Bishop William Laud who had influence at Court and also with the Duke of Buckingham who was the chief administrator of patronage during the reign of James I. Buckingham was unpopular with the public and Parliament due to his power

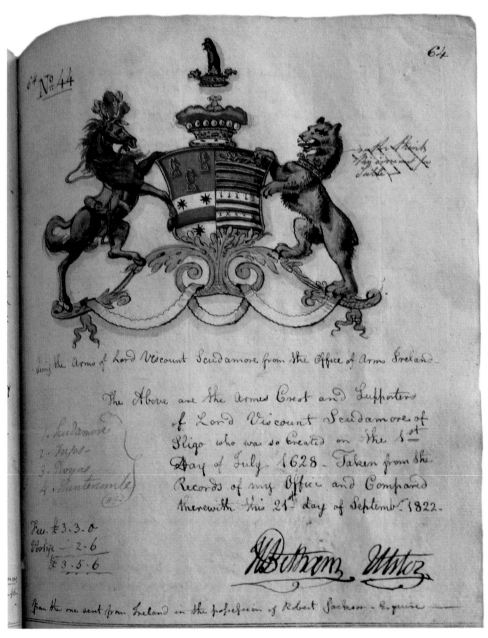

Arms of Viscount Lord Scudamore in 1628 as depicted in Collections of Herefordshire MSS
(*Herefordshire Archives*)

as a Court favourite, his erratic foreign policy and his disorganised command of poorly equipped men at Cadiz in Spain and La Rochelle in France.[4]

As a young teenager in 1614 John had married Elizabeth, the only daughter and heiress of Sir Arthur Porter of Llanthony,[5] Gloucestershire. The dowry consisted of considerable

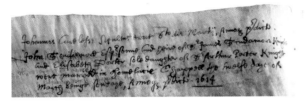

LEFT: Parish Register record of the marriage of John to Elizabeth Porter in 1614 (*Herefordshire Archives*)
RIGHT: Porter monument transcription, in Ralph Bigland's *Monumental and Genealogical Collections*, 1791

property in Gloucestershire including lands and tithes of Hempsted, which lay on the Severn near Gloucester.[6] Elizabeth's family had profited from the suppression of the monasteries as receivers of the lands of Llanthony Priory near Gloucester.[7] The marriage took place at the chapel in Holme Lacy House and, when John was in Herefordshire, the couple took residence at Caradoc in Sellack, the home of his great-uncle Rowland Scudamore. During the first few years of their marriage four infants were born but were buried before they reached a year in age. Whilst his grandfather was still alive and in a position of influence, John was appointed Captain of Horse in Herefordshire, a member of the Council in the Marches of Wales, and stood as the Member of Parliament for Herefordshire from 1620. At a young age John was frequently the host of Bishop Laud as he travelled to and from his diocese at St David's, and their correspondence shows a degree of love and affection between them. His other great friend was the Duke of Buckingham who had been drawn by John's qualities of 'address and abilities'.[8]

His grandfather Sir John died in 1623 at the great age of 81, and as his heir the young Sir John split his time between Caradoc and Holme Lacy, now the base of an extensive estate of 13,000 acres in Herefordshire and 1,840 acres in Worcestershire. Here the couple fortunately produced another son, James, who, out of nine children born to John and Elizabeth, was one of only two who survived into adulthood.

As a result of a family connection with one of the governors of the new colony of Virginia, John, before his grandfather died, had joined him in becoming an 'adventurer' in the Virginia Company, a trading company chartered by James I with the aim of helping to colonise the eastern coast of North America. Despite increasing prosperity, the role of the company became the subject of dispute between its shareholders and the king, who was unsympathetic towards the trend to popular government and of the colony's efforts to grow tobacco. After an investigation the Virginia Company was dissolved in 1624 and the two Johns had no further involvement in North America.[9]

Despite his full responsibility for Holme Lacy and its estate, his parliamentary duties, the distractions at Court and of London Society, Sir John still managed regularly to study history and theology, and follow his strong religious beliefs until his health began to fail. Only then did his friend Laud persuade him to take a rest from his studies and his hospitable life.[10] John returned to Herefordshire to stand in the Herefordshire election of 1625 but he failed to win and was forced to seek election at

Hereford. He won, but this success did not please him as this was only the third occasion that a Scudamore had not been returned for the county seats during the last 50 years. The same year King Charles succeeded to the throne and John became a loyal and devoted friend of the king, who later elevated him to the Irish Peerage as Baron Dromore and Viscount Scudamore of Sligo even though he had no estates or connection with Ireland.[11] By 1626 John's finances were under strain due to the marriages of four of his sisters – Ann, Elizabeth, Penelope and Frances – to various dignitaries. He also had to settle debts incurred by his mother and an unnamed uncle, and to cover these costs he sold his Worcestershire estates.[12] In 1626 John also received a letter from the Privy Council demanding he arrest two priests found 'lurking about the county and causing much mischief'. Bishop Godwin was determined to search for them with John's help, and one was found hiding at the Bodenham family's property at Rotherwas whilst the other appears to have escaped capture.[13]

The Scudamore tradition of martial courage and horsemanship was inherited by John who formed ideas for a more effective County Horse Troop, as set out in the draft of a speech intended to be used in 1627. He formed his company of 65 trained men and divided them by social distinction, with the gentry riding their own horses as a cavalry troop and the yeomen trained as foot soldiers. However, despite his enthusiasm the musters were not well attended.[14] In 1627 John supplied horses to the Duke of Buckingham for an expedition to Île de Ré in France and the following year joined the duke as a volunteer at Portsmouth to undertake a proposed expedition to La Rochelle, but outside an inn called the Spotted Dick, the unpopular duke was assassinated by a fellow officer, which put an end to the expedition. This unpleasant incident upset John, who stayed on and attended to the burial of his friend and reported the news to Bishop Laud. On his return John decided not to stand for re-election and put his energies into local matters.[15]

Meanwhile, the Ballingham branch of the Scudamore family began to rise to more prominence in national and local affairs by marrying into the Holme Lacy branch and receiving baronetcies. John of Ballingham had married Penelope, the daughter of Sir James of Holme Lacy in 1625 when two grants of rent were charged in trust, one to Sara, John's mother, and the other to the intended wife of John Scudamore of Ballingham.[16] After his marriage John of Ballingham travelled to Europe, was created a baronet but was killed in a duel in Bristol. With the later deaths of his sons, Sir John 2nd Baronet and Sir Barnaby 3rd Baronet, the representation of the family passed to another line when the title of baronetcy became extinct and Ballingham manor was eventually purchased by the Scudamores of Holme Lacy.[17]

The Carey islands in the river Wye at Ballingham had provided a natural site for a corn mill that had existed since at least the thirteenth century, and in 1627 the site had been chosen by partners Sir John Kyrle of Much Marcle, Sir John Scudamore of Holme Lacy and William Scudamore of Ballingham for an iron forge operated from the opposite side of the river at Fawley. Articles of Agreement were made and the forge

The site of the iron forge at Carey on the River Wye (*Landscape Origins of the Wye Project*)

An account of moneys paid out for carpenters and labourers at Carey Mill between 31 May and 28 June 1628 (*The National Archives*)

Carey forge accounts relating to cords of timber acquired in 1631 (*The National Archives*)

was completed in 1629 at the cost of £632 2s 9d. 'The Charge of making a ton of Bar Iron at Carey Forge' in 1630 was 15s 8d. The iron was transported to Bristol where smiths produced nails, horseshoes, tools, weapons and agricultural implements.[18] This was just one of several forges now operating on the lower Wye, and with concern over the amount of timber being felled in the Wye valley and Forest of Dean to fuel the industry, rioters protested about the loss of timber and inclosure of woods in the Forest of Dean. Aware of these riots, as their source of fuel ran low the Scudamore and Kyrle partnership tried to relocate the forge to Holme Lacy, but without success.[19]

This was a brief foray into industrial production, for John Scudamore of Holme Lacy was more concerned with religious beliefs as professed in rituals, and bore, from an early age, a guilt at having inherited monastic lands which now left him with a wish to do ser-

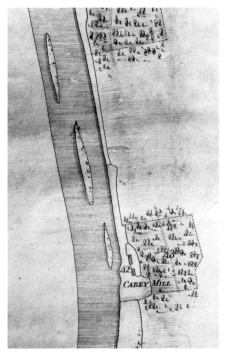

Map of Kings Caple c.1797 showing Carey Mill (*courtesy of Elwyn Brooke*)

vice to the Church. Guided by his friend Bishop Laud, he began by providing Holme Lacy church with an altar cloth, two silver flagons, one silver chalice and two silver patens, together with an iron chest with the traditional three locks, in which to keep them all safe. (Unfortunately, a few years later some church plate was stolen by one of the churchwardens, who fled to France and, suffering from self-pity, died in extreme misery.) John set about repairing the church, paving the floor, ceiling the roof and providing neat new seats for the parishioners. The tithes were another of his concerns, and as received two-thirds of the tithes he gifted them to the church for the support of the parish priest.[20] This was enabled by a License of Mortmain (dead hand of the church) which also allowed the release of the tithes to the churches at Hempsted, Abbeydore and Bolstone in 1631.[21]

Still burdened by guilt and also seeking to find a reason for the tragic loss of his infants, which caused his wife Elizabeth considerable grief, he decided to rebuild the ruined church at Abbeydore. The church was in such bad condition that the curate had to read prayers under one of the remaining arches to prevent his prayer book from getting wet. Accounts survive of the expenditure detailing the work carried out in the body of the church, the 'steeple' (then meaning gables) and the chancel, with sums paid to the masons, carpenters, tillers and others, and costs of stone, timber, tiles and ironwork.[22] The church was thereby transformed into a fine building with everything needed for Divine Service, including a beautiful screen, altar-piece and a stained-glass east window. The ancient altar had been buried in the ruins, then dug up and used for salting meat and making cheese, but was 'strangely' recovered by Scudamore and set upon three pillars supporting the twelve-foot long and four-foot wide stone. Three years later the consecration took place on Palm Sunday 22 March – the anniversary of John's baptism.[23] At the same time that John was busy rebuilding Abbeydore church he was enthusiastically involved with promoting the collection of funds for Laud's project to repair St Paul's Cathedral, and personally contributed £66 13s 4d.[24]

John inherited Caradoc from his great-uncle Rowland who died in 1630. According to the inventory, Caradoc was sparsely furnished although there were plenty of hogsheads of cider in the cellar, grain and livestock in the barn and a further stock of cider together with a fat ox, two market horses, a nag, 380 sheep, fodder and wains in the mill house. Rowland left silver plate, pewter dishes, his linen – in a trunk located in the Scudamore Chamber – and his wearing apparel, which included a black velvet coat and 'four paire of hatts'.[25] John and Elizabeth were still partly living at Caradoc and in 1631 a son named Rowland was born but sadly died the following year. With only one sickly child surviving, the parents were granted a licence by Richard Pritchard, the Vicar of Sellack, to allow their seven-year-old son James to eat flesh on prohibited days due to his sickness and infirmity. This was a similar request to that previously made by the wife of John Scudamore of Ballingham (*see Chapter 8*).[26]

By 1632 it appears that Holme Lacy had become the favourite place for the Scudamores to reside whilst in Herefordshire, described as 'the Lord Scudamore's ... stately and fair building ... sweetly seated on the hanging of a hill'.[27] During 1632 John Scudamore's steward kept a detailed account of all payments, which included repairs and improvements made to the house and grounds. A waterworks was installed to provide a supply of water, a wood house, offices, new thatched stables and a cider house were built, household furniture was purchased from London, and in the grounds a bowling green and a terrace walk were constructed. An impressive amount was also spent on a variety of wearing apparel. Travelling costs and delivery of letters were noted, but with only one mention of contact with the Scudamores at Kentchurch when 6d was paid for the footboy going there. Many charitable gifts were made to the poor and to churchwardens, which led to John becoming known as Good Lord Scudamore. That the family enjoyed a little light relief is shown by the gambling losses incurred at playing cards and shuffleboard. Against this, three funeral costs were recorded: one for the infant Rowland buried at Holme Lacy, another for John's mother Mary buried in Berkshire, and the third for his uncle George Scudamore of Treworgan at Llangarron.[28]

It must have been during 1632 that John Scudamore started to show an interest in producing cider, as there are entries in the accounts for 'carrying 6 hogsheads of sydar to London', 'for bringing down from London a dozen and half of bottles', '2 dozen and half of quart bottles', '1 dozen and half of pint bottles', '6 dozen of Corkes' and 'a lock for

ABOVE: An early cider press, as depicted in Hugh Stafford's *Treatise on Cider-Making* of 1753

LEFT: Redstreak apples, as depicted in the *Herefordshire Pomona* of 1876–1885 (*Logaston Press*)

BELOW: Orchards at Tump Farm, Holme Lacy, in 2008 (© *Landscape Origins of the Wye project*)

the sydar house door'. The cider house or cellar was situated in the park where water was available from nearby springs.[29] John is credited with introducing the Redstreak apple, originally called the Scudamore-crab, which he grafted and propagated to produce such a fine cider that its reputation reached London, to such effect that Charles I is reported to have preferred cider to the best wines. John was one of the first producers to bottle cider, as the process of making bottles from strong dark glass had just been invented by Sir Kenelm Digby in the Forest of Dean after his earlier experiments in London.[30] The bottles were stopped with corks and when the cork was drawn the drinker was regaled with the delightful nose of the Redstreak cider.[31] John introduced a number of cattle from Holland into Herefordshire. They were distinctively marked with red bodies and white faces and cross-bred with the local cattle. With selected breeding this led to the famous Hereford breed that was popular with the gentry, but the foreign animals with their large appetites did not impress the hard-working tenants.[32]

After a brief interval in the rural industries of cider and cattle, together with improving his home and landscaping his grounds, John was unexpectedly appointed by Charles I to serve as Ambassador to France due to Laud's patronage.[33] In 1635 he set out for France recording his transportation costs:

> *Myself and wife at two several times from Holme Lacy to London*
> *Myself and company from Greenwich to St Denis by way of Calais,*
> *Being 12 nights, including gifts to gards, drummers etc in towns* .   *£353*
> *Two carts for apparel. Etc necessary to be carried with me, being uncertain*
> *at the parting of my Barke from Greenwich where and when my first*
> *Audience would be, with horses of relay for part of my family*
> *Horses transported in three barkes and shaloopes for my company and goods*
> *Shipping and unshipping*
> *Goods with part of my family by long sea from Greenwich to Paris*
> *Goods from Holme Lacy to London* .   .   .   .   *£244*[34]

His years in France were not entirely satisfactory due to clashes of personality, political intrigue and religious conflict, which included shocking the Huguenots by introducing an altar in the embassy chapel. While in France he kept further accounts of his purchases and travels, his costly dress for formal occasions, bills of fare of the dinners, writing materials, postage and the purchase of valuable books.[35] John was joined by his wife Elizabeth, who had just given birth to her second daughter Mary. While in France in 1637 she gave birth to a son, who tragically died during a plague outbreak in Paris the following year.[36]

On the termination of his three-year appointment as ambassador in 1638/9, John returned to his estates in England, which now included properties at Petty France in London, Holme Lacy and Caradoc in Herefordshire and Llanthony in Hempsted, Gloucestershire.[37] John's steward at Holme Lacy continued to enter expenses in a series of account books detailing further work on the gardens and bowling green, carriage of bottled cider to London, generous gifts to the poor and needy, cost of food, wine and spices, wages to his workmen and a record of one year's income from his Herefordshire estates totalling £3,232 15s 7d. During this quiet period, it is claimed that John experimented in improving his cider by introducing cider fruit brought back by him from Normandy which was famed for its quality cider. John replaced the old and ruinous Holme Lacy vicarage with a handsome building near the church, for the cost of £400 or £500. Built between 1639 and 1643, the new vicarage replaced a building previously described as a 'dwelling house, barn, stable and other outhouses' at Holme Lacy, although there is also a puzzling record of the vicarage rents being termed as two 'founded in the Close of the Cathedral'.[38]

As John had been welcomed home so warmly by his friends and tenants and been granted the honour of serving as High Steward of Hereford City and Cathedral, in response he celebrated Christmas by keeping an 'open house' at Holme Lacy in a truly magnificent style between 23 December and 11 January. The lavish meals consisted of every type of meat, poultry, fish and game washed down with hogsheads of cider and beer, gallons of sack, bottles of claret and pints of Muscatel and white wine. The cooks were busy preparing pastries and fruit dishes with spices and nuts, the storehouse was brimming with delicacies and many loads of wood and coal were piled high for the fires. John presented gifts to the musicians, the singing boys, the cooks and kitchen staff and to the assistant brewer. Hay, oats and peas were provided in the stables for the guests' horses and a smith was on hand for shoeing. This extravagant Christmas Festival cost John a total of £338 3s 2d.[39]

By 1640 John and Elizabeth were just 40 with their two surviving children James aged 16 and young Mary, only five. James had accompanied his parents to France where he was educated under a private tutor, learning to fence, dance, read Greek, Latin and French before completing his education at St John's College, Oxford. During this period he kept an untidy and almost illegible account book, since badly damaged by damp.[40]

Further estate records show that daily life in the country continued despite the spirit of revolt caused by growing political tension between the king and members of parliament which was to result in the Civil War between king and Parliament. During the early years of the war Holme Lacy House escaped any direct involvement and Scudamore, a true royalist, made sure he was prepared with a supply of arms, ammunition, powder, horsemen's petronels (firearms used by cavalry), pikes and clubs, and that the larders were stacked with provisions.[41] John, however, was in Hereford when it was captured by Sir William Waller, who treated him with courtesy, ordering him to keep to his lodgings. Prior to being sent to London to appear before Parliament, John was granted a pass requiring all soldiers 'to permit the Lord Scudamore with his train to pass their guards'.[42]

At his home in London at Petty France John was kept a prisoner under the custody of the Sergeant of Arms for several years. He tried to redeem his liberty with a sum of money but found himself less fortunate than expected and spent the next few years in London with some allowances made for travelling.[43] Petty France was sequestered and all its goods and chattels were sold. The properties at Holme Lacy and Llanthony were also subsequently sequestered and badly treated, with buildings damaged, furniture destroyed and trees laid to waste. Lady Scudamore had appealed to Sir William Waller and received a reply 'worthy of the chivalry of earlier times', stating that no more trees should be felled and assuring her that the house had not been defaced and only that the tower of an old chapel had been pulled down. Despite his courteous letter, later that year Lady Scudamore was restrained at Llanthony in Gloucester without cause. By Christmas, however, she was probably at Holme Lacy, where she was recorded in 1644.[44] With John's son James also detained in London, Caradoc was vacant and in 1644 a party of Parliamentarian soldiers from Ross rode to Sellack intending to damage the churchyard cross and the stained glass window in the chancel, a gift from the Scudamore family. Fortunately the vicar, the Revd Prichard, detained them with such good hospitality that the soldiers forgot their sacrilegious intent and rode away with just one rider taking aim with his firearm and discharging a bullet through the lower part of the chancel window.[45]

As the war continued and spread, killing thousands in battles, skirmishes and plunders, John's younger brother Barnabas, who had been one of the first to join the Royalist army, was severely wounded in 1642. After recovering, he continued to serve the king and rose from the rank of captain to that of colonel by 1644. During the siege of Hereford in 1645 he was knighted for his courageous defence of the city. Later that year, however, when Hereford was taken by Colonel John Birch for the Parliamentarians, having managed to escape over the frozen Wye, he made his way to Ludlow, but was arrested near Oxford and accused of treachery. He defended the charge and was released. When Charles 1 marched from Hereford to the Golden Valley to meet and dine with supporters at Arthur's Stone in Dorstone, he changed direction and spent one night at Holme Lacy without the company of its owners who were imprisoned in London.[46] To regain his freedom John made every effort and used all his influences, though in vain as many of his friends were in favour of Parliament and he would not take the Negative Oath that Royalists needed to take in order to keep their land taken by Parliament. As the years passed and his health suffered he was eventually released in 1647 by the Gloucester Committee and his losses due to the Civil War were catalogued as follows:

LLANTHONY, NEAR GLOUCESTER	£
Household furniture	*600*
Trees	*1,200*
Besides sheds and mounts, that tenants quarrel	*"*
Pay and rent two Mansion Houses, with extraordinary outhouses ruined for ye	
Defence of Gloucester, which will not be got into the condition they were in	*10,000*
(for less than)	
Much of the materials being carried into Gloucester to make up their own	
Buildings there	
PETTY FRANCE	
Household Furniture, Clothes etc.	*700*
HOLME LACY	
Household Furniture. Linen, Books etc.	*1,200*
Horses	*500*
Sequestration my Estate in Gloucestershire, 4 years	*"*
Sequestration of my Estate in Herefordshire, 1 year, and	*"*
My son hath out of my Estate settled upon him pound £500 10s – at 15	
year's purchase is	*7,500*
Debts	*"*
Fine at Goldsmith's Hall (besides the Charges of Sequestration)	*2,790*

These figures totalled £24,490, but it was also recorded that the amount John suffered came to the value of 'thirty seven thousand, six hundred and ninety pounds'.[47]

Returning to Herefordshire John Scudamore found a changed society. His friend Laud had been executed, as had the king. He found the clergy very oppressed, many churches and Hereford Cathedral defaced and damaged. At the cathedral there was no bishop, dean, chapter or choir, no ordinations or confirmations and no prayer books or statutory services. In the parishes vicars were ejected in favour of 'preaching ministers'. One of these was the Revd Philip Price, ejected from his living in Ross to be replaced by the erudite, eloquent and learned John Tombs, who was described as a controversial neat-limbed man with a quick eye – who later befriended Scudamore.[48]

Life was changing for his family too. John's son James, of Caradoc, got into serious gambling debts playing at 'cards, dice and unlawful games' during the Commonwealth period and was sent abroad to keep him out of further trouble. However, James allegedly took a servant girl with him to France and, after visiting Paris, they travelled to

Padua and Venice and thence to Cairo and Tripoli. Having parted from the servant girl, he decided to return home, but crossing the Mediterranean his ship was captured by six ships from Naples. He was imprisoned for three days before being set ashore on a Greek island in the Ionian Sea where he fell ill and spent over three weeks in the 'pest house'. Upon recovering he returned home via Venice and served one year as a Member of Parliament for Hereford County before predeceasing his father.

As for John's brother Barnabas, who was married to Katherine, daughter of Francis Saunders of Shankton in Leicestershire, a story exists that he firstly married into the Brydges family of Wilton Castle. This seems unlikely, as during the war his troops had descended on Wilton Castle one Sunday morning, while the family were at church, and set fire to the castle, causing a sizeable breach in the masonry below the north-east tower, which led to its later collapse. Barnabas became impoverished by the war with debts at his death in 1652 paid by his brother.[49] William Scudamore at Ballingham had died and was buried in the chancel at Ballingham church. He left a long and interesting will bequeathing many charitable gifts to widows, workmen, a vicar at Yarkhill and to his family – leaving his young horse to John Scudamore of Holme Lacy, £50 a year to his wife Sarah, sums of money to his grandchildren and two coppice woods called Smith's Hill in Little Dewchurch to his wife's niece.[50]

Just below Smith's Hill Wood at Carey was the site of the Scudamores' iron forge which, since the Civil War, had ceased production probably due to lack of fuel, the breaking up of the partnership or having been damaged during the Civil War. As the

Ballingham church in 2018 (*Heather Hurley*)

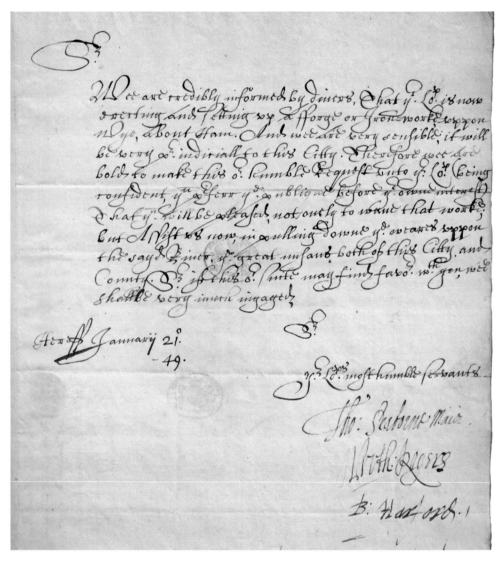

Petition against John Scudamore's proposed new forge at Hancock's Mill, upstream of Carey, due to perceived lack of wood, in 1649 (*British Library*)

forge had been a profitable venture John Scudamore considered constructing another forge in 1649 at Holme Lacy, upstream from Carey at the site of Hancock's Mill. As there was still a shortage of wood, the citizens of Hereford petitioned Parliament against the erection of the forge and to pull down the weirs as they complained that the county would be 'utterly ruined'.[51] This seemed to put an end to any further iron-making on this stretch of the Wye, and in 1653, during the Commonwealth, a petition was made by Hereford City for the removal of all weirs on the Wye and Lugg, followed in 1654 with an order from Parliament to make the Wye into a navigable river.[52]

By the conditions of his release, John Scudamore was restricted in his movements which may have meant that he was only allowed within the boundary of his estates. He pleaded for greater freedom by a letter in 1655 to the Governor and Commissioners and received a reply implying that the authorities had no 'cause of suspicion of any danger by him'. Obviously they were undecided though, as several months later John had to obtain a special order to visit London on account of his health, which was granted as follows:[53]

Saturday 6th March 1657
At the Councell at Whitehall

Ordered by his Highness Lord Protector and the Councell, that John, Lord Viscount, Scudamore, have liberty to Remayne in and about the citye of London and Westminster for recovery of his health, the late proclamation to the contrary notwithstanding.

HEN. SCOBELL, Clerk
of ye Councell

The monument of 1688 to Viscount John's son James in Holme Lacy church (*Logaston Press*)

10

The Restoration and Remodelling of Holme Lacy House, 2nd & 3rd Viscounts

> John succeeded to the title and estates of his grandfather; he
> married Frances, daughter of John Earl of Exeter, by whom
> he had issue three sons and three daughters; he died 22nd July,
> 1697, and was succeeded by his second son James, third and last
> Viscount who married, Frances, only daughter of Simon, Lord
> Digby ... In the early part of the reign of William III, the house
> was in great part rebuilt by John second Viscount Scudamore,
> but remained unfinished.
>
> Burke's **Visitations of Seats and Arms,** *1862*[1]

As John Scudamore 1st Viscount returned to a quiet life at Holme Lacy during the 1650s he generously bestowed gifts and pensions on the ejected cathedral clergy and poor parsons. Suffering from ill health, his wife Lady Elizabeth received some benefit from the waters in Bath, and before she died in 1651 she made a charitable gift for the 'poor sick' to receive free advice at Bath. As a widower John took a great interest in preserving his woods, in planting and grafting his orchards, attending his flock of sheep and improving his herd of cattle. The sheep and lambs' wool was stored in a large room set apart as a wool chamber in Holme Lacy House. He knew and was associated with John Beale, the Herefordshire scholar and agriculturalist, and John Evelyn, the diarist and agricultural writer, who both supported and encouraged cider orchards and promoted the Redstreak variety. Viscount Scudamore's cider was allegedly named 'vin de Scudamore' by an Italian prince visiting Oxford.[2]

At the Restoration of the monarchy in 1660, when Charles II took the throne, there was little evidence of celebrations at Holme Lacy or even in Hereford, where Nicholas Monk was consecrated as the new bishop. Monk died later that year and was succeeded by Herbert Croft, a popular choice, who came from the family ensconced at Croft Castle. He set about restoring the damaged cathedral by appealing to the nobility and gentry for funding, and received an immediate donation from John Scudamore of £100 towards the timber to repair the cathedral roof together with a gift of valuable books for the Cathedral Library which had been ransacked during the Civil War.[3] Indeed, the Restoration prefaced an age of 'good men' found amongst the 'church people' that included Isaac Walton, John Evelyn, Lord John Scudamore of Holme Lacy and John Kyrle of Ross.[4] John Scudamore visited London seeking medical treatment and kept in touch with government, but refused the offer of a parliamentary seat in Hereford in 1661 and took no active part in political affairs.[5] His home at Holme Lacy was taxed on 48 hearths in 1662 showing the extent of the house as compared with, for example, Sir Bennett Hoskyns' dilapidated house at Harewood, which had six 'decayed' hearths. The following year John Scudamore's military assessment was valued at £500, Henry Smyth's for Holme Lacy vicarage was £54 and Bennett Hoskyns' at Harewood was £120. Scudamore's charge was the equal largest in the county, his companion being the College of Vicars Choral in Hereford.[6]

Between 1666 and 1668, account books show that a certain amount of weekly work was carried out at Holme Lacy to the house, park and garden. Bricks were made, nails were purchased, tiles were mended, chimneys were swept, clocks were adjusted and the kitchen window was repaired. The Redstreak cider was made and bottled, beer was brewed and wool was spun in the outbuildings. In the garden and park, cords of wood were cut, bark was stripped, gates made, pumps mended, rabbits and deer killed and men were employed in ditching, fencing and sawing. In December 1667 William Vicks was paid 1s 2d for 'pitching stone in the highway by the slaughterhouse' and a footman was paid 1s for delivering a letter.

The parsonage at Holme Lacy, which was rebuilt in 1667 (*Heather Hurley*)

There was a certain amount spent on carriage of goods including cider, a box of hats and four boxes to London. Money was also spent on the vicarage to add an extra floor to the existing house that had been built on a raised plinth due to the site being liable to flooding. In 1668 eight women were employed to weed the formal 'walks' for a total of 7s 9d, while 22 men worked in the hop garden for a total of £2 10s 4d. The lower stable was mended by James Mayo for 10d, and Thomas Mayo was paid 1s for 'opening the vault and closing it again' in the chancel of the church for the burial of John's son James of Caradoc, who died at the age of 44. His fine marble monument in the church (*see p. 144*), erected by his wife Jane, bears a Latin inscription:[7]

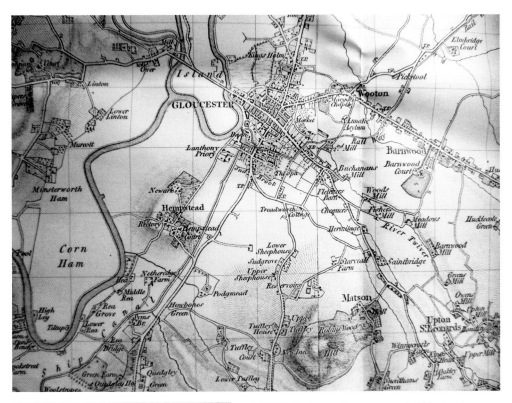

ABOVE: Ordnance Survey map of 1828, showing Hempsted, Llanthony Priory and Gloucester. LEFT: The door to Hempsted Vicarage. The inscription that curls above it reads: *Who'ere doth dwell within this door Thank God for Viscount Scudamore* (*Heather Hurley*) BELOW: Hempsted Vicarage, 1671 (*Heather Hurley*)

Hic jacet
Jacobus Scudamore
amiger natus
26 die Junii 1624
obit 18 die Junii
1668.

John was also turning his attention to Llanthony and Hempsted in Gloucestershire where he dealt with issues concerning the tithes, the church, the glebe and the rectory. He purchased the impropriated tithes and endowed them to the Hempsted rectory where a minister had not been in residence for a number of years as there was no garden, curtilage nor manse, and the church and churchyard were in a 'miserable condition'. During the late 1660s John repaired the church and began building a fine parsonage now known as Hempsted House which stands next to the church of St Swithun. The grateful rector, John Gregory, was so pleased with his fine new home that he inscribed over the doorway:

Who'er doth dwell within this door
Thanks God for Viscount Scudamore 1671[8]

This handsome rectory cost Scudamore £700 but he never saw the building completed as he died at Holme Lacy in 1671 in his 71st year, and was buried in the family vault at the church.[9] When the vault was opened in 1822, his lead coffin, shaped in the outline of a head and body, was discovered bearing a long description on a brass plate:

The Sacred remains of the Right Honourable John Lord Viscount
Scudamore who singularly illustrated that honour of his
Ancient family by his eminent and great virtues as
by his prudence & integrity expressed in the public
employment which he managed in native County
and that of ambassador to K Louis the 13th in the Court
of France

The lengthy inscription ended with:

this excellent person resigned his
Soul into his creator's hands this 9th May 1671
being aged 70 years two months and 23 days'.[10]

Aged just 22, John succeeded as the 2nd Viscount and heir to the Holme Lacy estate. However, The 1st Viscount had spent time in introducing John, his grandson, to the style of life he was expected to lead as his successor after the death of John's father, James, in 1668. John was born in London at Holborn in 1649, the son of the Hon. James Scudamore

Portrait of John 2nd Viscount (*Kentchurch Archives*)

and his wife Jane. Between 1661 and 1665 he attended Westminster School as a boarder and continued his education at Christ Church, Oxford where he matriculated in 1666 and attained an MA the following year. He followed the family tradition of becoming a Member of Parliament, and in 1672 he married Frances, the daughter of John Cecil 4th Earl of Exeter.[11] His wife earned a reputation of being 'one of the impudentest women as was ever known' and so became disliked. Later she was to be involved in a scandalous affair with Thomas Coningsby of Hampton Court, who became a Member of Parliament and was elevated to the Irish Peerage as Lord Coningsby.[12]

As the heir to Holme Lacy and with a new wife to impress, in 1674 John earnestly began to rebuild his house according to plans traditionally thought to have been drawn up by the 1st Viscount when he was ambassador in France, but the plans were set aside due to the unsettled times of the Civil War and Commonwealth. Articles were now prepared and agreed for the building, between the 2nd Viscount and Anthony Deane, a mason, for demolishing the existing mansion and building a house after the style of a French or Flemish chateau, though parts of the original building were retained and used as offices.[13] Hugh May, who was involved in the restoration of Windsor Castle, was employed as the architect and a Mr Hereford as clerk of works. Work began by adding two new fronts of reddish stone with the arms of the Scudamores impaling those of the Cecil family. A new staircase was inserted and all the ceilings of the principal rooms including the saloon, ante room and drawing room were richly plastered featuring the Scudamore and Cecil arms, shields and crests – which may still be admired today.[14] This large Palladian mansion consisted of a central block with cross-wings at the north and south ends with an orangery added at a later date. Throughout the house intricate wood carvings by Grinling Gibbons were used as wider frames for the portraits of the Scudamore family. Many were carved from lime and sycamore and featured fruit, shells, flowers, fish and birds.[15] The carvings were produced in the Gibbons' workshops and then inserted at Holme Lacy House once the builders, masons and carpenters had finished their work. Grinling Gibbons hailed from Deptford in Kent and his work dominated the interiors of English royal palaces, churches, cathedrals and country houses during the late seventeenth century.[16]

LEFT: Grinling Gibbons carvings framing a painting at Holme Lacy in 1910 (*Herefordshire Archives*). ABOVE: Plasterwork at Holme Lacy (*Heather Hurley*)

The pleasure grounds are understood to date from the rebuilding although some plantings, lawns, terracing, a yew garden and walks were already in existence, including the fish ponds and a bowling green where a pavilion or summer house had been erected. From the pavilion an avenue of trees was planted to create a linear walk, ride or drive to the banks of the meandering river Wye from which visitors could admire the views. A scattering of fragmented thick green bottle glass found near the pavilion, suggested that this may have been the site of John Scudamore's cider house, but archaeologists decided that the broken bottles were more likely to be evidence of a once 'merry' evening in the pavilion.[17]

During the late eighteenth century, when another John Gregory was the vicar at Holme Lacy church, John the 2nd Viscount instructed his gardener to plant a yew and a pine in the churchyard, an order recorded in the parish registers. Today, two yews remain and a group of pines stand opposite the church serving as a reminder of the past plantings. In 1691 Anthony Davies lived at Symonds Farm, and Burton House, next to the church, was leased along with several parcels of meadow and pasture land to George Preece, a baker from Hereford. Under the terms of the lease one half of its garden and herbage was for the yearly growing of apples and pears. The lease reserved to John Scudamore his right of free liberty and privileges to enter the demesne premises for fishing, fowling, hawking and hunting and for any other game, and to allow access to his servants, attendants and visitors in coaches or on horseback. It also allowed him to lead, drive or convey sheep, cattle, horses, wains and carts, and cut down and carry away willow and twigs from the banks of the Wye through the Broad Meadow and other named

TOP: Yews in the garden at Holme Lacy MIDDLE: Remains of the pavilion at Holme Lacy. BOTTOM: The Orangery at Holme Lacy House (*all Heather Hurley*)

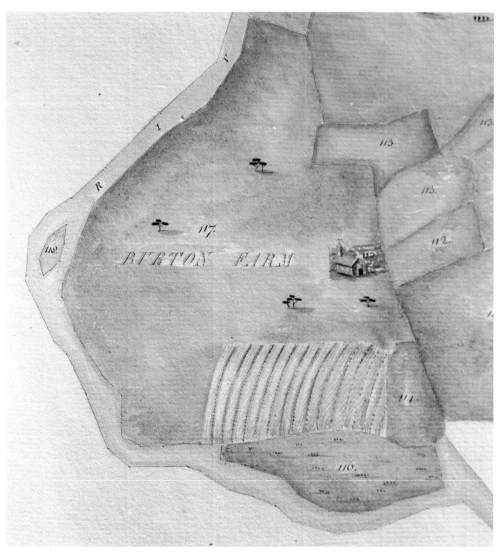

Map of Holme Lacy church and Burton Farm in 1780 (*Kentchurch Archives*)

fields. When George Preece sold his hay and crops he had to reinvest his profit into yearly replanting and to keep in repair ditches, hedges, gates, rails, fences and stiles.[18]

Although John and his wife Frances were not the perfect match, at least six children were born, but there was some doubt over the children's parentage due to Frances' affair and elopement with Thomas Coningsby after they met at a house party held at Holme Lacy House in 1681. Scudamore's servants succeeded in tracing the guilty pair to Banbury where they were 'caught in the act', and it was considered at the time that Coningsby 'has got all of my Lord Scudamore's children'. Three children were born in the 1680s – Cecil in 1681, who died in his fifth year; James in 1684, who was to succeed John Scudamore; and John in 1687, who inherited Caradoc at Sellack, whilst three daughters

Servants' wages at Holme Lacy and repairs at London in 1700 (*The National Archives*)

named Frances, Mary and Elizabeth were born during the 1670s before Frances' liaison with Coningsby.

The 2nd Viscount played an active but unfulfilled part as a Member of Parliament just at a time when politics was moving into a new age with the two-party system of Whig and Tory emerging during the last few years of Charles II's reign. John made no recorded speeches in the House and was a supporter of the Whigs, but moved away from the party after one of his followers had been bullied. It was during a meeting at John Scudamore's lodgings that a government informer, related to Thomas Coningsby, allegedly heard that Scudamore was offered the command of a revolutionary army, which he declined, saying he would never fight against the laws of the land. His political career was somewhat blighted, however, by the scandal over his wife's elopement with Thomas Coningsby. After the relationship with Coningsby ended, John welcomed back his wife.[19]

LEFT: Portrait of Frances 3rd Viscountess. RIGHT: Portrait of James 3rd Viscount (*Kentchurch Archives*)

In 1694 John became one of the undertakers of an Act for making the rivers Wye and Lugg navigable in the county of Herefordshire. In doing so he was in the company of other Herefordshire worthies such as Sir Herbert Croft, Sir Edward Harley, John Scudamore of Kentchurch, the Foleys – even Lord Thomas Coningsby, and others. Under the terms of the Act all weirs were to be removed except the Duke of Kent's at New Weir (Symonds Yat), and provision was made to build warehouses and storehouses in Hereford on the site of Hereford Castle.[20] While John was serving as Deputy Lieutenant of Gloucestershire, his wife Frances died at Holme Lacy in 1694, and his own death followed in 1697. The burials were in coffins placed in the vault of Holme Lacy church but when the vaults were reopened in 1822 (*see Chapter 12*) there was 'no appearance of any vault of the 2nd Vis.'; however, the churchwardens were in 'no doubt' that his remains lay in the inaccessible 6th or 7th vault.[21]

As the 2nd Viscount's son James was only a child when his father died, he was made a ward of his grandmother Jane Scudamore. She was the only senior member of the family resident at Holme Lacy between 1697 and 1703 when a sequence of accounts were made by Benjamin Mason that provide lists of rentals from tenants at Holme Lacy, Bolstone, Eaton Tregoz, Humber, Risbury, Yatton and Maud Bryan, all lying in Herefordshire. These record how daily life continued at Holme Lacy: the purchase of food; payments to servants, workmen and gardeners; the washing of bottles and the making and bottling of cider; glazing windows; cutting and carrying timber in the park; harrowing, ploughing, mowing, carting stone and barrels of lime, and payments in connection with funding the Wye and Lugg navigation, tax and supporting the poor and the church.

Entries for 1698 reflect the work on the Wye Navigation, recording payments 'for carrying Timber off the Park to Property by water', the timber being roped together to form a raft and floated downstream. In 1700, Jonas Jackson the coachman was paid £4 13s 6d; the groom was due £4 10s and John Nott was still owed £5 since the death of the 2nd Viscount.[22]

James had been born in Ireland at Shannon Park in 1684, the year Charles II died and was succeeded by his brother James II. After gaining his matriculation at Gloucester Hall, Oxford at the age of 11, James Scudamore spent time exploring the Continent, visiting galleries, churches and historic places such as Bologna, Parma, Rome, Naples, Genoa and Lake Lucerne. His cultural travels were well recorded in three volumes of handwritten journals. At his coming of age in 1705 he became the 3rd Viscount Scudamore and mar-

The yew tree that once gave shade to the ice house in the grounds of Holme Lacy House
(*Heather Hurley*)

ried Frances, the beautiful and cultured daughter of the 4th Baron Digby from County Offaly in Ireland. Under James, further improvements were carried out at Holme Lacy in the gardens, park and grounds, with payments recorded for digging stone, sawing timber, mowing, laying faggots, mending the park pale and weeding. The seasonal farming duties continued with the additional task of tusking pigs. In September 1708 £1 6s 6d was paid to 'men for fishing 55 days with ye long nett', 2s 6d 'for water to cure the mange of the dog', 1s 'for a quart of oyle for the gun', 2s 'for straightening my Lord's gun', 5s 6d 'for expenses at election' and a few months later £15 0s 3d was paid to William Davis for carrying 'the Lord's goods' to London, £2 2s paid for barley to feed the hounds, £5 7s 6d for a new cider mill, and £1 8s paid to Henry Lanwarne for 32 barrels of lime.[23]

It was at about this date that the deer park became fashionable as a delightful and scenic landscape for the Scudamores to entertain their guests and show off their estate, by following the mown paths on foot, on horseback or in carriages.[24] In order to keep food and drink cool for their guests, an ice house was constructed close to the fishing pool, and near this a yew was planted to provide shade in summer months. The tree still stands above the scanty remains of the ice house. In 1704 James purchased Ballingham manor from his relatives by means of a mortgage, and in 1715 had the rebuilt chapel at Holme Lacy consecrated by Bishop Bisse.[25]

James served as a Tory MP for Herefordshire from 1705 to 1714 during the reign of Queen Anne and in the first year of the Georgian period.[26] Whilst riding to Hereford

The monument of 1716 to James 3rd Viscount in Holme Lacy church (*Logaston Press*)

to attend some electioneering business James was seriously injured in a fall from his horse. He never fully recovered and died in 1716 at the age of 33 and was buried at Holme Lacy church, where he is commemorated with a large and elaborate monument inscribed with a Latin text:

M.S.
Praehonorabilis Jacobi Dni Scudamore
Vicecomptis de Slygo & Baronis de Dromore in Regno Hiberae
In uxorem duxit Franciscam filiam unicam
Praehonorabilis Simonis Dni Digby perquam filiam
Habuit unicam & haeredem Franciscam
Obit 2 die Decembris 1716
Aetatis 33

James and Frances had produced two children: James born in 1706, who died in childhood; and Frances, who was born in 1711. With no surviving male heir therefore, the title of viscount became extinct,[27] and James' unexpected death left his wife Frances as a young widow to run the estate and look after her young daughter.

As there was an increasing demand for timber by the Royal Navy, an agent by the name of Justus Durnford from Plymouth visited the Holme Lacy estate, possibly to procure suitable timber that could be felled and used to build ships.[28] As of 1717 large quantities of timber were purchased for the Navy from 'My Lady Scudamore'.[29] Bargemen such as William Morgan of Monmouth were employed by Thomas Foley and William Rea, a partnership associated with iron-making, to transport the timber down the river Wye from Holme Lacy Park to Chepstow. William Smith of Bewdley was employed to organise and bring men who were skilled floaters of timber on the river Severn to show the method to be used on the Wye. The felled timber was hauled from the park to a riverside meadow and the timber was lashed together to form a raft or floater which was navigated with danger and difficulty down the Wye to Chepstow before being trans-shipped onto seagoing vessels destined for the naval docks at Plymouth. Smaller timber for making hoops, laths and trenails (for ship-building) and cordwood were freighted in barges to Chepstow. Lime, coal and other goods were delivered to or exported from a wharf at the Withy Plantation by the

The former wharf near Holme Lacy church in 2018 (*Heather Hurley*)

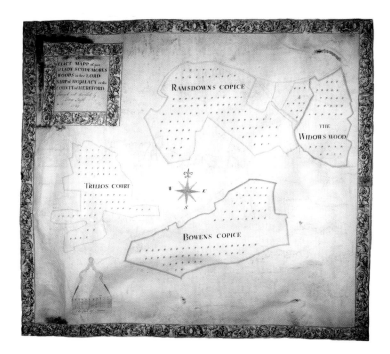

Map of 1723 showing
Ramsdowns and
Bowens coppices and
The Widows wood
(*British Library*)

Glebe Orchard a few hundred yards from the church. Another wharf at an equal distance from Holme Lacy House lay at Shipley from where agricultural produce including sacks of wheat and bags of barley were shipped to Bristol.[30]

Rudimentary maps of this period reveal a rough plan of the Glebe and show various field names around the church and mansion with its outbuildings and home farm; another outlines Ramsdowns Coppice, Widows Wood and Bowens Coppice surveyed by George Smyth in 1723. The pavilion, bowling green and the avenue of trees leading to the Wye are shown on a slightly later plan.[31]

Lady Frances Scudamore was not just involved in the management of the house and estate and in bringing up her daughter, for she was also a patron of literature and used to entertain the emerging literati of the eighteenth century. She had been introduced to the poet Alexander Pope by her relative Robert Digby, who shared her love of classical and English literature. During the 1720s Pope visited Frances at Holme Lacy on at least two occasions when John Kyrle, known as the Man of Ross, may have been present together with John Gay, a notable poet and dramatist, and Lord Bathurst from Cirencester Park. Pope represented the English landscape movement, of replacing formality with a natural appearance in gardens and grounds, and shared much in common with Kyrle who, by his public-mindedness, had beautified the town of Ross and its surrounding landscape. Kyrle transformed the town's Prospect into a garden with a fountain and a water supply, and created a walk along a wooded escarpment from the Prospect to a summer house overlooking the Wye. A year after Kyrle's death in 1724, Pope accompanied by his friends visited Frances at Holme Lacy where they were engaged in planning various landscape improvements to be undertaken in the grounds. Frances Scudamore was certainly influenced by Kyrle, becoming known as a 'rural lady embracing the pastoral idyll – the female prototype of John Kyrle', and according to Pope she was 'imbued with an Arcadian naturalness and simplicity very contrary to the artificial habits of town ladies'.[32]

In 1727 Matthew Gibson, the rector of Abbeydore and vicar of Holme Lacy, researched, wrote and published *A View of the Ancient and Present State of the Churches of Door, Hom-Lacy and Hempsted Endowed by the Right Honourable John, Lord Viscount Scudamore*. The book was dedicated to Frances Viscountess Scudamore in grati-tude of enjoying so large a share 'of the Lord Scudamore's Bounty to the Church'. His rather obsequious dedication explains that he wrote the contents 'out of pure gratitude to John Scudamore's memory

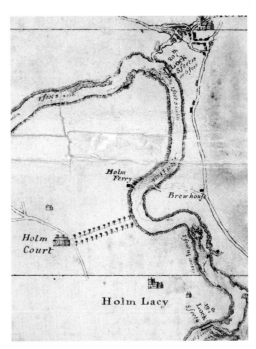

The tree-lined avenue leading from Holme Lacy House to a bend in the Wye, as shown on Taylor's map of 1763

and to revive some particulars of a life so eminent for piety and charity', signing him-self 'Your Ladyship's Most Obliged Beneficiary, and Most devoted Chaplain'. Matthew Gibson hailed from Westmorland, was educated at Queen's College, Oxford, gained his MA in 1703, and from 1708 served as the vicar of Holme Lacy and domestic chaplain to the 3rd Viscount at Holme Lacy House. In 1722 he became rector of Abbeydore where he remained until 1741 under the patronage of Lady Frances. His book has remained a standard book of a history of the Scudamore family and the churches they were associ-ated with at Abbeydore, Holme Lacy and Hempsted with a brief mention of Bolstone, Bredwardine, Bosbury and Little Birch, together with an appendix of Latin documents.[33] Matthew Gibson knew the antiquarian Thomas Hearne and John Kyrle, whose niece he married. When Hearne asked Gibson about Kyrle he replied that he knew him as a chari-table and generous man but cruelly implied that it was all out of vanity and ostentation. At a later date Hearne was to describe Gibson as a 'crazed and stingy man'.[34]

The opening of the Wye as a navigable waterway was partly due to the wretched state of the roads churned into mud by horses' hooves, deeply rutted by wheeled vehicles and almost impassable during the winter months. As trade and transport increased for a growing population at the beginning of the eighteenth century, attention was paid to improving the roads by establishing turnpike trusts. Holme Lacy was situated on an ancient route leading from Hereford via Hoarwithy to Ross, which was in a dangerous state and inconvenient for passengers and carriages on account of its steep ascents and descents. In order to improve the six-mile route from Hereford to Hoarwithy Passage it was turnpiked by the Hereford Turnpike Trust in 1729, a time when this route from Hereford led from Rotherwas over Dinedor Hill to Holme Lacy, skirting the Scudamores' house, and continued up and past Tump Farm and across Ballingham Hill to Carey and Hoarwithy. It was later replaced by an easier route, leaving the original road difficult to trace but shown on contemporary maps.[35]

In 1729 Lady Scudamore, whilst at her London home in Albemarle Street, was taken ill with smallpox which she had probably contracted from her favourite Digby cousin, who had recently died of the disease. At first the physicians were hopeful of her recovery and made sure that the street outside her house was

Part of the former turnpike road at Dinedor in 2011 that led from Hereford to Hoarwithy
(*Fenny Smith*)

covered in straw to prevent the noise of carriages and carts making a disturbance; the townspeople were also requested to 'hinder any of their usual cries'. Tragically, the illness took its toll and within a matter of days she died in 1729 at the age of 44, leaving her only child Frances as heiress. In her will the Viscountess left bequests mainly to the Digby side of her family, together with ones to charities including £1,000 for the maintenance of five poor widows at £10 per annum, gifts to her servants and £50 to her favourite lady's maid. Money was also 'laid out' for her daughter Fanny, but the only charity local to Holme Lacy that received a bequest was Lord Scudamore's seventeenth-century charity, a fund reused at a later date to provide for schools in Hereford.[36]

Lady Scudamore's body was taken to Holme Lacy church where she was buried in the first vault on the south-east side of the chancel. She was laid in an outer wooden coffin with a brass plate on the leaden inner coffin bearing the Scudamore and Digby arms and an inscription 'The Right Hon'ble Frances Viscountess Scudamore died 8th May 1729 aged 44 years'. At the death of Frances, Pope, in his first draft of *The Essays of Man* penned 'and Scudamore ends her name', although it was not ended. Even so, at her death Caradoc at Sellack, which had been left to Frances by the 3rd Viscount, passed from the Scudamores to the Digbys on her side of the family.[37]

11

The Heiresses Lady Frances Scudamore and her Daughter the Duchess of Norfolk

> the heiress married first in 1729, Henry Duke of Beaufort,
> from whom she was divorced, and marrying again Col Charles
> Fitzroy, (natural son of the first Duke of Grafton) was mother of
> Frances her heir, married in 1771, to Charles, the present Duke
> of Norfolk, to whom she brought this, and other large estates in
> this neighbourhood for life.[1]
>
> *Revd S. Shaw*, A Tour to the West of England, *1788*

F RANCES Scudamore, known as Fanny, the daughter of the 3rd Viscount and his wife Frances, was born in London on 14 August 1711 and at only 18 was left a desirable and 'pretty' heiress after the death of her father in 1716 and her mother in 1729. Prior to the death of Viscountess Scudamore, the Foley family from Stoke Edith paid a visit to Holme Lacy in the hope of arranging a marriage between their son Thomas and Fanny. The young Tommy and Fanny seemed to be 'in earnest' but were overshadowed by a grander match in the person of the Duke of Beaufort, son of the influential Gloucestershire family whose land included large estates in Gloucestershire stretching to the Welsh Borders.[2] Alexander Pope had described young Fanny as 'most innocent and the least warped by idle fashion and custom', but she was also known to have a vile temper and the licentious disposition of her grandmother, the daughter of John Cecil (*see Chapter 10*). Within two months of her mother's burial at Holme Lacy, Fanny duly married Henry Somerset, 3rd Duke of Beaufort, at Holland House in London. In 1730 the Duke took the name of Scudamore by an Act of Parliament and succeeded in her right to Holme Lacy and the other Scudamore estates.[3] This private Act of 1730 was for 'obliging Henry Duke of Beaufort and Frances Duchess of Beaufort and her children to take the additional Surname and bear the arms of Scudamore pursuant to a Settlement made by James late Lord Scudamore'.[4]

Before Fanny's marriage to the Duke of Beaufort a number of transactions had been made between her mother, relating to leases of tenant's property and land in Holme Lacy,

Upton Bishop, Much Marcle, Yatton, Sollers Hope, '2 messuages, cottage and garden in Bolstone' and a 'parcel of land in Hempsted', but after 1740 the estates were 'devised' by the Duke of Beaufort to trustees. The marriage between the temperamental Fanny and the Duke was an unsuccessful match causing them to live separately and to divorce in 1744 after she eloped with William Talbot, later Earl Talbot of Glamorgan, with whom, it was suggested, she gave birth to an illegitimate child in 1742, allegedly named Frances Matthews Talbot. The transcription of the private Act to dissolve the marriage stated that the Duke was unable to marry again and was 'occasioned by her Ladyship's pranks with Lord Talbot'.[5] Less than a year after the divorce the Duke died aged 37 after unknown 'complications of disorders' and coping with the 'mettlesome' Fanny.[6] In 1748 Fanny entered into a second marriage 'held in her own chapel' with Colonel Charles Fitzroy, the 'natural' son of the 2nd Duke of Grafton. Again, a private Act enabled the couple to use the name and bear the arms of the Scudamore family. Charles Fitzroy had attended Westminster School, worked his way up the ranks in the army and over time served as Member of Parliament for Thetford in Norfolk between 1733 and 1754; for Hereford between 1754 and 1768; for Heytesbury in Wiltshire between 1768 and 1774, and again for Thetford between 1774 and 1782, the year of his death, having become Father of the House during the preceding year. Fitzroy's unusual royal

TOP: Portrait of Frances Duchess of Beaufort (*Kentchurch Archives*). BOTTOM: One end of the tomb in Holme Lacy church of Frances who died in 1749, and of her daughter, also Frances, who died in 1820 (*Heather Hurley*)

appointments during the Georgian period included Master of the King's tennis courts, a groom porter and deputy cofferer, the latter having responsibility for paying wages to servants 'below the stairs'.[7]

Living at her husband's estate at Badminton or in London, Fanny's absence from Holme Lacy meant that the estate was somewhat neglected. Large amounts of timber had already been felled and transported down the Wye (*see Chapter 10*) and matters would not have been helped when Fanny died in childbirth in 1749, leaving a motherless infant also named Frances to be brought up by her father. Fanny was buried in a coffin bearing the inscription 'Frances Fitzroy Scudamore died Feb 15th 1749 aged 38 years' and placed in the vault at Holme Lacy church. She was later commemorated on a tablet in the church.[8] During his daughter's minority it seems that Fitzroy was mostly concerned with generating income from the Holme Lacy estate, for he 'did infinite injury to the place, by cutting down £15,000 worth of timber'.[9]

With little documentation found for the years between 1749 and 1769 it is difficult to be certain as to the life the young Frances had, her father being preoccupied with parliamentary duties and royal offices. In 1752, during the reign of George II, a private Act of Parliament was obtained empowering Fitzroy, as her guardian, to 'make building leases of her estates' in the county of Surrey, but apart from this minor piece of information the story moves to the late 1760s when young Frances was soon to reach her coming of age and a future husband was to be found. Fitzroy had left his Hereford seat for Heytesbury in Wiltshire, so was still concerned with matters away from Herefordshire when, from 1769, a series of rentals, valuations and incomes were produced of the Scudamore estates, showing tenants and field names, and detailing the work of felling, stripping bark and hauling timber in Widow's Wood, Ramsden Coppice and Birch Grove in Holme Lacy, and in Gilbert's Hill Wood in Abbeydore.[10] The accounts were made in preparation of a marriage settlement drawn up in 1771 between Frances and the Honourable Charles Howard the Younger, documenting all her estates in Herefordshire, Gloucestershire, Monmouthshire, Buckinghamshire, Surrey and London. The lawyers made sure nothing was missing, listing all the tenants' names together with all 'houses, outhouses, erections, buildings, barns, stables, mills, wharves, orchards, gardens, backsides, curtilages, meadows, pastures, feeding grounds, commons and common of pasture, wastes, heaths, moors, marshes, woods, under-woods, trees and the ground and site thereof waters, water courses, ditches, mounds, fences, free boards, ways, paths, passages etc.'[11]

The Honourable Charles Howard, Earl of Surrey, later to become the 11th Duke of Norfolk, was born into a Catholic family in 1746 and educated in France before his first marriage in 1767 to Marian, the daughter of John Coppinger of Cork, who died in childbirth the following year. His second marriage, to Frances, took place on 2 April 1771 at St Georges, Hanover Square in London, at which Frances broke out into a fit of hysteria after the vows were exchanged – an early sign of her nervous temperament that

LEFT: Portrait of Frances Duchess of Norfolk (*Kentchurch Archives*). RIGHT: Portrait of Charles Howard
11th Duke of Norfolk (*Herefordshire Libraries and Herefordshire History website*)

led to her future madness.[12] Charles Howard was a typical English nobleman, being both peer and politician, but as an MP he was independently-minded, sometimes supporting the Tories; at other times the Whigs. He had family 'seats' at Arundel Castle in Sussex, Worksop Manor in Derbyshire and Deepdene in Surrey, as well as at Holme Lacy. Although known to have neglected his estates, he favoured Holme Lacy, and in 1773 spent time and money on repairs to the house, garden and stables, and purchased furniture, bedding and cooking utensils as well as harnesses for his horses. There must have been a large number of horses, for working, riding and driving carriages, as the smith was kept busy forging many shoes and nails.[13] From this date it appears that the mentally disturbed Duchess Frances was kept locked away while her husband Charles Howard enjoyed the company of several mistresses. These included Mary Ann Gibbon, who is reputed to have become his third wife having secretly married the Earl in 1796 even while Fanny was still alive, producing five children fathered by him including two sons: Matthew Howard-Gibbon and Edward Howard-Gibbon who became officers in the army. Although a staunch supporter of Catholicism he eventually conformed to the Church of England, and when in parliament voted for Catholic Emancipation.[14]

At Holme Lacy in 1776, the vicar Revd Bagnall Gibbons noted in the parish registers 'a great natural Curiosity that the great Pear tree upon the Glebe adjoining the Vicarage house; produced, this year, fourteen hogsheads, each hogshead containing one hundred gallons'. The remarkable pear tree covered nearly a quarter of an acre, forming an orchard of itself, and for many years continued to yield from 12 to 16

Mem. It is likewise inserted, as a great natural Curiosity, that the great Pear-tree upon the Glebe, adjoining to the Vicarage house; produc'd, this year, fourteen hogsheads; each hogshead containing one hundred gallons. ——

TOP: A record of 1776 concerning 'the great pear-tree' on the Glebe land by the Vicarage, which produced 1,400 gallons of juice (*Herefordshire Archives*). MIDDLE: Pear trees at Holme Lacy today (*Heather Hurley*). BOTTOM: The new coach road made into the estate by Charles Howard and called the Green Drive, photographed in 2018 (*Heather Hurley*)

hogsheads of perry. Another account recorded that a large branch broken by the wind fell to the ground with its butt still attached to the trunk. Sometime later it took root and formed a scion, encouraging the vicar to order other layers to be made from the tree in a similar manner.[15] Lying north of the Vicarage between the withy plantation and the river Wye is the Glebe in Stank Orchard field where a clump of leaning and aged pear trees have fallen and re-rooted, and which may date from this original great pear tree.[16]

In 1780 maps were produced from a survey made by Richard Frizell of the Hereford, Gloucester, Buckingham and Monmouth estates of the Earl and Countess of Surrey named as Frances, the Countess, and Charles Howard, the Earl, at a time when Frances was going through a lucid period. By December 1782, however, she was suffering from being a 'Lunatic and did not enjoy Lucid Intervals'. The Glebe fields are listed in the schedule and depicted on the map near the church, surrounded by the lands of Burton Farm.[17] Shortly after this survey, Charles Howard created a new coach road into his estate named the Green Drive which led from the south-west corner of Holme Lacy at a small settlement called Newtown. For his guests arriving from Ross and Monmouth this provided a scenic drive across the park before arriving at Holme Lacy House. The Green Drive leading through fields, across parkland and past the mansion to the village has survived, but only as a public footpath with little sign of this former and grand coach road.[18]

Having conformed to the Church of England in order to pursue his parliamentary career, Charles Howard stood for Carlisle in 1780 and addressed the freemen in a 'very gentleman-like manner'. Throughout his career he always spoke in favour of parliamentary reform and, in 1780, successfully stood for Carlisle and for Arundel in 1784 but failed to win at Hereford. Known as a 'lively, affable, talking man' with 'very good sense and competent knowledge' Charles Howard succeeded to the title of the 11th Duke of Norfolk in 1786, with Frances becoming the Duchess.[19] As Frances had been diagnosed as a 'lunatic' and he had no immediate heirs, the Duke was curious to search for a legal heir by examining the name plates on the coffins in the vaults at Holme Lacy church to ascertain what additional information they might contain. In order to carry this out, a bizarre and extraordinary occurrence took place during the late 1780s when a group of lime burners from the Hop Lawn Lime Kiln at Fownhope carted a load of lime to the church in return for a payment of '2/6 allowed for liquor, with which 4 Gallons and an half of beer was purchased'. Once the lime was placed in the church the lime burners were ordered out. The lime was to serve two purposes: one was to smother the smell, and the other so an iron chest, which had stood in the 'Hall in Hom House', could be sealed in the vault, once a cavity had been made, with brick, stone and mortar. The chest clearly contained family papers which the Duke did not want to be seen. Meanwhile a lawyer from London and the churchwardens took the plates off the coffins and also recorded the ages and maiden names of members of the family from

the parish registers. There was concern that this undercover work was a 'hanging matter' but the lime burners understood that a gentleman sitting in parliament 'can do anything' and were warned 'to keep their council'. A few days later the church was reopened and the bells 'burst out a ringing', announcing the Duke's return to Holme Lacy from London.[20]

The Duke occasionally enjoyed entertaining at Holme Lacy House which, in 1788, was described as a plain, dark stone building with wings and approached through the park to the west front. The hall was old, magnificent and lofty, with paintings and gilt bronzes hung from the ceiling. Apart from a fine portrait of Charles I, there was

TOP: Painting of Holme Lacy House and grounds in 1832 by T.N. Webb. BOTTOM: Remains of a tower at the cottage known as the old schoolhouse (*Heather Hurley*)

a painting of Sir James Scudamore, son of Sir John, dressed in armour and ready for a tilt, Sir John Packington, his wife Lady Packington, and over the chimney a 'curious flower piece' framed by a carving by Grinling Gibbons. From the hall there were two small drawing rooms displaying further portraits, and a tall staircase, hung with old pictures, led to a suite of unfinished rooms and a chapel no longer used for 'divine service'.

The area around Fownhope and Holme Lacy as shown on Bryant's map of 1835

The gardens in the south front were in the style of King William's fortifications, known as a Dutch or Battle Garden descending between great banks of yew around a terraced glade. The yew hedges were cut in a variety of forms, and the view from the west lawn was 'sweetly picturesque' overlooking a small tower, a church spire and a white house. Terraces ascending the hill into the park, 'the charming and varied scene', offered views of the meandering river Wye and the distant hills in Gloucestershire, Monmouthshire and the Black Mountains below the branches of the venerable oaks that had survived from the 'destructive' felling by Fitzroy, the father of Frances the Duchess of Norfolk.[21]

It was during the 1780s that access to and through Holme Lacy was further improved by road and water. In 1789 a Turnpike Road Act was passed for 'making and keeping in Repair, the Roads from the said City of Hereford to Hoarwithy Passage' which skirted the western boundary of Holme Lacy parish, giving access to the newly created Green Drive. On the eastern side the same Act enabled a new toll road from Hereford through Lower Bullingham, Rotherwas, Dinedor and Holme Lacy to Little Dewchurch and Hoarwithy to replace the former toll road because of it being 'dangerous and inconvenient to Passengers and Carriages on Account of the Ascent and Descent' over Dinedor Hill. (The old road remains as an example of a narrow and sunken eighteenth-century route.) On the opposite eastern side of the river Wye a major toll route from Gloucester to Hereford was improved by the Hereford Trustees when they allotted a sum of £80 to be spent from the top of Eign Hill in Hereford to Mordiford and Fownhope. For travellers from Gloucester and Ledbury this toll road provided an easy and convenient access to several ford and ferry crossings over the Wye to Holme Lacy House.[22] From the turnpike road at Fownhope a short walk through the meadows led to the Shipley or Hom Ferry which conveyed goods, horses and vehicles to and from Holme Lacy House. After visiting Nathanial Purchas at his Fownhope Brewery, George Lipscomb wanted to take the opportunity to visit the Duke of Norfolk's house across the Wye at Holme Lacy and was directed to a ferry, where a boat was kept 'for the purpose of conducting passengers over the Wye', but the wind frustrated all their efforts to make themselves heard by the boatman, and therefore they had to return by the same road to Mordiford.[23] From the Old Mill at Fownhope there was an ancient ford leading across the Wye to the opposite bank where a path passed Holme Lacy Vicarage and led through a former avenue of elm and thorn trees to arrive at a southern entrance into Holme Lacy House.[24] As there was no known inn, public house or a beer or cider retailer in Holme Lacy, Bolstone and Dinedor since the last drinking house was closed at Dinedor in the late seventeenth century, the villagers crossed the Wye at Even Pits to access the Anchor Inn at Fownhope. It was traditionally known that the Scudamores did not encourage any drinking houses on their estates, although the cellars at Holme Lacy House were stocked with wine, beer and cider.[25]

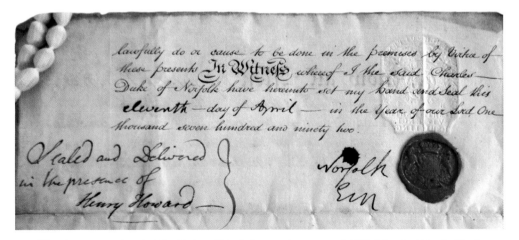

The signature and seal of the Duke of Norfolk on a document of 1792 (*Herefordshire Archives*)

View of Holme Lacy House in 1802 (*Herefordshire Libraries*)

As the Duke had no intention of living permanently at Holme Lacy, in 1792 he appointed Thomas Braithwaite, already in his employ, as his agent and manager of all his 'Messuages, Farms, Lands and Hereditaments in the County of Hereford and in the County of Monmouth', an appointment confirmed by the Duke in the presence of his relative Henry Howard.[26] Braithwaite was to receive all rents and arrears that were due from the tenants and to give proper receipts. Fulfilling his role with integrity and clear judgement, as well as being known for his 'simplicity of manners and propriety of his behaviour', Braithwaite was employed for 30 years 'in the management of the extensive property of the Duke and Duchess of Norfolk' before he died aged 62 in 1819 and was commemorated in the church.[27]

When at Holme Lacy on short visits the Duke entertained a rich assortment of guests who feasted on 'venison and turtle' and watched the playing of sports and sparring matches. It was here that the young Tom Winter (later named Spring) from Fownhope was invited to join a troupe of boxers who sparred on the front lawns and was talent-spotted as a future bare-knuckle boxing champion. As Frances was unable to be present at social occasions in her delicate mental state, the Duke would often choose two of the prettiest maids and button them 'close packed and smiling' into one of his capacious waistcoats to provide him with female comfort. As the entertainments and dining came to a close the Duke's laughter 'echoed along the corridors' of the unfinished mansion house (*see Chapter 10*).[28] In September 1798 the Three Choirs Festival held a concert with an orchestra playing in the saloon at Holme Lacy, which was attended by Lord and Lady Oxford, Mr and Mrs Clive, Sir Hungerford Hoskyns, Sir George Cornewall, Richard Payne Knight, Uvedale Price, Charles Rotherham, Major Symonds, Mr Scudamore and other ladies and gentlemen who were invited by the Duke of Norfolk. Over 200 people enjoyed the concert which was followed by a ball and a concert on the next day. Afterwards the audience alighted onto barges for a pleasing trip down the 'wild and romantic scenery' of the river Wye to Monmouth. Uvedale Price shared his enthusiasm and promotion of the picturesque landscape with the Duke and as a regular visitor to Holme Lacy was invited to create a path featuring the views and veteran trees. This became known as Price's Walk, as marked on a contemporary map.[29] It was recorded in 1802 that due to the good taste of the Duke of Norfolk his mansion at Holme Lacy was allowed to remain unaltered 'as a perfect specimen of the style preferred by our immediate ancestors'. The old garden on the

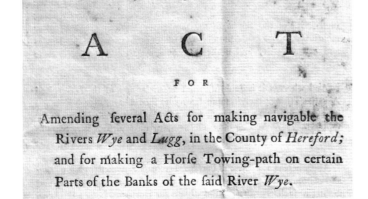

ABOVE: Part of the survey of the Wye in 1805 by Henry Price, prior to the making of a towing-path (*Herefordshire Archives*)

LEFT: Part of the title page for the Horse Towing Path Act of 1809 (*Landscape Origins of the Wye project*)

The River Wye at Holme Lacy in 1909 (*Kentchurch Archives*)

south front was said to be 'formed on the model of Hampton Court, in Middlesex', the yew trees originally clipped into grotesque shapes were left to regain their foliage and the pear tree near the Parsonage was still yielding 12 to 16 hogsheads of perry.[30] A view in 1800 depicts a far reaching scene of the meandering Wye from Holme Lacy Park.[31]

In 1805, during the long reign of George III, plans were taken to improve the navigation on the Wye by clearing the channels through the principal shoals and for making a horse towing path between Hereford and Tintern. The surveyor Henry Price produced a detailed plan which showed the extent of the Duke of Norfolk's property bordering many miles of the Wye at Holme Lacy, Bolstone, Ballingham and Kings Caple. This was followed in 1809 by the Horse Towing Path Act which made provision for a towing path from Hereford to Lydbrook, with stables for the horses and houses where a toll of sixpence a mile per horse would be charged.[32] At Holme Lacy and Ballingham the line of the path followed the right bank of the Wye through the land owned by the Duke, which was let out to tenants including John Elliott, who had renewed his lease for the farm 'called or known as Ballingham Hall' together with other lands.[33] In 1814 the Duke renewed a lease with William Coleby for several messuages and tenements at Hollington and Gannah farms lying in the parish of Holme Lacy with all 'houses, out-houses, buildings, barns, stables, folds, yards, gardens, orchards and the lands, meadows, leasows, pastures, feedings, rough grounds' and a cottage known as Wheeler's occupied by Margaret Suff. The Duke kept his customary rights to use the quarries, for his servants and workmen to haul timber by horses, to fish by drawing out and landing nets upon the banks of the river Wye and to hunt fowl and shoot over the premises. The rent was £602 of 'lawful British money' paid in equal portions twice a year on the first day of August and the second day of February.[34]

Within the grounds of Holme Lacy the Duchess of Norfolk remained in seclusion due to her 'unremitted malady'. She was cared for by Miss Jessitts and Miss Layton, with the help of two nurses during extreme cases of her mental disorder. As early as 1797 the inheritance of Frances's estates at Holme Lacy and Llanthony, valued annually at £8,000, was discussed over dinner at the Herald's Office by the Duke's secretary who had been informed of the difficulties ahead due to the Duchess's mental incapacity, and of the numerous claimants and descendants, and suggested that the aid of the Court of Chancery would be needed.[35] Her doctor confirmed her condition in 1782 when an affidavit enabled the Duke to administer her affairs with the assistance of her father Charles Fitzroy, although Fitzroy died later that year. On infrequent occasions the Duke visited her and spent a few days at Holme Lacy during the spring and the month of August on his way from the North to London. Apparently she appeared pleased with his attention and hearing about her neighbours, whose names she remembered. After many years of seclusion, the Duke, advised by her physician, organised a change of 'air and scene' at Graystock, his seat in Cumbria, where she resided for some seven or eight years, but at her request returned to her home in Herefordshire before 1815.

That year the Duke held a 'very large party of Nobility Male and Female' at his restored Arundel Castle where all his 'Relatives of the Noble family of Howard' were invited. The dissolute and portly Duke managed to carry out the 'honours of the table' and consumed wine at a dinner that included up to 60 ladies. Now aged 70, his constitution was 'unequal to the fatigue in his health', a symptom which led to his subsequent loss of appetite which never recovered. In August 1815 he met the Marquis of Stafford at Trentham Hall in Staffordshire where the Marchioness gave him every care and attention. He then returned to Holme Lacy for a fortnight, where he had a premonition that he would never return. As he left Holme Lacy the Duchess was 'extremely anxious' to go with him to the stable yard where his carriage was waiting, as she now sensed that this was the last time she would see him. During his last months the Duke was looked after by Mrs Frisby, an old servant, and Miss Ann Wood, an accomplished young lady who also served as a companion to Frances at a salary of £240 a year. The Duke died on 15 December 1815 at St James Square, London and was buried at Dorking in Surrey. When her physician, Dr Blount, broke the sad news to Frances she said 'I thought Lord Surrey was unwell when here last as he did not eat as he used' and she 'went to the window, took out her handkerchief and put it to her eyes', but her concern was momentary.[36]

In 1816 Frances's health deteriorated, which caused concern to the Duke's executors. She could recollect many past events but could not deal with her own affairs, so a commission and inquisition of lunacy was applied for but deferred for six months by the executors who endeavoured to put her affairs in order, no doubt with the help of the Scudamores' lawyer Thomas Bird, based in Hereford. Before the six months were up, Frances was in such a state that 'every lucid appearance had entirely vanished', so a Commission of Lunacy was issued in 1816 under Mr Wingfield and Lord Digby. The family papers, consisting of deeds, books, papers and writings, were conveyed in wagons from Holme Lacy to London, subject to Chancery supervision to protect her inherited estates and those who might benefit. For the remainder of her life Frances was paid every attention and was made comfortable, until the spring of 1820 when, despite being in 'tolerable good health', she succumbed to the 'last, and almost only illness of her life, when some rays even of religious light and presentiment of dissolution, occasionally darted through the cloud which had so long obscured and deranged her mental powers'.[37] She rapidly declined and was attended by her physician Dr Blount and twice by Dr Warren from London. They decided her pain could be treated by medicines, but by 16 October it was unlikely she would 'live over the night'. Medicinal skills and 'unremitted attention' in fact kept her alive until 22 October when she died uttering 'Mercy, Mercy!'[38] A rumour exists that, until her death in 1820, Frances did not actually live in Holme Lacy House, but possibly in the Keeper's Lodge near the Upper Deer House.

A painting of the Duchess of Norfolk's coffin in 1820, covered in crimson velvet and various ornamentations (*Kentchurch Archives*)

The day after Frances's death, her body was laid out in a mahogany shell lined and tufted with rich white satin, and because of the heat of the weather a leaden coffin was prepared and soldered up. The following Saturday an 'outward coffin' made of British oak was taken in a hearse to Holme Lacy mansion and placed on tables in the saloon. The coffin was covered with crimson Genoa velvet ornamented with gilt nails and a gilt memorial with a ducal crown and brass plate inscribed 'Frances Duchess of Norfolk ob 22 Oct 1820 aged 70'. The coffin was attended by the butler and others in the saloon lit by large wax candles in the chandeliers. The funeral was a lavish affair but was not attended by any members of the Duke's family of Howard, the Scudamores from Kentchurch or any notable landowners. The three mourning coaches and the hearse were each drawn by six horses displaying the Scudamore arms. The order of the funeral was as follows:

First coach conveyed Revd Richard Walwyn, vicar of Holme Lacy
Revd John Duncumb, vicar of Dore, late domestic chaplain to Duke of Norfolk
William Blount, physician
John Griffiths, apothecary
Second coach was the empty chariot of her Grace with the blinds drawn attended by
the stewards wearing hatbands and scarves
Next the hearse drawn by six horses
Followed by fifty principal tenants on horseback
Third coach conveyed the chief mourners, William Wingfield and George Digby
Labourers and tradesmen followed on foot clad in mourning provided for
the occasion

In the churchyard the clergy led the procession, followed by the medical men, stewards and professional men, as the coffin covered with black velvet and gold tassels was placed on trestles. Revd Walwyn read an impressive service before the coffin was placed in the vault containing the remains of Frances' mother. The funeral was attended by the whole household of Holme Lacy House and the gardener, keeper and steward all dressed in 'handsome' mourning with the working men provided with short stockings. Liquor and 'proper refreshments at the mansion' were offered to those giving their respects and to many 'who had the management of her estates after the Duke's death in Dec 1815, the establishment having been kept up to as great an extent as the Rules of the Court of Chancery would allow'. The solemn ceremony was held in keeping with her Grace's 'peculiar situation having lived in seclusion nearly 40 years'.[39]

Of the clergy who attended the funeral, Richard Walwyn served 23 years as vicar of Holme Lacy before he died three years later at the age of 55 whilst 'in the discharge of his duties as a Christian minister' and was buried at Holme Lacy church. John Duncumb is well remembered for his contribution to the *Collections towards the History of Herefordshire*. He had been engaged by Charles Duke of Norfolk at £2 2s a week with extra payments for travelling outside the county. He later entered into holy orders, lived to the age of 74 and was buried at Abbeydore where he served as vicar under the patronage of the Duke of Norfolk.[40]

The week after the funeral the *Hereford Journal* reported that at Holme Lacy 'all in the course of a week, three individuals residing within 200 yards of one another, whose united ages made 228 years: the Duchess of Norfolk, 71; Mr Hudson, 83; and an old woman who had lived as servant of the latter gentleman; and died same day, 71'. (In fact the Duchess was 70 and the total should be 225!) Mr Hudson was a gentleman who spent his youth in industry and was described as a man of integrity with cheerful manners who showed kindness to all around him.[41] The death of Frances the Duchess of Norfolk was recorded by the family as a 'rare instance of one person possessing a family estate 70 years – she and her late mother having been proprietors for 103 years'. She was the last of the true Scudamores at Holme Lacy but not the end of the story.[42]

SACRED TO THE MEMORY OF
FRANCES FITZROY SCUDAMORE,
WIFE OF COLONEL FITZROY SCUDAMORE,
AND THE ONLY DAUGHTER AND HEIRESS OF
JAMES THE THIRD AND LAST VISCOUNT SCUDAMORE,
WHO WAS BORN 14. AUGUST 1711 AND DIED 27. FEB. 1749. O S
AGED 38 YEARS.

AND OF HER DAUGHTER
FRANCES DOWAGER DUTCHESS OF NORFOLK
WIDOW OF THE MOST NOBLE CHARLES DUKE OF NORFOLK
WHO WAS BORN 10. FEB. 1749 O S AND DIED 22ᵗ OCTʳ 1820.
AGED 70 YEARS.

THIS TABLET WAS ERECTED BY HER COHEIRS
SIR EDWIN FRANCIS STANHOPE, *BARONET*,
LINEAL DESCENDANT OF MARY WIFE OF
SIR GILES BRIDGES, *BARONET*,
THE ELDEST DAUGHTER OF
SIR JAMES SCUDAMORE, *KNIGHT*,
AND SISTER OF THE FIRST LORD SCUDAMORE,
VISCOUNT SLIGO AND BARON OF *DROMORE*,

AND JOHN PARSONS, *ESQUIRE*,
ANN SUSANNA DAVIS,
AND MARY THE WIFE OF LIEUT. GENERAL BURR,
THE LINEAL DESCENDANTS OF
FRANCES WIFE OF
JOHN HIGFORD, *ESQUIRE*,
ANOTHER DAUGHTER OF
SIR JAMES SCUDAMORE
AND SISTER ALSO OF THE FIRST
LORD SCUDAMORE.

Plaque erected in Holme Lacy church by the coheirs of Frances Dowager Duchess of Norfolk
(*Logaston Press*)

12

Scudamore-Stanhope, the Earls of Chesterfield and the 1909 Sale

It was decided in the Court of Chancery that since all of the issue of the 1st viscount was now extinct the estate should go to the descendants of the eldest sister Mary, wife of Sir Giles Brydges, Bt., and Frances, wife of John Higford. The partition deeds were dated 13 May 1829 and Holme Lacy passed to Sir Edwyn Francis Stanhope (father of the 9th earl of Chesterfield) as the senior representative of the elder daughter. Holme Lacy and the other estates in Herefordshire were sold by the 10th earl of Chesterfield in 1909. Sir Edwyn assumed the additional surname and arms of the Scudamore family by Royal Licence on 17 January 1827.[1]

Warren Skidmore, *edited by Linda Moffatt, 2015*

A FTER her death and funeral Frances was commemorated with her mother on a black marble tomb in Holme Lacy church, and at a later date the various coheirs erected a plaque on the church wall to show their legal rights as inscribed (*see opposite*). This was the result of a lengthy Chancery case that involved the huge array of documents that Thomas Braithwaite, the steward of the late Duke and Duchess, had collected. He then asked the Scudamores' Hereford solicitor Thomas Bird to use the collection to compile an inventory after the death of the Duke of Norfolk in 1815. When the widowed and childless Frances died in 1820 the documents were still deposited in London and formed the papers for the long legal case to prove her coheirs. There were many petitions from those who claimed to be related and hoped to benefit from the large estates and properties in Herefordshire, Gloucestershire, Worcestershire, Monmouthshire, Buckinghamshire, Cambridgeshire and Southwark in Surrey.[2] It took the lawyers almost seven years from 1821 to reach their decision that Sir Edwyn Francis was the main heir together with four minor heirs including Mary Burr, wife of Lt Gen. Daniel Burr, who served 35 years in the Indian army and who may have initiated the case.[3] In 1822 it became necessary to

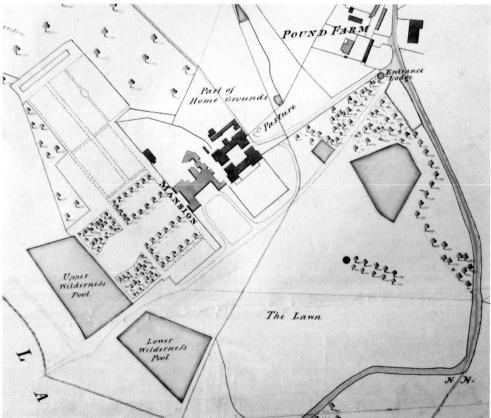

TOP: Holme Lacy House in 1800, showing the stables, coach house and steward's house that were demolished *c.*1827, by Wathen (*David Whitehead*). BOTTOM: Plan of Holme Lacy House and garden, showing the stables and offices prior to their demolition (*Herefordshire Archives*)

reopen the vaults at Holme Lacy church to view the name plates on the Scudamore coffins to confirm the succession. Many were found to be loose, some lost and others 'without plate or inscription', but the group of men, including the vicar Revd Walwyn and at least two attorneys, continued their investigations until they were 'completely satisfied'. They also agreed on a fee for the men breaking the ground and opening the vaults – two guineas for those under the raised chancel and one guinea each for those in the other part of the church. As Thomas Bird was suspicious of the previous meddling with the vaults, he interviewed under oath one survivor from among the former workmen, although no conclusions were reached.[4]

Between 1822 and 1825 the properties of the 'Coheirs of Her Grace the Late Frances Dowager Duchess of Norfolk' were surveyed by Henry Garling, who produced several large volumes containing the perambulations of the numerous manors and parishes. Holme Lacy estate consisted of 2,214 acres and produced an income of £2,760 per annum.[5] The park, containing a herd of 150 fallow deer, was estimated to extend to around 450 acres.[6] The perambulation was carried out by a surveyor who was accompanied by the steward John Braithwaite, Benjamin Morris an estate carpenter, James Harris a woodman and John Mason the gamekeeper of 56 years of age who had lived all his life at Holme Lacy. An earlier rental was taken into consideration, which listed names of the tenants including John Hudson Jun. at Lower Bogmarsh, James Stevens at Hollington and Gannah Farms, John Smith at the Bower, Benjamin Morris at Shipley, George Cutter at the Blacksmith's Shop, Richard Andrews and John Morgan at Tars

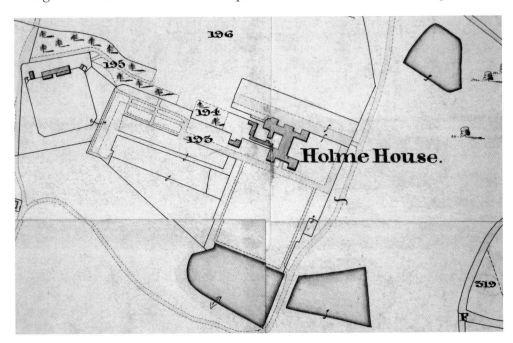

Plan of Holme Lacy House and grounds as shown on the 1840 tithe map, after the stabling and offices had been demolished (*compare with plan on p. 178*)

Mill Cottages and also names the cottagers at New Town. In Bolstone and Ballingham James Smith was at Bolstone Court Farm, William Townsend at Hancock's Cottage and Phillip Elliot at Ballingham Hall Farm. The valuable woods including Widow's Wood, Ramsdown Coppice, Smith's Hill Wood, Bolstone Wood and Gilbert's Hill Wood were named, showing their acreage and the year of being last cut.[7]

Sir Edwyn Francis Stanhope, the main heir, was born in 1793, the only son of Sir Henry Edwyn Stanhope 1st Baronet of Middlesex. As a young man Edwyn succeeded as 2nd Baronet, served as a captain in the Royal Navy and married Mary Dowell from Devon. When it was confirmed in 1827 that he was the heir to the Scudamores of Holme Lacy he assumed by Royal Licence the name of Scudamore, becoming Sir Edwyn Scudamore-Stanhope 2nd Baronet.[8]

At the time he inherited Holme Lacy House, the rather neglected building was approached from the north through a gateway between an entrance lodge and Pound Farm, where a drive led to a block of antiquated buildings containing stables, coach houses, laundry, larders, brew house and cider house. An archway led into a courtyard to access the 16-stall stables with harness and saddle rooms, 'terminated' with a clock turret and the brew and cider houses topped by a bell turret. There was a good Steward's house, lofts in abundance and accommodation for the grooms and stable lads. This building was known to have been in good repair, of 'unusually solid construction', with four-feet-thick walls built of 'splendid bricks' made in the nearby Brick Kiln Wood, and stone from Perrystone Hill near Ross. This 'beautiful and useful building' stood exactly opposite the north front of the house, divided by the terrace, with the Steward's House facing a wing containing the servant's hall. Sir Edwyn wasted no time in demolishing this block of buildings before updating, modernising and enlarging the mansion to be approached by a new sweeping drive.[9]

Edwyn commissioned the architect William Atkinson to carry out his proposals of demolition and to create a new north front with an imposing porch approached from the road along the drive through gate piers beside a lodge. At this date Holme Lacy House was described as having 'steep roofs after plans of French palaces and chateaux', with a carved oak cornice covered with lead to prevent decay and to 'carry off rain and melting snow which it did very well', but Edwyn had this taken down and burnt. Instead, a balustrade was added around the pitched and slated roof, and, on the east side, where deer had wandered up to the dining room windows, a terrace was created. Part of the plan was to construct a new range of outbuildings to contain a larder, laundry, dairy, brew house and kitchen to be built on the site of an earlier chapel that had been used as a dining room by the Duke of Norfolk to entertain the 'freemen' of Hereford. Although in good repair, this was 'destroyed' and Sir Edwyn and his architect made interior alterations, converting the pantry into a hall, the housekeeper's room into a billiard room, the existing chapel into a tenant's hall, the state bedroom into a library and a bedroom into a study. Panelling was removed from the ground floor rooms, the Grinling Gibbons

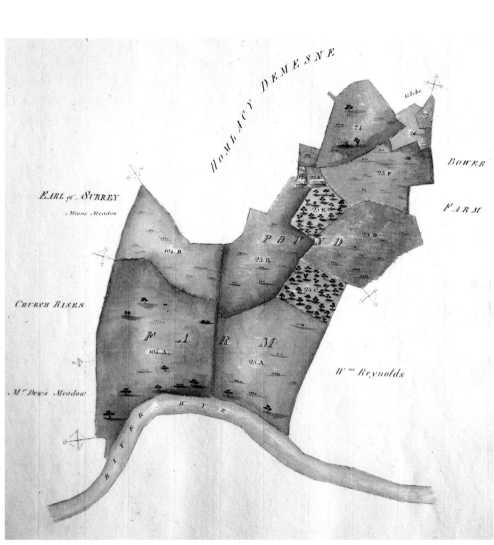

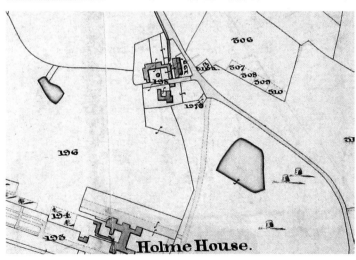

ABOVE: Frizell's map
of Pound Farm in 1780
(*Kentchurch Archives*)

LEFT: Plan of Pound Farm
on the 1840 tithe map

carvings were taken down, repaired and rehung, and other alterations were made 'quite out of character' – including replacing the main oak staircase with one from Hampton Court, Herefordshire. The majority of the pictures and furnishings remained in the house except for the personal effects of Frances. These were inherited by Lord Digby of Sherborne Castle in Dorset and other members of the Digby family. The valuable pictures were listed by Sheffield Grace in 1828 in a 'Catalogue of Portraits at Holme Lacy'. Some remained in the house when Sir Edwyn took possession; others were taken by the coheirs. The subsequent history of the paintings is rather muddled. Some seem to have passed through the hands of Thomas Bird and Robert Phillipps of Longworth, while some found their way, via various auctions, to the British Museum and the National Portrait Gallery. Of the family portraits, several remain at Sherborne Castle and many finally found their way to Kentchurch Court.[10]

ABOVE: Pound Farm stables (*Heather Hurley*)
RIGHT: The dovecote at Pound Farm in 1957 (*Robert Walker*)

As Sir Edwyn had demolished the stabling and coach houses, he arranged for stone and tiled stables to be built at Pound Farm, the home farm. The stables were formed around three sides of a large square yard and contained five stalls, four loose boxes, two spacious coach houses, a harness room and a groom's cottage with accommodation in the village for the coachman.[11] A stone-built circular folly, built as a dovecote, stood in the centre of the courtyard and dated from the same period, together with the 'Offices, Yards and Gardens'.[12] Sir Edwyn then turned his attention to enhancing the park and gardens by planting shelter belts, groups and groves of deciduous trees, creating new woodland with European Larch, and introducing specimen conifers and many 'exotics'. In the gardens a Coastal Redwood, a Cedar of Lebanon, a Wellingtonia Mammoth and a Turkey Oak were planted among earlier trees. The north terrace of 700 feet in length and the south terrace of 88 feet provided a pleasant walk around the house, offering far-reaching views and led to the old yew walks, the formal gardens and paths to two pools renamed as Lower and Upper Wilderness Pools. To the west a walled kitchen garden was constructed with outbuildings and accommodation for the gardener.[13]

It was not until July 1832 that Sir Edwyn and his family officially moved into Holme Lacy House, an event which was reported with enthusiasm in the *Hereford Journal* as a 'rapturous and universal welcome home'. Upon reaching Hoarwithy the party were greeted as they passed under an archway of evergreens and over strewn flowers on the Hoarwithy to Hereford turnpike leading to the Caldicot turn and Newtown where the coach road led through their estate to the park gates. Here they were met by 'hundreds of horsemen, consisting of the tenantry headed by the steward and several gentlemen and tradesmen from Hereford and the neighbourhood'. The crowd of admirers was estimated at 2,000 to 3,000 in a cavalcade with horsemen taking the lead in pairs, followed by pedestrians walking six abreast. On approaching the north front Sir Edwyn and his family alighted and proceeded to the balcony where, according to the *Hereford Journal* reporter, Sir Edwyn said: 'Friends and Gentlemen – in the name of Lady Stanhope and myself, I beg you will accept our most sincere and grateful thanks for this highly flattering reception on our return to Holme Lacy. We feel it, be assured, most deeply; and the more so, at a time like the present, when attempts are being every day made to set landlord and tenant at variance with each other: you have to but look around you to feel convinced that I have returned to you the first moment that I could: my greatest happiness, believe me, consists in living here among you, and in contributing as far as lies in my power to your welfare and your comfort.' He concluded that after his long journey he could no longer detain them from the refreshments of a roasted ox, half a dozen sheep, a wagon load of bread, several hogshead of strong ale and cider and a dessert of pineapples and melons. At dinner further toasts and addresses were conveyed including one from the young 'Heir apparent, a fine lad, who, in the name of his brothers and himself, returned thanks, in a manner that drew down the warmest applause'. Music summoned the crowd to the terraced walks where quadrilles and country dances commenced, only disturbed by one incident of a 'saucy boor' intoxicated with cider who insulted the mayor and was punished by a beating 'amid the cheers of the bye-standers'.[14]

The heir apparent, Henry, who was in time to succeed, had been born in 1821 and was followed in quick succession by Chandos, Berkeley, Edwyn, William, Arthur, Philip and one daughter, Anna-Eliza, who died as an infant.[15] Three sons went into the church and two followed a military career, while Arthur died as a young man.

During Sir Edwyn's residency at Holme Lacy a number of alterations and improvements took place in the parish, which involved Sir Edwyn as either a magistrate, sponsor or supporter. In September 1833 a notice, prepared by William Bird, Clerk to the Magistrates, was displayed on the church door on three successive Sundays announcing that a Special Session of Highways was to be held at Pound House to view a certain highway intended 'to be stopped up as useless and unnecessary' and that three footways were to be diverted through the lands of Sir Edwyn Scudamore-Stanhope in the parish of Holme Lacy. The plans of the road and footway diversions were displayed at several points along the footpaths to inform the local users. Despite Sir Edwyn being a magistrate and powerful landowner the public road was not rerouted, but the footpaths did suffer some alterations.[16] It is not known what benefit these orders would have made to Sir Edwyn or to the public except that they cleared the footways from within sight of the house – and perhaps Sir Edwyn had prior knowledge of plans for the forthcoming railway and road bridge over the Wye.

During the 1830s Brunel surveyed a route for a railway line connecting Hereford to Gloucester through Ross but it was not until 1850 that he gained financial support which led to the incorporation of the Hereford, Ross & Gloucester Railway Company at a meeting held at the Green Dragon in Hereford in 1851. Plans were submitted, engineers contracted, money raised and compulsory powers obtained for the 30-mile route of which many miles traversed Sir Edwyn's property at Holme Lacy, Bolstone and Ballingham and land belonging to the Company of Proprietors of the River Wye and Lugg Navigation and the Horse Towing Path.[17] The opening of this railway in 1855 with a station at Holme Lacy 'had a dramatic effect on communications between the east and west banks of the Wye' due to the construction of a road bridge over the Wye, enabling the inhabitants of Fownhope a safe access across the Wye to the railway.[18]

The Fownhope and Holme Lacy Bridge Company was formed in 1856 'For Effecting a Communication with the Railway Station at Holme Lacy' by erecting a proposed bridge at or near Even Pitt. The Prospectus, offering shares at £10 each, appealed for investment from hop growers, lime and coal merchants, expected developers of villas and the local landowners. As the landowner on the west bank, Sir Edwyn donated the land on that side of the Wye, valued at £600, and gave £30 towards expenses. Other donations were collected and shares were purchased by many tradesmen, farmers, businessmen, clergy and landowners. The prospectus pointed out the importance of coal and other goods delivered to the neighbourhood by the new railway 'now that the Wye Towing Path and Navigation had virtually ceased' and that the bridge would benefit those living and working on the eastern side of the Wye.[19] The Fownhope and Holme Lacy Bridge Act was passed in 1857 with a right for the Company to 'take and hold the Ancient Ferries' at Even Pitt and Shipley Boat, and to stop up the Ox Ford and Old Mill Ford. The Act authorised the building of a good and substantial bridge with abutments of stone, brick, iron or other durable materials that was to commence on the western side of the river in a field belonging to Sir Edwyn and to terminate on waste land lying between the turnpike road and the river on the eastern side. The bridge opened the following year as a toll bridge with charges ranging from one farthing for small animals, one halfpenny for foot passengers and two shillings and sixpence for steam carriages.[20]

HEREFORD, ROSS, & GLOUCESTER RAILWAY.
First General Ordinary Meeting.

NOTICE is hereby given, that the FIRST GENERAL ORDINARY MEETING of the SHAREHOLDERS in the HEREFORD, ROSS, and GLOUCESTER RAILWAY COMPANY, will be held at the GREEN DRAGON HOTEL, in the City of HEREFORD, on THURSDAY, the 4th day of SEPTEMBER, 1851, at One o'clock in the Afternoon, for the Election of Directors and Auditors, and for the transaction of the General Business of the Company.

By Order of the Board of Directors,

JOHN NASH, Secretary.

August 2nd, 1851.

HOLME LACEY. 267

HOLME LACEY.

HOLME LACEY, or Holm Lacey, a large Parish six miles S.E. of Hereford. Holme Lacey House, the seat of Sir E. F. Scudamore Stanhope, Bart., is a noble mansion surrounded by a fine park.

THE CHURCH, which stands on the banks of the River Wye, is an old edifice, with two aisles and a large square tower, containing eight bells. In the Church there are several fine monuments, erected to the memory of the ancient Scudamore family. The gallery and organ was erected in the year 1833, by Lady Stanhope, and presented to the Parish. The Rev. Francis Lewis, Vicar; the Rev. Selo Brigstock, Curate; Mr. Francis Ward, Clerk. Service—11 a.m. and 3 p.m.

A FREE SCHOOL for Boys and Girls. Mary Gaymes, Mistress.

The SUNDAY SCHOOL, for Boys only, is a neat stone building, erected 1833 by Lady Stanhope. Mr. Wm. Wellington, Teacher.

CLERGY, GENTRY, TRADES, FARMERS, ETC.

Stanhope Sir Edwin Francis Scudamore, Bart., Holme Lacey House
Brigstock Rev. Selo, Curate, Vicarage House
Barrett Edwin, farmer, Holinton
Bonner John, farmer, The Bower
Downing John, farmer, Lower Bog Marsh
Green George, farmer, The Tump
Magness Matthew, blacksmith
Morris Richard, farmer, Shiply
Mutlow John, farmer, Upper Bog Marsh
Pain Isaac, farmer, Billingsley
Powell George, farmer, Cannow Dales
Ward Francis, Letter Receiver, Parish Clerk, shopkeeper, and farmer

POST OFFICE.—Francis Ward, Receiver. Arrival, 10 a.m.; dispatch, 2 p.m.

TOP LEFT: Notice in the *Hereford Journal* advertising the first meeting of the Hereford, Ross and Gloucester Railway Company in September 1851. TOP RIGHT: Details of Holme Lacey parish as given in a directory of 1851. ABOVE: Holme Lacey station in 1901 (*Kentchurch Archives*)

In Holme Lacy village the growing population of the mid nineteenth century was served by the Revd Francis Lewis and a curate at the church, Mistress Mary Gaymes at the Free School, Mr William Wellington at a Sunday School for boys only, Francis Ward a shopkeeper and letter receiver, Henry Pearce the station master, two carpenters, a blacksmith, a wheelwright and a nail maker. In the church, Lady Mary Scudamore-Stanhope had presented the gallery and organ in 1833 when she founded the Free School which once stood opposite Pound Farm. The school was later replaced with a larger building erected by Sir Edwyn. Tarrs Mill had ceased milling, leaving two cottages inhabited by James Morgan and Elizabeth Hodges, but flour was available from William Wheatstone the miller at Dinedor Mill also on the Tarrs Brook.[21]

There is little information about the life of Sir Edwyn and his family while living at Holme Lacy House. Apart from serving as a Justice of the Peace and Deputy Lieutenant, Sir Edwyn was not much involved in local or national affairs. In 1841 his son Arthur died aged 18, and in 1846 his long-serving butler of 17 years died at the age of 65, leaving 'a disconsolate widow to mourn the affectionate husband and friend'. In 1851 his eldest son Henry married Dorothea, daughter of Sir Adam Hay, and in 1855 another son, Edwyn, died while serving as a captain in the 59th regiment in Hong Kong after three days of fever.[22] His son William took over as incumbent of Ballingham and curate of Bolstone, and son Berkeley, vicar of Bosbury, married Caroline Arkwright of Hampton Court, Herefordshire in 1858 after Sir Edwyn had written to her father John Arkwright expressing his pleasure at the announcement.[23] The wedding was one of the last events that Edwyn's wife Mary would have attended as she died that year aged 60 and was buried in the graveyard at Holme Lacy church. In fact the whole family apart from Berkeley, Philip and Anna-Eliza were to be commemorated on plaques, windows and monuments in Holme Lacy church bearing Biblical inscriptions.[24]

During the mid nineteenth century the Scudamore-Stanhopes employed a large staff at Holme Lacy House, consisting of a butler, footboy, housekeeper, housemaid, cook, lady's maid, dairy maid, kitchen maid, laundress, groom and a coachman, with little reduction in the total after the death of Mary.[25]

In 1874 Sir Edwyn died aged 81, leaving his heir Henry to succeed him at Holme Lacy as the 3rd Baronet Stanhope. Henry had been educated at Winchester College and graduated at Balliol College, Oxford, with a Bachelor of Arts degree in 1841. His marriage to Dorothea in 1851 produced five sons – Edwyn, Henry, Claude, Chandos and Evelyn.[26] At Holme Lacy he followed his father as a Justice of the Peace and Deputy Lieutenant and became a member of the Travellers and Brooks's Clubs, two fashionable clubs in London with a limited membership.[27] During his ownership, Sir Henry opened his extensive estate to the public to enjoy the commanding views, the old garden on the south front with its spacious terrace and the old yew trees, and in 1879 made an agreement with the Great Western Railway to erect telegraph wires on his land.[28]

In 1883 Sir Henry succeeded to the title of the 9th Earl of Chesterfield from the 'disreputable' George Philip Stanhope, the 8th Earl (his fourth cousin once removed).[29] As Sir Henry, his wife and eldest son continued to reside at Holme Lacy House they kept on a staff of ten for household and outside duties. Sir Henry employed Edward Jakeman as head gamekeeper and John Smith as his bailiff, the tenant farmers growing hops, wheat, barley and oats. In the village there was a woodward, grocer, coal merchant, wheelwright, blacksmith, postmaster, station master, schoolmistress teaching 45 children and, at the vicarage, William, Sir Henry's brother, was living as incumbent of Holme Lacy church.[30] With Sir Henry's interest in the Scudamore family he continued as scribe of the Holme Lacy MSS Book containing pedigrees, monumental inscriptions and family history. His was the last entry signed 'Chesterfield' 1884.[31]

LEFT: The previous garden gates of Holme Lacy House re-erected in Holme Lacy churchyard (*Heather Hurley*). RIGHT: A gatepost at Holme Lacy House in 1901 (*Kentchurch Archives*)

Three years later he died at the age of 65 while staying at a hotel in St Leonards-on-Sea in Sussex. The will was a long document referring to trustees, mortgages, freehold and leasehold property and bequests to his wife, eldest son and family including 'my Deer in the Park', works of art, glass, gold and silver items, books, plate, wines, carriage horses, shares in the Fownhope and Holme Lacy Bridge Company and included a gift of £100 to the Hereford Infirmary, free of legacy duty. A codicil listed many of his personal belongings left to his wife Dorothea, eldest son Edwyn (known as Edly), his other sons and brothers Berkeley and William who were the trustees. The document noted that he was worth £13,620 14s 0d at his death.[32]

His tomb of three tiers stands in a burial plot for the Scudamore-Stanhope family in the churchyard at Holme Lacy. The plots are enclosed by hedges and entered by two gates that stood originally in the gardens of Holme Lacy House.[33] After Sir Henry's death a Furniture Inventory of Holme Lacy House was produced listing all the contents of the 5 servants' rooms, 18 bedrooms, 2 dressing rooms, the gallery, 2 halls with oil paintings and tapestries, the library and its books, the kitchen, butler's pantry, dairy, laundry and housekeeper's room. All glassware, cutlery, china and linen were itemised, together with seven hogsheads and nine casks of cider in two cellars. The saddle room and coach house contained a long inventory of harnesses, bridles, three carriages, one cart and a stabled carriage mare and gelding.[34]

In 1888 Sir Henry was succeeded at Holme Lacy by his eldest son, Edwyn, who became the 10th Earl of Chesterfield and 4th Baronet of Stanhope. Sir Edwyn had been born in 1854 and was educated at Eton and Brasenose College, Oxford where he graduated in 1877, and then practiced at the Inner Temple as a Barrister-at-Law. In 1900 he married the beautiful Enid, second daughter of Charles Wilson, MP, a ship owner from Hull, Yorkshire. Edwyn led a busy and active life, holding prestigious positions as Treasurer of HM's Household, Captain of the Corps of Gentlemen-at-Arms, Lord Steward, Master of the Horse, a Justice of Peace in both Hereford and the North Riding, Deputy Lieutenant of Herefordshire and Captain of the 4th Battalion of the Shropshire Regiment. In his later life he was awarded the Order of the Red Eagle, 1st class (a Prussian order of chivalry), the Danish Grand Cross of the Dannebrog, and the Grand Cordon of the Order of King Leopold of Belgium. After his father's death he took his seat in the House of Lords and served in the Liberal government under Gladstone.[35] During his life he gained a reputation as 'one of the best dressed, best mannered and best looking men in the kingdom', and his wife Enid was known as 'witty, clever, artistic to her fingertips and adept at whatever happened to be the most fashionable sport or game'.[36]

The year 1891 saw the death of Revd William Stanhope aged 64, Edwyn's unmarried uncle who served for 20 years as vicar of Holme Lacy church and was buried in the graveyard.[37] It appears that Holme Lacy House was let out during the 1890s to an auditor by the name of Richard Oliverson, his wife, daughter and two sons from Hyde Park, as Sir Edwyn was living at Grosvenor Gardens near his London Clubs of Brooks's, Turf, Marlborough and Bachelors'. Richard Oliverson was a barrister and a Justice of the Peace in Lancaster, and kept a household staff of ten at Holme Lacy, with Charles Taverner the coachman/groom, William Humphries the head gardener and Thomas Wall the estate's agent at Pound Farm.[38] To celebrate Queen Victoria's Diamond Jubilee Sir Edwyn allowed a day of 'Athletic Races' to be held in the park for the parishioners of Holme Lacy, Ballingham and Bolstone. The programme included races for men, ladies, children, and for those mounted on bicycles, donkeys, horses and ponies. Prize money did not exceed 5s except 10s for the Tug of War. The sports commenced after the Men's Dinner at 1 pm, and women and children were served tea at 4 pm. The day was organised by Revd Jenkins, vicar of Ballingham, and Mr Hodskiss of Lower Bogmarsh Farm, Holme Lacy.[39]

The Holme Lacy estate in 1899 was 'famous for its charms' and its prospects that were enjoyed by the tourist travelling along the Wye. The landscape 'composed of hills in endless varieties, descending to the glorious river, was truly English in its rich luxuriance, full of charm as clouds passed over and

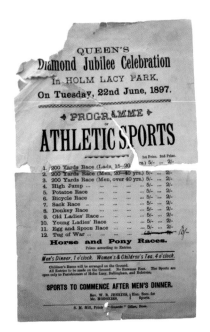

Poster advertising the Queen's Diamond Jubilee sports to be held at Holme Lacy in 1897 (*Herefordshire Archives*)

CLOCKWISE FROM TOP LEFT: Monkey Puzzle; and Scots Pines planted in the grounds of Holme Lacy House in Victorian times (*Heather Hurley*); the Monarch tree in 1866 (*Woolhope Club Transactions*); the Monarch tree in 2018 (*Heather Hurley*); cordon pears inside the walls in 2018 (*Heather Hurley*); cordon pears shortly after being planted in 1865, from H. Bull's *A Sketch of the Life of Lord Vis Scudamore*, 1894

LEFT: Portrait of Enid Wilson as Countess of Chesterfield (*National Trust*). RIGHT: The Earl of Chesterfield as his picture appeared in *Herefordshire Portraits*, printed by Jakeman and Carver in 1908

fleeting bursts of sunshine lit up its woods and meadows'. The gardens were 'simple and good' with various styles blending and contrasting in a pleasing way. The house was seen from the park beyond a broad lawn rising from the lakeside amid a wealth of foliage, firstly discovered by the visitor at the entrance gate where great elms overhung the drive. Many varieties of forest trees were admired in the park where oak, elm, ash, beech, cedar and a few coniferous trees were said to blend in beautifully. The splendid Monarch Oak had a circumference of 21 ft 10 in. and the Trysting Tree was found to be 'grander', whereas the Orangery was 'clustered with magnolias'.[40] In 1866 the Woolhope Club had visited the ridge of Holme Lacy where 'oak trees grew in great perfection', noting in particular the Monarch Oak and the Trysting tree which they measured and photographed.[41]

By 1900 the time was almost overdue for the eligible Sir Edwyn, 10th Earl of Chesterfield, now aged 46 to get married. He chose the beautiful 21-year-old Enid Wilson, second daughter of Charles Wilson 1st Baron Nunburnholme, whom he married at St Mark's church in Mayfair on 15 February. Although his bachelor life had ended he was residing at Grosvenor Street in London whilst she was at Holme Lacy entertaining Bernard Gunston, an army captain and her brother-in-law Evelyn, Chief Police Constable of Herefordshire. Enid was amply provided for in the house with a cook, lady's maid, three house maids, laundry maid, kitchen maid, scullery maid, two butlers and three general servants, with outside help from Thomas Hayward the head gamekeeper, William Humphries the head gardener and Thomas Wall the agent at Pound Farm.[42] Family photographs of 1901 depict Holme Lacy House with heavily furnished rooms typical of the Victorian period, a formal garden, a park with its trees, family groups and a smart two-horse-drawn carriage. The album includes personal images of Queen Victoria, the Prince Consort and King Edward VII who ascended the throne in 1901.[43]

By 1903 Sir Edwyn had become a patron of St John's Hospital for Diseases of the Skin, founded in Soho in London in 1863 and where the School of Dermatology was established in 1885. In 1896 in-patient wards were opened in Hammersmith, and in 1903 Sir Edwyn appealed for further funds for the rebuilding of the out-patients department in Soho. At a later date St John's became a London University postgraduate hospital and Sir Edwyn's name is remembered in the Chesterfield Gold Medal awarded to outstanding postgraduates.[44]

In 1907 Sir Edwyn applied to the Charity Commissioners to amalgamate the various Holme Lacy Charities under a scheme to benefit selected people under the age of 60 who for two years had not received Poor-law Relief, as it appears that some earlier charities had been lost whilst others had been incorporated into the 'Charity of the Honourable Jane Scudamore' and the 'Charity of Viscountess Scudamore, otherwise Duke of Beaufort's Charity'.[45]

One possible blot on the character of Sir Edwyn was his involvement with the Wye Free Fishery case which started in 1906 to prevent the free fishermen's rights of fishing a stretch of the Wye. Lord Chesterfield (as Sir Edwyn was referred to in the case) and Mrs Alice Foster each owned one bank of the Wye opposite one another for a stretch of some 3 miles and claimed that they owned the whole fishery along that stretch of the river. The defendants in the case, a Mr Harris and a Mr Bailey, claimed that the fishery for this stretch and more of the river was vested in the Hundred or Manor of Wormelow subject to the rights of freeholders in the Manor or Hundred to a common right of fishery, as had been the case for at least 700 years. In 1907 the local magistrates upheld the defendants' rights and the following year Lord Chesterfield and Mrs Foster appealed the decision which was heard in the High Court. This accepted the claim of long and uninterrupted rights of the freeholders of the Manor or Hundred to fish this stretch of the river but was reversed when taken to the Court of Appeal that same year. The judges came to the conclusion that the Hundred of Wormelow was an irrelevance as it covered too wide an area; that all the documentation from Domesday onwards could not prove that the Manor of Wormelow had any rights to the soil of this stretch of the river; that an unending right to fish commercially (which Harris and Bailey had been doing, netting and selling fish in local markets and on the fish board at Hoarwithy) was illegal in law, and finally that a private right to fish could not have been granted them as they were not freeholders 'of any ancient messuage'. At

The saloon in Holme Lacy House in 1909 (*Kentchurch Archives*)

the subsequent appeal by Messrs Harris and Bailey to the House of Lords heard in 1911, the Court of Appeal's judgement was upheld by a majority of four to three of the law lords hearing the case. By this time, however, Sir Edwyn had sold up and moved away to Scudamore House, Regent's Park near Buckingham Palace where he was a member of the Royal Household on the 'Board of the Green Cloth'. Later he retired to Beningbrough Hall in Yorkshire.[46]

xx.   *Supplement to COUNTRY LIFE.*   [June 19th, 1909.

TELEGRAMS:
"GALLERIES, LONDON."

KNIGHT, FRANK AND RUTLEY.
Offices: 9, CONDUIT STREET, LONDON, W.

TELEPHONES:
1942 GERRARD.
497 MAYFAIR.

By Direction of the Right Honourable the Earl of Chesterfield.
IMPORTANT ANNOUNCEMENT of the
SALE BY AUCTION
on THURSDAY, July 29th, 1909, at Two o'clock,
by Messrs.
KNIGHT, FRANK & RUTLEY,
of the HISTORICAL DOMAIN

"HOLME LACY"

(between Ross and Hereford), for centuries the home of the
Scudamores, and unquestionably one of the most beautiful
seats in England.

The Estate extends to about **5,504 ACRES**, and is situated
in the midst of the picturesque hills rising to 700ft. above sea
level, and descending into the

RIVER WYE, with NINE MILES OF SALMON FISHING.
The Property will be divided as follows:
Holme Lacy portion, 5,018 acres.   Outlying portion, 486 acres.
Few estates possess the varied attractions of Holme Lacy
with its Mansion, beautiful in its simplicity, the gardens and
grounds with their famous giant yew hedges and specimen
forest trees, the exceptional shooting and fishing facilities, and
the many historical associations connected with the Property.
Holme Lacy lies about five miles south-east of Hereford,
in the parishes of Holme Lacy, Ballingham, Bolstone, Little
Dewchurch, Hentland, Little Birch, and Aconbury, and has
two railway stations on the Estate.
Placed on a plateau about 250ft. above sea level, on gravel
soil, with glorious views over the Wye Valley, and surrounded
by the

TOP: The dining room in Holme Lacy House in 1909 (*Kentchurch Archives*). BOTTOM: An advertisement in *Country Life* for the sale of the Holme Lacy estate in 1909 (*Herefordshire Archives*)

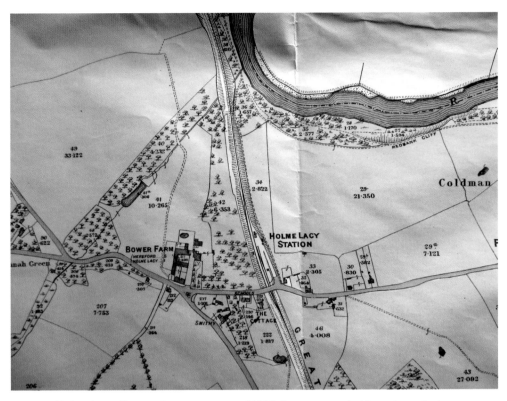

Holme Lacy village as shown on a map of 1909 that accompanied the sale particulars
(*Kentchurch Archives*)

It may have been partly due to this expensive Wye Free Fishery case, combined with the costs of releasing the entailment of Holme Lacy (so removing a restriction placed on the house of limiting the inheritance to the owner's lineal descendants and so preventing its sale), and the lack of family fortunes that forced Sir Edwyn to sell the Holme Lacy estate in 1909, the same year that *Country Life* featured the house in three parts under 'Country Homes, Gardens Old & New'.[47] The agents, Knight, Frank and Rutley of Mayfair in London, first advertised the 'Freehold, Manorial, Sporting and Agricultural Domain' on a two-page illustrated spread in April, then on full-size pages each month in *Country Life* before the auction on 29 July. The lavish and bound sale particulars with a separate wallet for the estate plans were sent out to prospective purchasers. These detailed the 5,578 acres and described the house with its vestibule, four reception rooms, billiard room, music room, smoking room, study, gun room and domestic offices on the ground floor, along with 37 bedrooms and dressing rooms with four bathrooms on the upper floors. The house was provided with an abundant supply of water gravitating from a reservoir on the estate, which was stored in cisterns for a hot water system. In the grounds there was stabling for nine horses at Pound Farm, a 23-acre garden with a walled kitchen garden, a 288-acre deer park with 150 fallow deer, nine miles of salmon fishing on the Wye and 772 acres of woods and plantations. The sale also included the Advowson of Holme Lacy and Ballingham, 18 farms, 11 smallholdings, 71 cottages, three private houses, a timber yard and a stone and sand quarry.[48]

At the auction the reserve price was not met, and so Sir Robert Tooth, a wealthy Australian banker and brewer, agreed to purchase 3,396 acres of the estate for £140,000 of which £8,000 was paid as a deposit with the remainder due on completion in February 1910. The remaining land and farms were subsequently successfully auctioned off. The Grinling Gibbons carvings were not included in the sale and were to be removed by Sir Edwyn 'making good any damage done to the Mansion'.[49] The sale of the other contents of Holme Lacy House not retained by the Chesterfields took place over four days commencing on 31 January 1910.[50]

The departure of Lord and Lady Chesterfield ended the Scudamores' association with Holme Lacy that had lasted for hundreds of years, but it is not the end of the Scudamore story – for at Kentchurch Court Lady Patricia, daughter and sole heir of the 12th Earl of Chesterfield married Lt Cmdr John Lucas Scudamore of Kentchurch Court in 1947 (*see Chapter 6*), and during her married life at Kentchurch was able to acquire many family portraits, items of furniture and Grinling Gibbons carvings that had formerly hung at Holme Lacy House to display at Kentchurch.[51]

The early Ancestry of the Scudamores of Kentchurch is involved in much obscurity
(Charles Robinson, 1872)

SCUDAMORES OF KENTCHURCH & HOLME LACY: A TIMELINE

NATIONAL EVENTS	DATES	KENTCHURCH: family members living, and key events	HOLME LACY: family members living, and key events
Norman Conquest (1066)			
Domesday Survey (1086)	1086	*Ralph*; Ralph at Corras, Kentchurch	
Henry I became king (1100)			
	1120	*Reginald*	
Stephen became king (1135)	1138	*Walter*	
Henry II became king (1154)	1148	*Sir Walter*	
	1195	*Walter*	
Magna Carta sealed (1215)	1227	*Ralph*	
	1230	*John 1*	
Edw. I became king (1272)	1281	*Vincent*	
	1300	*John 2*	
Edw. III became king (1327)	1337	*John 3*	
	1370	*Sir John 4*	
	1382	. . . .	*Philip*; Philip of Hollington, Holme Lacy
	1383	*Sir John 5*	
	1386	*Sir John 6*; Kentchurch fortified; Jack of Kent living at Kentchurch	
Hen. IV became king (1399)	1398	Scudamores raid Dore Abbey	
Owain Glyndwr rebellions (1400–15)	1400s	Sir John married Alice Glyndwr	
	1409	. . . .	Raid on William Hamm of Holme Lacy
Hen. V became king (1413)	1411	. . . .	*George*
Battle of Agincourt (1415)			
	1430	*Sir John 7*	
	1442	. . . .	*Philip*
Wars of the Roses (1455–86)			

NATIONAL EVENTS	DATES	KENTCHURCH: *family members living,* and key events	HOLME LACY: *family members living,* and key events
Bat. Mortimers Cross (1461) Rich. III became king (1483) Hen. VII became king (1485)			
	1489	*James*	*William*
Hen. VIII became king (1509)			
	1521	*Joan & Philip*; Marriage linking Kentchurch & Holme Lacy branches	
Dissolution of the monasteries began (1536)	1536	. . . .	*John* augmentation receiver of monastic lands
	1538	. . . .	Site for Holme Lacy House chosen
	1541	. . . .	*Sir John (1541–1623)*
	1546	Park formerly belonging to Knights Hospitallers purchased	Holme Lacy House completed, and Chapel consecrated
Act of Uniformity (1552) Mary became queen (1553) Eliz. I became queen (1558)	1547	. . . .	*John*
	1562	Marriage linking Kentchurch to Holme Lacy	
Papal Bull of excommunication (1570)	1569	. . . .	Sir John takes the Oath of Supremacy
	1572	. . . .	Sir John Usher and Gentleman Pensioner at Court
	1580	Mills on the Monnow dispute	
	1584	*John*; Manors seized by Crown	
	1596	. . . .	Sir James at tilts before the queen
James I became king; Bye Plot conspiracy (1603)	1600	. . . .	*John 1st Viscount (1600–71)*
Gunpowder Plot (1605)	1605	Whitsun riots in Monnow valley	
	1607	*Thomas*	
	1616	*John*	
Charles I became king (1625)	1624	*John*; First mention of Court	Virginia Company dissolved
	1627	. . . .	County Horse Troop
England made peace with France and Spain (1630)	1629	*John*	Carey Forge partnership of Kyrle and Scudamores

National Events	Dates	Kentchurch: family members living, and key events	Holme Lacy: family members living, and key events
	1632	. . . .	House repairs; Redstreak cider
	1635	. . . .	John, Ambassador to France
	1637	Llancillo iron forge	
	1639	. . . .	New Holme Lacy Vicarage
Civil War began (1642)	1642	. . . .	John captured during Civil War
Siege of Goodrich castle (1646)	1647	. . . .	Losses due to Civil War
Charles I executed;	1649	. . . .	*John 2nd Vis. (1649–97)*
Commonwealth (1649)	1650	Miles Hill accounts	
Restoration of monarchy; Charles became king (1660)			
Great Plague (1665)	1665	Pontrilas forge	
Great Fire of London (1666)	1672	Llancillo forge	
	1674	. . . .	Rebuilding of house
Titus Oates, Popish Plot (1678)	1678	. . . .	
	1679	Father Kemble executed	
	1680	*William (1680–1741)*	
James II became king (1685)	1684	. . . .	*John 3rd Vis. (1684–1716)*
Glorious Revolution (1688)			
Battle of the Boyne; William and Mary became king and queen (1689)	1691	Inn at Kentchurch recorded	
Anne became queen (1702)	1695	Trees felled	Wye and Lugg Navigation Act
Queen Anne's Bounty; Battle of Blenheim (1704)	1711	. . . .	*Lady Frances Fitzroy (1711–49)*
George I became king (1714)	1717	. . . .	Timber accounts
South Sea Bubble (1720)	1725	. . . .	Alexander Pope visited
George II became king (1727)	1727	*Col John (1727–96)*	
	1729	Hereford Turnpike Trust	Hereford Turnpike Trust
	1749	. . . .	*Frances Duchess of Norfolk (1749–1820)*
Change of calendar (1752)			
	1754	Bark stripping	
George III became king (1760)	1757	*John (1757–1805)*; County Militia	
American War of Independence (1775)	1773	Anthony Keck reconstruction	
	1776	. . . .	Great pear tree production
Wars of Spanish Succession (1780)	1780	. . . .	Maps by Frizell

National Events	Dates	Kentchurch: family members living, and key events	Holme Lacy: family members living, and key events
	1786	. . . .	Charles becomes Duke of Norfolk
Napoleonic Wars started (1793)	1793	. . . .	*Sir Edwyn Scudamore-Stanhope (1793–1874)*
	1795	Plans undertaken attributed to Nash	
Act of Union with Ireland (1801)	1798	*John Lucy (1798–1875)*	Three Choirs Festival Concert
	1809	River Wye & Lugg Towing Path Act	
End of Napoleonic Wars (1815)	1815	. . . .	Duke of Norfolk dies
	1816	. . . .	Family papers subject to Chancery
George IV became king (1820)	1820	Restoration by Thomas Tudor	
	1821	. . . .	*Sir Henry Scudamore-Stanhope 9th Earl of Chesterfield (1821–87)*
	1822	. . . .	Vaults reopened in church
Catholic Emancipation (1829)	1827	Tramway established	Sir Edwyn Stanhope became main heir
William IV became king (1830)			
	1831	*Laura Adelaide Lucas (1831–1912)*	
Reform Act (1832)	1832	. . . .	Sir Edwyn moves in
Victoria became queen (1837)			
Abolition of the slave trade (1838)	1840	Garden improvements	
	1850	Lucas of Castle Shane	
Crimean War started (1853)	1854	. . . .	*Sir Edwyn Scudamore-Stanhope 10th Earl of Chesterfield (1854–1933) left Holme Lacy in 1910*
	1855	. . . .	Hereford, Ross & Gloucester Railway opened
Indian Mutiny (1857)			
	1859	Church rebuilt	
	1853	*Edward Lucas Scudamore (1853–1917)*	
	1854	GWR opened via Pontrilas	
	1857	. . . .	Fownhope and Holme Lacy Bridges Act
	1876	Kentchurch Court tenanted	

National Events	Dates	Kentchurch: family members living, and key events	Holme Lacy: family members living, and key events
	1883	. . . .	Sir Henry succeeds to 9th Earl of Chesterfield
	1890	. . . .	House tenanted
Edw. VII became king (1901)	1902	*John Harford Lucas-Scudamore (1902–76) married Lady Patricia, only child of 12th Earl of Chesterfield, living at Kentchurch in 1960*	
	1906	. . . .	Wye Free Fishery Case
Geor. V became king (1910)	1910	. . . .	Sale of house and contents completed
WWI started (1914)	1920	Castle Shane fired and burnt down	
Outbreak of Irish Civil War (1922)	1927	Family returned to Kentchurch Court	
Edw. VIII became king then abdicated; G. VI king (1936) WWII started (1939)	1937	Opened gardens to the public	
Elizabeth II became queen (1952)	1959	Flooding of the Court	

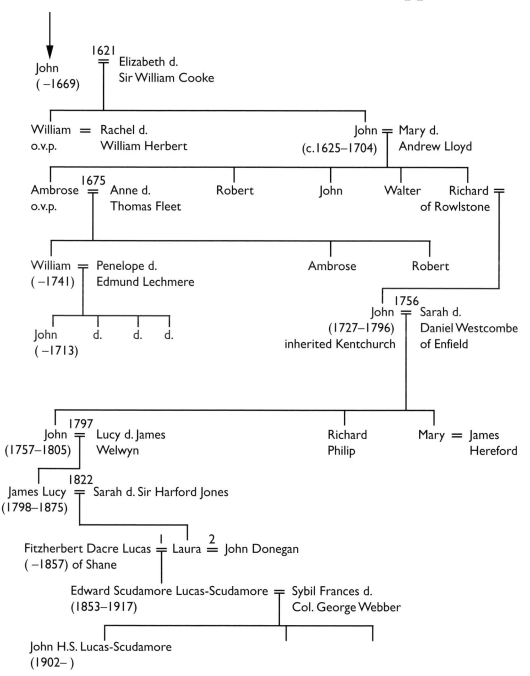

Family tree, as submitted by Sybil Lucas-Scudamore to the National Library of Wales in 1942 (*HAS NLW v III*)

BIBLIOGRAPHY

Atherton, I., *Ambition and failure* (1999)

— *John, 1st Viscount Scudamore* (1993)

Bigland, Ralph, *Monumental and Genealogical Collections* (1791)

Bull, H.G., *A Sketch of the Life of Lord Viscount Scudamore* (1894)

Coates, S. & Tucker, D., *Water-Mills of the Monnow* (1978)

— *Water-Mills of the Middle Wye Valley* (1983)

Dugdale, W., *Monasticon Anglicanum* (1830)

Duncumb, J., *General View of the Agriculture of Herefordshire* (1805)

— *Wormelow Hundred Lower Division* (J.H. Matthews) (1913)

— *Wormelow Hundred Upper Division* (J.H. Matthews) (1912)

Faraday, M.A., *Herefordshire Militia Assessments of 1663*

Fleming-Yates, J., *The River Running By* (2005)

Gibson, M., *Churches of Dore, Home-Lacy and Hempsted* (1727)

History of Parliament, printed and online, various dates

Hodges, G., *Ludford Bridge & Mortimer's Cross* (2001 edition)

— *Owain Glyn Dwr* (1995)

Hughes, P. & Hurley, H., *The Story of Ross* (2009)

Hurley, H., ed., *Landscape Origins of the Wye Valley* (2008)

— *The Green Lanes of Herefordshire* (2010)

— *The Pubs of Monmouth, Chepstow and the Wye Valley* (2007)

— *The Pubs of Ross & South Herefordshire* (2001)

— *Trackway to Turnpike* (2nd edition 2007)

Hurley, Jon, *In Search of John Kyrle* (2013)

Johnson, A. & Shoesmith, R., eds. *The Story of Hereford* (2016)

Leonard, J., *Herefordshire Churches through Victorian Eyes* (2006)

Lipscomb, George, *Journey into South Wales* (1802)

Little Birch History Group, *Little Birch on Aconbury Hill* (2006)

Moir, A.L., *Bishops of Hereford* (1964)

M.N.J., *Bygone Days in the March Wall of Wales* (1926)

Palmer, K., *The Grosmont Map* (2013)

Pevsner, N. & Brooks, A., *The Buildings of England, Herefordshire* (2012)

Price, J., *City of Hereford* (1796)

Richardson, John, *Local Historian's Encyclopaedia* (2nd edition 1986)

Robinson, C., *Castles of Herefordshire* (1869)
 — *Mansions and Manors of Herefordshire* (1872)

Ross, David, *Royalist, But ...* (2012)

Ross-Lewin, G.H., *Lord Scudamore* (1900)

Rowley, T., *The High Middle Ages* (1988)
 — *Landscape of the Welsh Marches* (1986)

Seaton, Revd, *History of Archenfield* (1903)

Shoesmith, R., *Hereford* (1992)

Shoesmith, R. & Richardson, R. (eds.), *Dore Abbey* (1997)

Skidmore, W., *Scudamores of Upton Scudamore* (1989)
 — *Scudamores of Holme Lacy* (ed. Moffatt, W.) (2015)

Thorn, F. & C., *Domesday Book, Herefordshire* (1985)

Timmins, H., *Nooks and Corners of Herefordshire* (1892)

Walker, R., *Dovecotes and Pigeon Houses of Herefordshire* (2010)

Webb, John, *Memorials of the Civil War Vol I & II* (1879)

Whitehead, D., *Historical Landscape Appraisal* (2003)

Whitehead, D., *Holme Lacy Parkland Plan* (2013)

Victoria County History (VCH), Herefordshire (1908)

ENDNOTES

ABBREVIATIONS

AL40 Kentchurch Court Papers
      & Documents at HAS
BGAS Bristol and Gloucestershire
      Archaeology Society
BL   British Library
BLG   *Burke's Landed Gentry*
GRO   Gloucester Record Office
GSIA Gloucestershire Society
      for Industrial Archaeology
HER   Herefordshire Historic
      Environment Record
HAS   Herefordshire Archive Service
HCA   Hereford Cathedral Archives
HCL   Hereford City Library
JP   Joseph Powell map *c.*1798 KA

KA   Kentchurch Archives
MNR   National Monuments Record
NLW   National Library of Wales
LOWV Landscape Origins
      of the Wye Valley
OS   Ordnance Survey
RCHM Royal Commission
      on Historic Monuments
TNA   The National Archives
TWNFC *Transactions of the Woolhope
      Naturalist's Field Club*
VCH   *Victoria County History*
WS   W. Skidmore, *Burke's Landed Gentry*
      (extract 1972)

1 Origins of the Scudamores at Kentchurch

1   WS, (1989) p 1
2   WS, (1989), F & C Thorn ed., *Domesday Book, Herefordshire* (1985), *Domesday Book*, Penguin edition (1992), pp 180 & 512
3   HER website, TWNFC (1989) pp 194–196
4   AL40, C14th
5   KA, Misc. papers. Recent research suggests the bear's paw denotes a second son
6   *Monasterii Sancti Petri*, Vol 1, p 280 (printed 1863), TWNFC (1989) p 194
7   Duncumb (1912) p 11
8   AL40 (1257), TWNFC (1989) p 208
9   WS (1972), Skidmore, W., *Some Notes on the Skidmore Family* (2010)
10 Ancient Deeds 1 HAS AL2/6, printed p 9
11 AL40 1299
12 AL40 1299
13 Duncumb (1912), Scudamore Family Tree online p 12

14 TWNFC (1989) p 208
15 Pat Rolls 14th century HAS AL2/3 printed p 253
16 Skidmore 1989, RCHM, Herefordshire Vol 1 p 153–154
17 National Parks, Thirlwall Castle leaflet (nd)
18 List of Kentchurch Rectors in Duncumb (1912) p 6
19 Hurley, H., Kentchurch Tour notes (2011), Palmer, R., *Herefordshire Folklore* 2002 pp 25–27
20 TWNFC (1912) pp 122–123
21 Pat Rolls 1401–1450 HAS AL2/4 printed pp 45–46
22 Royal Commission Survey 1926, NMR
23 Bridge Inn sign at Kentchurch, Hurley (2001) p 247–248
24 History of Parliament online, 1386–1421
25 Shoesmith, R. & Richardson, R. eds., *Dore Abbey* (1997) p 27
26 Shoesmith, R., *Goodrich Castle* (2014) p 47, Pat Rolls HAS AL2/3 14th century printed p 304, Close Rolls, KA 1351–1400 printed p 214, Hodges 1995 p 143
27 *Dictionary of Welsh Biography* online (1959)
28 *Monmouth Review*, Vol 1, No 3 (1933) p 245, Hodges (1995), preface p x
29 Griffiths, R., *Conquerors and Conquered in Medieval Wales* (1994) p 268, Herald's Visitation *c*.1634 HAS B56/1, Burke (1972)
30 Griffiths, R., *Conquerors and Conquered in Medieval Wales* (1994) p 268, Hodges (1995) pp 163–166
31 Thompson, E.M., translation of *Chronicon Adae de Usk* (1377–1421), printed 1904 p 237, tun equals 252 wine gallons, from Mendelsohn, O., *Dictionary of Drink and Drinking* (1965)
32 Griffiths, R., *Principality of Wales* (1972) p 360
33 Llywelyn ap Gruffydd Fychan Memorial leaflet 2001
34 *History of Parliament* online 1386–1421
35 Barker, J., *Agincourt* (2006) p 422, Skidmore, W., *Herefordshire and the Welsh Marches* mss (1983) KA
36 *Duchy of Lancaster Book*, translated from the French and framed at KA, Pat Rolls 1401–1450 HAS AL2/4, printed p 85
37 Duchy of Lancaster Books 11 Hen VI (1432) extract KA
38 Robinson (1872)
39 Members of Parliament KA
40 Johnson, A., & Shoesmith, R. eds., *The Story of Hereford* (2016) p 112, *Dictionary of Welsh Biography* online (1959)
41 AL40 1451
42 Hodges (2001) pp 45 & 56, Burke (1972), William Worcester printed 1969 in HAS CC60/1/2, *Dictionary of Welsh Biography* online (1959)
43 Thompson, E.M., translation of *Chronicon Adae de Usk* 1377–1421, printed 1904 p 113, Johnson, A., & Shoesmith, R. eds., *The Story of Hereford* (2016) p 171
44 Ancient Deeds 1 HAS AL2/6 printed
45 WS (1972), AL40 1456
46 KA (nd)
47 Duncumb (1912) p 15

48   AL40 1473, Skidmore, W., *Herefordshire & the Welsh Marches* (1983) KA

49   Rental HAS A63/111/23/1 with transcription from Joan Thomas, Phillipps notes HAS B56/6

50   AL40 1504

51   AL40 *c.*1521, WS (1972), Petitions 1409 TNA SC/8/186/9261

52   BLG (1937)

2 The Dissolution and Effect of the Reformation

1   Rowley, T., *The High Middle Ages* (1988) pp 315–316

2   Robinson (1872) p 177, Cooke, W.H., notes CF50/105, Duncumb (1912) p 10, 1535 *Valor Ecclesiasticus* J64/31

3   Royal Commission Survey (1926) MNR

4   Dugdale, W., *Monasticon Anglicanum* (1830) Vol 7 p 786, Hurley, H., 'Historic Harewood' in *Historical Aspects of Ross* (2000) p 185

5   Rowley, T., *Welsh Marches* (1986) p 181, Rental of Hospitallers HAS A63/111/23/1 with thanks to Joan Thomas for transcription

6   Cooke, W.H., notes HAS CF50/105, Duncumb (1912) p 12, Phillipps, R.B., HAS B56/6, Robinson (1872) p 177, Skidmore, W., *Herefordshire & the Welsh Marches* (1983) KA

7   Cooke, W.H., notes HAS CF50/105 in Latin, kindly transcribed by Philip Bouchier, archivist at HAS

8   Whitehead, D. & Lovelace, D., *Parkland Report* (2012), Duncumb (1912) p 12

9   *VCH Herefordshire* (1908) p 250, Royal Commission survey 1926 MNR, HER website

10   Shoesmith, R. & Richardson, R., *Dore Abbey* (1997), chapters XIV–XV

11   AL40 1560 Covenant, Alcock, N., Old Title Deeds (1986) p 44

12   Duncumb (1912) p 7

13   Cooke, W.H., notes HAS CF50/105

14   Fleming-Yates, J., 'Catholic Martyrs of the Wye Valley' in *Historical Aspects of Ross* Vol II p 37

15   Duncumb (1912) p 8, TNA website

16   List of MPs, KA

17   Griffith Davies, J., 'The Catholic Nonconformists' in *Monmouthshire Review* Jan 1934

18   Timmins, H.J., *Nooks and Corners of Herefordshire* (1892) pp 129 & 134

19   Master Harvey's Exhibition 1999

20   Robinson (1872) p 177, Skidmore, W., *Herefordshire & the Welsh Marches* (1983) KA

21   AL40 1582/1584 Rentals and Leases, Rees, W., *The Order of St John* (1947) p 91, Duncumb (1913) p 55

22   Phillipps, R.B., notes HAS B56/6

23   *Ducatus Lancastriae*, printed 1823 Vol III HAS J64/45, AL40 1595 grant

24   Exchequer records 36 Eliz 1594 TNA E112/17/101 (kindly obtained & transcribed by David Lovelace)

25   Visitation of Herefordshire 1634 printed p 142

26 AL40 1599 Grant
27 Nicholls, M., 'Treason's Reward' in *Historical Journal* Vol 38, No 4, Dec 1995 pp 821 & 838–841
28 Duncumb (1912) pp 8–9
29 Skidmore, W., *Herefordshire & the Welsh Marches* (1983) KA, AL40 1607 Surrender
30 Skidmore, W., *Herefordshire & the Welsh Marches* (1983) KA
31 Cooke notes HAS CF50/105
32 STAC records TNA 8/70/3
33 AL40 1616 will (kindly transcribed by David Lovelace). Amy was the daughter of John Starkey of Darlie Hall, Chester
34 Eighteenth-century notes HAS CF50/107
35 Kentchurch church monuments, Robinson (1872) p 178, the tomb was vandalised in 1991, *Hereford Times* 1 Aug 1991
36 AL40 1621 grant, JP map KA, BLG (1937)
37 AL40 1625 award, first known mention of Court in 1624
38 Robinson (1872) p 178, *Herald's Visitation* Vol III (1634) HAS BS6/1, *Alumni Oxonienses* Vol III 1968 pp 1327–1328
39 AL40 *c.*1650 Llancillo Forge
40 Llancillo forge visited in 2017; further history in chapter three
41 AL40 1637 lease, Coates, S. & Tucker, D., *Water-mills of the Monnow* (1978) pp 46–47, Rowley, T., *Welsh Marches* (1986) pp 228–229
42 Coates, S. & Tucker, D., *Water-mills of the Monnow* (1978) pp 45–46, HAN 24 (1972)
43 JP map KA, Master Harvey's Exhibition 1999

3 Civil War and Aftermath

1   TWNFC (1912) pp 121–122
2   AL40 surrender & lease 1640
3   Webb (1879) Vol I p 7 & 9, Jervoise, E., *Ancient Bridges* 1936 p 122, Fleming-Yates (2005) p 196, 1770 plan M26/8/131
4   Little Birch History Group, *Little Birch on Aconbury Hill* (2006) p 47
5   Atherton, Ian, *John, 1st Viscount Scudamore* (1993) p 179
6   Webb (1879) Vol II p 398
7   Ross, David, *Royalist, But...* (2012) p 128
8   Skidmore, W., *Herefordshire & the Welsh Marches* (1983) KA, Webb (1879) Vol II p 408
9   Webb, J., *Memorials of the Civil War* Vol II p 406
10 AL40 Grant 1648/9 , Robinson p 178
11 Miles Hill MSS 1650 HCL PC2506
12 Duncumb (1912) p 10, Webb, J., *Memorials of the Civil War* (1879) Vol II p 410
13 AL40 Deed 1657
14 Militia Assessments 1663 p 125
15 Hearth Tax 1665 AM21/9, AL40 Articles of Agreement 1665, Coates & Tucker (1978) p 46, JP 1798 KA, Bryant map 1835

16   AL40 documents

17   Lease 1672 Gloucestershire Archives D1677/GHe/72, Coates & Tucker (1978) p 46, *VCH* Gloucester Vol v p 97

18   Duncumb (1912) p 9, Bowen, G., *The Jesuit Library in Hereford Cathedral* (1965) pp 24–25, *History Today* online

19   M.N.J., *Bygone Days in the March Wall of Wales* (1926) pp 223 & 231–232

20   Seaton, Rev., *History of Archenfield* (1903) p 95 (Combe is Cwm in Llanrothal)

21   Seaton, Rev., *Seaton* (1903) p 95 (Kemble was canonised as a saint in 1970)

22   Webb 1879 Vol II p 428, AL40 documents

23   M.N.J., *Bygone Days in the March Wall of Wales* (1926) p 223

24   Webb (1879) Vol II p 428

25   Bromage, R.R., *Father John Kemble* (1902) p 34 HAS X61

26   AL40 1686 transfer of trust

27   Hughes & Hurley (2009) p 85–86

28   *BBC History* online

29   AL40 Commission 1689, Kentchurch archives

30   Kentchurch Parish Registers MX131

31   AL40 1691 lease, Navy Board records 1695 TNA ADM106/461/87 & 106, 106/480/166,106/482/77

32   Hurley, H., *Herefordshire's River Trade* (2013) p 46

33   AL40 1701 Deed, the forge was reassigned in 1702 Bristol Archives 31963/53

34   Kentchurch Parish Registers HAS MX131,

35   AL40 documents and 1701 Will

36   1713 Charity HAS L10/6, Charity Commissioners Report 1819–1837 p 315

37   Charity Commissioners Report 1819–1837 p 302

38   AL40 documents 1730 to 1733, Commission & Inquisition of Lunacy 1736 TNA C211/23/S61

39   Johnson & Shoesmith (2016) p 216, Hereford Road Act 1729 HCL PLC386, Hurley 2nd edition (2006) p 50

40   AL40 Mortgage 1740

41   AL40 list of burials 1686–1802

42   BLG (1972)

43   AL40 Letters and Papers 1741–44

44   AL40 Survey, Rental and Remarks 1742

4 Colonel John Scudamore and Keck's Remodelling of Kentchurch Court

1   HAS CF50/105

2   AL40 letters 1744–45

3   AL40 Letters and Papers 1641–44, Robinson (1872) p 176, TWNFC (1980) p 98, AL40 Bennarth 1750

4   Lincolns Inn website, Middle Temple Guide (2013) p 24

5   AL40 title & mortgage 1750

6   AL40 will 1750 (almost illegible due to damp)

7   Rents 1752–54 HAS M26/8/132, AL40 acreage 1750

8   AL40 mortgage & accounts 1754, Hurley, H., *Landscape Origins of the Wye Valley* (2008) p 128

9   AL40 documents 1750

10   Assignment 1727 HAS M26/2012

11   Inventory 1736 HAS M26/20/14

12   KA, Richardson, S., Correspondence with Sarah Westcombe 1808

13   AL40 commission of deputy lieutenant 1757

14   Brecon Road Act 1759 HCL LC386, AL40 Turnpike Act 1756

15   Bills 1757–59 HAS M26/15/2

16   Williams, E.N., *Life in Georgian England* (1962), Johnson & Shoesmith (2016) p 192

17   Kissack, K., *Monmouth* (1975) p 270

18   AL40 Commission 1760, Richardson (1989) p 201

19   Hopkinson, C., *Herefordshire Under Arms* (1985) p 101

20   AL40 tenants rents 1760

21   AL40 Llangua Mill Lease 1762

22   Coates & Tucker (1978) p 52, Herefordshire Through Time website, Rowlestone Tithe Map 1839, Palmer, K., *The Grosmont Map* (2013) pp 46–49

23   Bills 1765 HAS M26/15/3-5, AL40 Servant's wages 1764

24   *History of Parliament* Vol III p 419, Williams, E., *Georgian England* (1962) pp 11–14

25   Heath, C., *Excursion Down the Wye* (1828) no pagination, thanks to Judy Stevenson for enquiring about the skull

26   Proposals 1770 HAS M26/7/229

27   Lovelace, D. & Whitehead, D., Kentchurch Park Report (2012)

28   HAS M26 passim

29   HAS M26/14/124, M26/8/102, M26/6/108

30   Bills HAS M26/15/5, Charity Commissioners Report, Herefordshire Charities 1819–37 p 330

31   HAS M26/9/177–215, *History of Parliament* Vol III p 419, Richardson, S., Correspondence with Sarah Westcombe (1808)

32   Richardson, R., Correspondence with Sarah Westcombe (1808), Carpentry 1771 HAS M26/ 15/8, *Herefordshire Directory 1784*

33   Brooks, A. & Pevsner, N., *Herefordshire* (2012), Colvin, H., *English Architects* (1954) pp 332–333

34   Francis Thomas proposals 1773 HAS M26/6/14, D. Whitehead, TWNFC (1992)

35   Margam Park guide (nd) pp 6–7

36   AL40 Insurance 1774, AL40 letter 1777

37   *History of Parliament 1754–1790*

38   AL40 letter, Letter from Milborne to Harley 1774 HAS F37/238, *History of Parliament 1754–1790*

39   Shoesmith, R. & Eisel, J., *The Pubs of Hereford City* (2004) p 145

40   AL40 burials

41   Letter 1776 HAS M26/7/231, AL40 Appointment 1778, Expenses 1778–79

42   AL40 admission & articled 1779

43   Letters HAS M26/15/77–79

44 AL40 Oath 1789, Commission of DL 1807

45 Byng, J., *Torrington Diaries 1781–1794* (1954 edition) pp 38 & 61

46 Letter HAS M26/6/102, catalogue details HAS M26/14/95–96, M26/14/114

47 *Hereford Journal* 15th Mar 1787

48 AL40 Rents 1785, bark 1785, 1789, acreage in 1781, bark 1791 HAS M/26/92–3, M26/6/61

49 AL40 accounts 1794, *Hereford Journal* 20th Feb 1793, Lovelace D. & Whitehead, D., Kentchurch Park Report (2012)

50 AL40 In Chancery 1786

51 Letters HAS M26/15/144

52 Letter 1787 HAS M26/8/90, wine info Jon Hurley

53 Letters HAS M26/6/107–115

54 Letters HAS M26 passim.

55 Letters 1793–94 HAS M26/8/34–8

56 Hurley, H., *Harewood End Agricultural Society* (2015) p 1

57 Portrait by J.A. Oliver at Kentchurch Court

58 Davis, T., *John Nash* (1960) pp 25 & 90, Price, J., *City of Hereford* (1796) p 72

59 Whitehead, D., 'John Nash & Humphrey Repton', TWNFC (1992), Cornforth, J., Kentchurch Court Part 1, *Country Life* (1966) p 1633, the earliest reference to Nash & Kentchurch is in Neale, J.P., *Views of Seats* (1828) and by Samuel Meyrick in 1835 HAS CF50/105

60 *History of Parliament 1790–1820*

61 AL40 Burials, Havergal, F., *Monumental Inscriptions* (1881) p 62 (the monument has been moved and could not be found in 2016)

62 Lucas-Scudamore, Lady Patricia notes (nd) KA, portrait by J.A. Oliver

63 AL40 Burials, Will HAS M26/6/34

5 John Lucy Scudamore, John Nash's Legacy and Thomas Tudor

1 Duncumb, J., (1912) pp 10–11

2 BLG (1972), Pre-nuptial 1797 AL40

3 Inventory 1797 HAS M26/6/100

4 Rentals 1797 AL40, Rentals 1797 HAS M26/9/52, Burials AL40

5 Joseph Powell maps *c.*1798 KA

6 Burgh of Ayr 1798 AL40, *History of Parliament 1790–1820*

7 Proc of Court Martial 1800 online passim, Burgh of Ayr 1798 AL40

8 Tablet in Kentchurch church

9 Accounts & letter 1799 AL40

10 Kentchurch Land Tax 1799 HAS Q/REL/8/18/1–37

11 AL40 Rental 1803, Survey 1803 AL40

12 AL40 Memo 1800

13 *History Today* Vol 61 (2011)

14 Heath, C., *Excursion Down the Wye* (1824) (no pagination)

15 Her Jnl 10th Feb 1802, Hurley, H., *Herefordshire's River Trade* (2013) p 14

16 *History of Parliament 1790–1820*

17 Chancery 1806 TNA C101/2263, *History of Parliament 1820–1832*

18 Deputy Lieutenant 1807 AL40, Wye & Lugg 1810 AL40

19 Chancery C101/2260 TNA, notes KA, *History of Parliament 1820–1832*

20 BLG 1972, Brasenose College Registers 1909 p 444, *Hereford Journal* 29th March 1820

21 Jennerian Society 1820 AL40, Centre for the History of Medicine online

22 Powys History Project online, Harford Jones assumed the family surname and arms of Brydges, *Burke's Peerage* (1888)

23 Letters, accounts 1821–1822 AL40

24 No letters or plans of Kentchurch from Nash have been located

25 AL40 timber valuations & sales 1823–24, Hurley, H., *Herefordshire's River Trade* (2013) pp 32 & 133, Waters, I., *About Chepstow (*1952) p 24

26 accounts & letters 1824–25 AL40

27 letter 1823 AL40, major work 1825 AL40, notes KA

28 letters Bird, Harford Jones, Tudor 1823–24 AL40, *Wye Tour and its Artists* (2010) guide

29 accounts & letters 1822–1826 AL40

30 Brayley, E. & Britton, J., *The Beauties of Britain (c.*1805), AL40 1824 repairs

31 letter 1825 AL40

32 account 1828 AL40, Kentchurch Rentals 1827–30 KA, Owen N., *History of the Landscape* (2004) pp 9 & 26 KA, Lovelace, D. & Whitehead, D., Kentchurch Parkland (2012) pp 21 & 40

33 Release 1828 AL40

34 letters 1824–28 AL40

35 Gatehouse built in 1840s but Rev M.G. Watkins dates it *c.*1860 in *History of Kentchurch* (1891) p 73 KA

36 AL40 letter 1826, Owen, N., *History of the Landscape* (2004) KA, info from Tristan Gregory in 2017, Watkins, M.G., *History of Kentchurch* (1891) p 69

37 letter 1826 AL40

38 letters 1828 AL40, Case over River Monnow 1832 AL40

39 survey 1827 AL40, Hurley, H., *Herefordshire's River Trade* (2013) p 158, Tram Road Act 1826 HAS BC79/14/1c

40 letters 1828 AL40, Hurley, H., *Trackway to Turnpike* (2nd edition 2007) p 50

41 report 1828 AL40

42 Eisel, J. & Bennett, F., *The Pubs of Hay on Wye* (2005) pp 51–55, AL40 Monmouth Cap 1830–33, Grosmont mill 1829–36 AL40

43 Turnpike road plan 1832 HAS Q/RWt/27

44 turnpike roads & highways 1835–38 AL40, Fleming-Yates, J., (2005) pp 190–209, (the stopped-up road remains as a ROW and HAS Q/SR/126–127 1839 was not traced)

45 George Bentham notes 1993 KA

46 Scudamore letters 1832–38 KA

47 Portrait KA, Hurley, H., notes (2007)

48 Census 1841

49   accounts 1840 AL40, Hurley, H. (2001) p 250
50   assignment of mortgage 1846 AL40, vouchers 1840–1848 AL40, Bryant map
     1835, Road plan 1832 HAS Q/RWt/27, Letters 1846–47 HAS A95/v/EB/1183–1219
51   vouchers 1843–48 AL40, Watkins, M.G., *History of Kentchurch* (1891) p 75
52   Scudamore notes (nd) KA
53   *Herefordshire Directory 1851*
54   Census 1851

6   Laura Adelaide, the Lucas Family and the Colourful Twentieth Century

1   Robinson (1872) p 176
2   Census 1851, Family journal (nd) KA, BLG 1837
3   Lucas Diary 1820–1825 Xerox copy KA (transcribed by Jon Hurley)
4   Portrait at Kentchurch KA, Scudamore letters 1856–57 KA
5   Lucknow Residency website, Memorial inscription KA, *The Times* 10th Feb 1858,
     Irish War Memorials website
6   Letter 1857 KA
7   Journal (nd) KA, letters 1856–57 KA
8   Letter 1860 KA
9   Census 1861
10   Journal (nd) KA, Harford Jones died in 1847, Land Improvement Loan AL40 1860
11   Family Search website
12   *Herefordshire Directory 1867*, Parsonage (1866) HAS HD10/25, Hurley (2001)
     pp 249–250
13   Letter 1869 KA
14   Census 1871, Family Search website
15   Death Registration 1875, Family Search website, Watkins, M.G., *History of
     Kentchurch* (1891), KA
16   Inventory 1875 HAS M5B/153/2
17   Hurley notes (2011), Much Marcle church guide (nd)
18   *Herefordshire Directory 1876*, Watkins, M.G., *History of Kentchurch* (1891) KA
19   *Herefordshire Directory 1876*, Hurley, H. (2001) p 151
20   UK County Families 1879 (with thanks to Joan Fleming-Yates)
21   Census 1881
22   Particulars 1881 found in Cooke's Notes HAS CF30/105
23   Census 1881, Cooke's Notes HAS CF30/105, Kentchurch Tithe map 1839, Watkins,
     M.G., *History of Kentchurch* (1891), Parish Council minutes (1973) HAS AS97/1
24   Land Improvement Loan AL40 (1890)
25   *Herefordshire Directory 1900*, Watkins, M.G., *History of Kentchurch* (1891) KA
     (extracts have been transcribed HAS AT43), Census 1891
26   Information from Joan Fleming-Yates (2017)
27   *Monmouthshire Directory 1895*, Monmouth Museum, Release AL40 (1893)
28   Letters from Edward to Sybil (1900) KA
29   Unnamed newspaper cutting 1900 KA, Cracroft's Peerage online

30   BLG (1894), 1891 census, photograph of Jack at Cap House 1903 KA, Ancestry details from Joan Fleming-Yates

31   Watkins, M.G., *History of Kentchurch* (1891) KA, the oaks have not survived

32   *Hereford Journal* 22 Feb 1907 KA

33   *Herefordshire Directory 1905*, photograph of Panhard (1905) KA

34   *Herefordshire Directory 1902, 1905*, Pontrilas Court sale (1919) HAS M5/16/6

35   Herefordshire Portraits (1908), poster (1906) KA

36   Photographs 1907–09 KA, *Herefordshire Directory 1905, 1913*, Census (1911)

37   Architect's plans (1912) HAS E44/1

38   Wolfson College online, Sybil's Memoirs extracted and transcribed by Rosie Watts KA

39   BLG (1978), *Monmouthshire Beacon* 27th Apr 1895, Monmouth Museum, *Evening Express* online 1901, *Weekly Mail* online 23rd June 1906, Death of Laura Adelaide and Passenger lists (1913) kindly produced by Joan Fleming-Yates, Sybil's Memoirs KA

40   British Red Cross website, Sybil's Memoirs KA, Women's Health Association letter (1919) KA, *London Gazette* 30th March 1920

41   Statement (1923) KA, Lucas Trust (1923) KA

42   Sybil's Memoirs KA, Cross in Kentchurch graveyard, *Herefordshire Directory 1914*, Castle Shane photos 1917–19 KA

43   Pontrilas court sale particulars (1919) HAS M5/16/6, Pontrilas Sale summary (1919) KA, Kentchurch sales (1920) KA

44   Report in unnamed Irish newspaper 21st Feb 1920 KA, (the cause of the fire was not recorded)

45   Sybil's list (1912) KA, *Castle Shane Inventory 1889, 1912* KA, Murphy, N., 'The Incunabulum in the Castle', Northern Sound radio programme 2015

46   Contemporary press cuttings (unnamed and undated) KA

47   *The Northern Standard* 27th Aug 1943

48   Letters to Sybil (1920) KA, photograph of Noble (nd) KA, Reports and letters to Sybil 1920–22 KA

49   Sybil's Memoirs KA, BLG (1972)

50   Sybil's Memoirs and memorabilia KA

51   Sybil's memoirs KA, Letters from Shaw to Sybil 1926–27 KA, amount of game killed 1913–26 KA

52   Sybil's Memoirs, *Herefordshire Directory 1934*, *Who's Who in Herefordshire 1933*

53   Unnamed newspaper cutting (1937) KA, Sybil's memoirs KA, RNVR list 1939, 1945 online

54   Plans of rooms for auxiliary hospital 1941 HAS AB97/4-6, Letter to Sybil 1945 KA, NLW Annual Report 1942–43 KA (AL40 collection was later transferred to Hereford Archives)

55   Sybil's Memoirs KA, Cornforth, J., *Country Life* 22nd Dec 1966 p 1688, Daisy Rees grave in Kentchurch churchyard

56   *Hereford Times* May 1959, 21st March 1998, Sybil's Memoirs KA

57   Letters and notes 1959, 1960 KA

58   Kentchurch Court website 2017

7 The de Lacys and the Early Scudamores at Holme Lacy

1   Sale particulars 1909 HCL914.244
2   *Burke's Visitations*, Holme Lacy (1862) HCA 39.4 9
3   LOWV website (2008), Thorn (1983)
4   Gibson 1727 pp 141–142, Registers of the Priory of Llanthony, BGAS (2002) p xiv
5   Martin, S.H., 'Holme Lacy', TWNFC (1952) p 277, summary of the grant in Freeman, J., Charters of the de Lacy family, TWNFC (2016) p 51, Whitehead (2003) pp 9–10
6   Lucas-Scudamore, Lady Patricia, St Cuthbert Parish Church (nd), Hillaby, J., *Clients of the Jewish Community* TWNFC (1985) p 197, Grant 1225 HCA 3240
7   Grant 1200–1241 HCA 483
8   Robinson (1869) p 120, Strong, G., *Heraldry of Herefordshire* (1848) pp 70–71, Hillaby, J., 'Walter II de Lacy' TWNFC 2016 p 79
9   Robinson (1869) p 71, Whitehead (2003) pp 10–11
10 Whitehead (2003) p 10, Scudamore Map of Lands 1723, BL G24
11 Whitehead (2003) p 10, Endowment 1332 HCA 2507
12 Martin, S.H., TWNFC (1952) p 277, Moir (1964) p 22–23
13 Lease 1266 HAS AS/2/38, AS58/2/32
14 Calendar of Inquisitions Vol VLLL pp 63–64, Bishop's Registers 1327–1344 transcribed by Capes, W. p III, Gibson 1727 pp 121–122
15 Royal Commission Survey (1927) NMR, choir stalls seen in church 2017
16 Cook, G.H., *Medieval Chantries* (1963) pp 7, 8 & 86
17 Herefordshire Council Sites and Monuments Records online, Royal Commission Survey (1927) NMR
18 Moir (1964) p 29, Rowley p 173
19 Bishop's Registers 1344–1361 transcribed by J.P. Parry
20 Seaton (1903) p 46
21 Bishop's Registers 1344–1361 transcribed by J.P. Parry (1910)
22 Endowment 1364 HCA 209
23 Scudamore family tree online, Skidmore (2015), Gibson 1727 p 60, Atherton (1999) p 25
24 Skidmore (2015), Extracts from deeds HAS CF50/107, Petition 1409 TNA SC 8/186/9261
25 Calendar of Probate & Administration Acts printed 1407–1550, Wye Free Fishery Case documents HAS AS58/8/26, Seaton (1903) p 46
26 Whitehead (2003) p 11, Lease 1409 HCA 1259
27 Hunt, J., Scudamores of Ballingham mss HAS AP71/1
28 Skidmore (2015)
29 Skidmore (2015), Whitehead (2003) p 11
30 Robinson (1872) p 155, Whitehead (2003) p 11
31 Bishop's Registers 1504–1516 printed, edited by A.T. Bannister (1819)
32 *History of Parliament 1509–1558* online, Whitehead (2003) p 11, Skidmore (2015)
33 Draft thesis by W. Tighe KA, Description of Holme Lacy (1862) HCA 39.A.9
34 *History of Parliament 1509–1558*

35   *History of Parliament 1509–1558*

36   Johnson & Shoesmith (2016) pp 177–178

37   Atkyns, R., *State of Glostershire* (1712) p 472, Gibson (1727) pp 164–166

38   Hughes & Hurley (2009) p 93

39   Seaton (1903) p 46, Whitehead (2003) p 11, Faraday M.A., 'Herefordshire Taxes' 2005 pp 78 & 143, *Valor Ecclesiasticus* 1535 J64/31, *History of Parliament 1509–1558*

40   Endowment 1536 HCA1985, Wye Free Fishery Case AS58/2/9, Skidmore (2015)

41   Gift 1538 HAS AD2/ii/130

8   John Scudamore, Sir James and Sir John Living at Holme Lacy House

1   *Burke's Visitation of Country Seats and Arms, Holme Lacy* (1862) HCA

2   Shoesmith & Richardson (1997) pp 149–150 & 153

3   Robinson (1872) p 36, LOWV website translated from rental 1505 HAS A63/III/23

4   Gibson (1727) p 61, Taylor map 1754, Taylor Navigation plan 1763, Whitworth Navigation plan 1779, OS 1815

5   Robinson (1872) p 155, Price (1796) p 200, Herefordshire Through Time website, Extracts HAS CF50/106, Moir (1964) p 41

6   Robinson (1872) p 155

7   Whitehead, D., 'Some connected thoughts on Parks and Gardens', TWNFC (1995) p 217

8   Saxton map 1577

9   Skidmore (2015)

10   *Parliamentary Papers 1509–1558* online, Gibson (1727) p 61

11   Grant 1553 HCA 568

12   Skidmore (2015)

13   Sale of woods in 1560 HCA1256, Wool tithes 1563 HCA 5177

14   *Parliamentary Papers 1509–1558* online, Tighe, W., draft (1984) KA

15   Holme Lacy MSS book KA

16   Skidmore (2015), Hurley (2008) p 65

17   Tighe, W., draft MSS (1984) KA, Holme Lacy MSS book KA

18   Skidmore (2015), *Parliamentary Papers 1558–1603*, Tighe, W., draft MSS (1984) KA

19   *Parliamentary Papers 1558–1603*

20   Skidmore (2015), Gibson (1727) p 62

21   Tighe, W., Two Documents Illustrating the marriage of Sir John Scudamore, in TWNFC (1984) pp 423–26

22   Scudamore Papers Vol 1 BL MSS, Bridge Act 1597 HCL LC 385, Hurley, H., 'River Crossing at Wilton' in *Historical Aspects of Ross* (2000) pp 31–33

23   Hurley (2008) p 65, Hurley, Canon Barn notes, LOWV (2005)

24   Parliamentary Papers 1604–1629, Strong, R., *Cult of Elizabeth* (1972) pp 159, 209–211

25   Whitehead (2003) p 14, Scott, C., *Maligned Militia* (2016), online no pagination, Parliamentary papers 1604–1629, Appointment of Cus. Rot. 1612 TNA C115/62

26   Skidmore (2015), Parliamentary Papers 1604–1629

27 Fleming-Yates (2005) pp 135–137, Parliamentary Papers 1604–1629, also see Matthias, R., *Whitsun Riots* (1963)

28 *RCHM* Vol 1 (1931), LOWV website

29 Ballingham Church Records HAS BD1/1

30 Parliamentary papers 1604–1629, Will 1619 TNA PROB 11/133/536

31 Linton steel-work HAS E12/vi/D, Coates & Tucker (1983) p 62

32 Herefordshire Archaeology online. LOWV project, no evidence found in 2018

33 Holme Lacy MSS book KA, Holme Lacy Parish Registers HAS AL17/1

34 Whitelock, A., *Elizabeth's Bedfellows* (2014) pp 225–226

35 Tighe, W., draft (1984) KA, Moffatt (2015)

36 Holme Lacy MSS book KA, Livery of lands 1628 TNA C115/34

9 Sir John 1st Viscount – Civil War, Holme Lacy, Dore Abbey and Hempsted

1   Gibson (1727) pp 63–64

2   *History of Parliament 1604–1629*, Bull (1894) KA

3   Bull (1894) KA, List of MSS of Lord Scudamore sold in 1954, Belmont Abbey

4   *Alumni Oronienses* (1968) p 1327, Bull (1984) KA, *Britannica* online

5   Holme Lacy parish registers HAS AL17/1

6   Atkyns, R., *Gloucestershire* (1712, reprinted 1974) p 472, Feoffment 1615 TNA C115/30

7   British History online

8   Bull (1894) KA, Members of Parliament KA, Skidmore edited by Moffatt, Ross-Lewin (1900) KA

9   Skidmore (2015), *Britannica* online, *History of Parliament 1604–1629*

10 Bull (1894) KA, Ross-Lewin (1900) p 5

11 *History of Parliament 1604–1629*, Atherton (1993) p 80

12 *History of Parliament 1604–1629*

13 Bull (1894) KA, catalogue of MSS in the Phillipps library 1892 of Lord Scudamore sold in 1954, Belmont Abbey

14 Gibson (1727) p 67, Atherton (1993) pp 61–62, List of MSS sold in 1954, Belmont Abbey, Bull (1884) p 65 KA

15 Bull (1884) KA, *History of Parliament 1604–1629*, Atherton (1993) p 82

16 Two Grants 1625 TNA C115/6

17 Skidmore (2015), Robinson (1872) p 22

18 Carey forge TNA C115/35, Hurley, H., notes LOWV (2006), Taylor, E., 'Seventeenth-Century Iron Forge', TWNFC (1986) pp 450–468

19 Atherton (1993) p 91, *VCH* Gloucester (1996) Vol v p 222, Scudamore Papers BL Add MSS 11052

20 Ross-Lewin (1900) pp 7–8, Atherton (1993) p 55, Holme Lacy Church guide (nd) p 4

21 Gibson (1727) p 166

22 Tonkin, J., in Shoesmith & Richardson (1997) pp 163–172, Gibson (1727) p 36

23 Ross-Lewin (1900) p 10

24 *History of Parliament 1604–1629*

25   Inventory 1630 TNA C115/62/5513 transcribed by the late Elizabeth Taylor HAS BN83/131

26   Bull (1894) KA

27   Reade, H., 'Tours & Travels' in TWNFC (1924) p 35

28   Steward's Accounts (1632) HCA 6417, transcribed by Morgan, F.C. in TWNFC (1949) pp 155–184

29   Steward's Accounts (1632) HCA 6417, Bull (1894) p 67

30   *Herefordshire Cider Tradition* (1972) KA, Chapman, J. in GSIA 'The Cider Industry and the Glass Bottle' (2012)

31   Stafford, H., *Treatise on Cyder-Making* (1753) p 62, according to modern cider makers, Redstreak has not survived in its original variety and Red Foxwhelp could be derived from it. Information from Brian Robbins & friends

32   Macdonald, J., *History of Hereford Cattle* (1909) p 256, Heath-Agnew, E., *A History of Hereford Cattle* (1983) p 12

33   *History of Parliament 1604–1629*

34   Bull (1894) KA

35   For a full account see Atherton (1993) chapter 5 and Lewin (1900) pp 12–16, Scudamore accounts 1635–37 HAS CF60/4, Reade, H., 'Some Account Books' TWNFC (1924) pp 119–122

36   Skidmore (2015)

37   Atherton (1993) p 154

38   Gibson (1727) p 129, Herefordshire Cider Route (c.2017), Rents (1619) TNA C115/65, Vicarage (1927) NMR, HAS HD2/5

39   Bull (1894) KA, Ross-Lewin (1900) p 19, Christmas festivities 1639 transcribed by D. Chapman (1886) HCL 647.1

40   Skidmore (2015), James Scudamore account book 1639 HAS CF60/1

41   Scudamore accounts HAS CF60/5–6, Reade, H., 'Some Account Books', TWNFC (1924) pp 123–128

42   Bull (1894) KA, 1643 pass, catalogue of MSS in the Phillipps Library (1892) sold in 1954, Belmont Abbey

43   Bull (1894) KA, *History of Parliament 1604–1629*

44   Webb (1879) Vol I p 265, Ross (2012) pp 59, 68 & 80

45   Webb (1879) Vol II p 428, Ross (2012) p 64

46   Skidmore (2015), Atherton, I., *Sir Barnabas Scudamore's Defence* (1992), Ross 2012 pp 113 & 137, Webb (1879) Vol 2, p 231

47   Bull (1894) KA, Gibson (1727) p 109

48   Hughes & Hurley (1999) p 39, Bull (1894) KA, Moir (1964) p 51

49   Skidmore (2015), List of MPs KA, Hurley, H., Wilton Castle notes (2016)

50   Duncumb, J., *Hundred of Wormelow* (1912) pp 18–19

51   Petition (1649), Scudamore Papers BL ADD MSS 11052, Taylor, E., 'Seventeenth-Century Iron Forge', TWNFC (1986) p 464

52   Hurley, J., *In Search of John Kyrle* (2013) p 7

53   Bull (1894) KA, catalogue of MSS in the Phillipps Library (1892) sold in 1954, Belmont Abbey

10 The Restoration and Remodelling of Holme Lacy House, 2nd & 3rd Viscounts

1   *Burke's Visitation of Seats and Arms* (1862)
2   Bull (1894), Archive of Cider Pomology, Heref. Cider Museum, Atherton (1999) p 56
3   Moir (1964) pp 52–53
4   Ross-Lewin (1900) p 23, Hurley, J., *In Search of John Kyrle* (2013)
5   *History of Parliament 1604–1629*
6   Hearth Tax 1662, Militia Assessments 1663
7   Accounts 1667–68 HAS CF50/268, Royal Commission Survey (1929) NMR
8   Gibson (1727) pp 168–170 & 73–75, Hempsted church history online, inscription on door of Hempsted House
9   Atkyns, R., *State of Glostershire* (1712) p 472
10 Bull (1894) KA, Holme Lacy MSS book, KA
11 Bull (1894) KA, Skidmore (2015), Smith, E., *Scudamores of Westminster School* (2018), KA, *Alumni Oronienses 1500–1714*
12 Skidmore (2015), Robinson (1862) p 169
13 Articles TNA C115/102, Robinson (1872) p 156
14 Whitehead, D., 'Holme Lacy House', Essays in Honour of Jim & Muriel Tonkin (2011) pp 73–76, *Country Life*, June 1909 p 908 KA
15 Holme Lacy House Royal Commissioners (1927) NMR, *Country Life* 12th June 1909 p 870, 19th June 1909 p 911
16 Esterly, D., *Grinling Gibbons* (1998) pp 62–64, cover notes
17 Whitehead, D., 'Holme Lacy House', Essays in Honour of Jim & Muriel Tonkin (2011) p 80, information from Jeremy Milln, Conservation archaeologist (2018)
18 Note in parish registers HAS AL17/1, copy of lease 1691 HAS AS58/2/47, some field names may be identified on the 1723 map and schedule BM G24, and 1840 tithe map
19 *History of Parliament 1660–1690*, Skidmore (2015)
20 Wye Navigation Act 1695 K38/CE/vi/4a, Hurley (2013) p 8
21 Skidmore (2015), Holme Lacy MSS book KA
22 Scudamore accounts 1697–1703 TNA C115/114
23 Scudamore accounts 1708–1709 HAS CF50/268, TNA ADM 106/662/52
24 Whitehead, D., 'Holme Lacy House', *Essays in Honour of Jim & Muriel Tonkin* (2011) p 83
25 Historic Tree Trail, Holme Lacy House (nd), Robinson (1872) pp 22 & 156
26 Skidmore (2015), *Alumni Oronienses 1500–1714*, James Scudamore Diaries HAS CF60/3. List of MPs KA
27 Holme Lacy MSS book KA, Skidmore (2015)
28 Navy Board Records (1711) TNA ADM 106/662/52
29 Scudamore accounts (1717) TNA C115/68
30 Hurley (2013) pp 43–46 & 111–112, also see Hurley (2008) pp 89–91 transcribed by David Lovelace
31 Plan 1729 BM, Exact map of Lady Scudamore's Woods 1723 BLG22, Particulars of land BMG24

32 Erskine-Hill, H., *The Social Milieu of Alexander Pope* (1975) pp 38, 136, Hurley, J., I*n Search of John Kyrle* (2013), Whitehead (2003), *Country Life* 19th June 1909 p 914

33 Gibson (1727), *Oxonienses Alumni 1500–1714*, Bannister, A. *Institutions* (1923)

34 Erskine-Hill, H. *The Social Milieu of Alexander Pope 1975* pp 32–33, Hurley, J., I*n Search of John Kyrle* (2013) p 95

35 Hurley (2nd edition 1992) pp 68–69, best followed on Price's map 1817

36 Rogers, P., *Life and Times of Lord Coningsby* (2011) pp 219–220, Holme Lacy MSS book, TNA Account book C115/114, Charity Commissioners Report 1819–37 pp 347–349, Tonkin, J. & M., *The Book of Hereford* (1975) p 114

37 *Country Life* 19th June 1906 p 914, Robinson (1872) p 283

11 The Heiresses Lady Frances Scudamore and her Daughter the Duchess of Norfolk

1 Shaw, S., *A Tour to the West of England* (1788) p 172

2 Palmer, P., *The Life and Times of Lord Coningsby* (2011) pp 92 & 211

3 Skidmore (2015), Palmer, P., *The Life and Times of Lord Coningsby* (2011) p 216

4 Holme Lacy MSS book KA

5 Holme Lacy MSS book KA

6 Skidmore (2015), Cracroft's Peerage online

7 Holme Lacy MSS book KA, *History of Parliament 1754–1790* online

8 Whitehead (2003) p 24, Holme Lacy MSS book KA

9 Shaw, S., *A Tour to the West of England* (1788) p 174

10 Rentals 1769 TNA C115/R23, R31

11 Marriage Settlement 1771 HAS AS58/6/13

12 Skidmore (2015)

13 Whitehead (2003) p 25, Accounts 1773 TNA C115/35

14 History of Parliament 1754–1790 online, Alchetron encyclopaedia online

15 *Herefordshire Directory 1858*

16 Holme Lacy parish registers HAS AL17/2, Brayley, E & Britton, J., *The Beauties of England and Wales* (1802) p 506, Holme Lacy tithe map 1840

17 Holme Lacy maps 1780 KA, Chancery notes 1822 KA

18 Whitehead (2013) pp 9 & 16, Holme Lacy tithe map 1840

19 *History of Parliament 1754–1790* online

20 Deposition *c*.1786 on display at Fownhope History Display (2007)

21 Shaw, S., *A Tour to the West of England* (1788) pp 170–175, Price (1796) pp 200–202, Warner (1995) p 20, some of these paintings are now at Kentchurch Court

22 Hurley (2nd edition 2007) pp 65–66 & 40–44, 1726 Road Act HAS K38/Ce/vi/6, 1789 Local Acts Vol 1 HAS 346

23 Lipscomb (1802) p 70

24 A. Lamont, 'Fords and Ferries of the Wye', TWNFC (1922) p 86

25 Hurley (2008) p 183, Hurley (2001) p 155

26 Letter 1792 HAS N80

27 Monumental Inscriptions HAS AS88/224

28 Hurley, J., *Tom Spring* (2002) pp 17–18

29 *Hereford Journal* 12th Sept 1798, Whitehead (2003) p 25, Whitehead (2013) p 11

30 Brayley, E. & Britton, J., *The Beauties of England and Wales* (1802) pp 505–506

31 View from the park 1800 HAS S40/44

32 Hurley (2013) p 14

33 Richards, N., *Navigation of the Wye and Lugg* MSS (1969) 942.44 at HAS, Lease (1804) HAS A58/2/29

34 Lease (1814) HAS AS58/2/30

35 Report of legal division HAS BD25

36 Holme Lacy MSS book KA

37 Duchess of Norfolk Deeds information TNA, Commission of Lunacy 1816 TNA C211/17/N36, Holme Lacy MSS book KA, Report of research KA, Skidmore (2015), *Hereford Journal* 1st Nov 1820

38 Holme Lacy MSS book KA, *Hereford Journal* 1st Nov 1820

39 Holme Lacy MSS book KA

40 Monumental Inscription HAS AS88/224, copy from DNB HAS P174

41 *Hereford Journal* 1st Nov 1820, 8th Nov 1820

42 Holme Lacy MSS book KA

12 Scudamore-Stanhope, the Earls of Chesterfield and the 1909 Sale

1 Skidmore, Warren, *The Scudamores of Holme Lacy* (2015) edited by Linda Moffatt

2 The Duchess of Norfolk, Deeds, Master Harvey's Exhibits, Introduction to C115 TNA, Charles Fitzroy, Petition 1828 HAS R8/35/17–18

3 Burr, Daniel, *Memoir* (1821), The matter of the Duchess of Norfolk papers 1821–27 KA

4 Holme Lacy MSS Book KA, Family Records (1822) HAS D55/1

5 Duchess of Norfolk Coheirs Vol v (1825) KA, Burr Memoirs (1821)

6 Whitehead (2003) p 26

7 Duchess of Norfolk Coheirs Vol v (1825) KA, Burr Memoirs (1821)

8 *Burke's Peerage 1953*

9 Holme Lacy MSS Book KA

10 Skidmore, W., The Scudamore Portraits Once at Holme Lacy (nd), Holme Lacy MSS Book KA, Letter 9 July 2018 from Ann Smith, Archivist Sherborne Castle

11 Holme Lacy MSS Book, Whitehead, D., 'Holme Lacy House', Essays in Honour of Jim & Muriel Tonkin (2011) pp 86–87, Holme Lacy Sale Particulars 1909 KA

12 Walker, R., *Dovecotes and Pigeon Houses of Herefordshire* (2010) pp 94–96, Tithe Map 1840

13 Whitehead (2003) p 27, Historic Tree Trail, Holme Lacy Hotel (nd), Whitehead (2011) p 88, 1833 map HAS Q/SR/120, Holme Lacy Tithe Map 1840, Warner, Holme Lacy Hose (1995) pp 19 & 23

14 *Hereford Journal* 18th July 1832

15 *Burke's Peerage 1953*

16 Quarter Sessions HAS Q/SR/121 (1833)

17   Smith, W., *Herefordshire Railways* (1998) p 10, Reference Book HAS Q/RW/R9c, Notice HAS AL88/35

18   *Hereford Journal* 20th Aug 1851, Hurley (2008) p 176

19   Fownhope & Holme Lacy Bridge Company Prospectus, letter & Share List 1856 HAS AC97/11

20   Bridge Act 1857 House of Lords, Hurley (2008) pp 153–155

21   *Herefords. Directory 1851, 1867*, Holme L. Tithe map 1840, Notes LOWV project (2006)

22   Monumental Inscriptions, Herefordshire Family History Society HAS AS88/224

23   1857 letter A63/iv/9/7, Beale, C., *Champagne and Shambles* (2006) pp 31–32

24   Monumental Inscriptions, Herefordshire Family History Society HAS AS88/224

25   Census Returns 1851, 1861

26   *Burkes Peerage 1953*, Peerage online

27   *Herefordshire Directory 1886*, London Clubs, Oxford University (1996)

28   *Herefordshire Directory 1876*, Agreement 1879 TNA 2515 210 Box 32/1

29   *Burke's Peerage 1953*, Letter TNA CR2747/90A

30   Census Return 1881, *Herefordshire Directory 1885*

31   Holme Lacy MSS book KA, the last entry apart from Lady Patricia who purchased the book in 1958 for Kentchurch Court, LOWV p 214

32   Peerage online 2015, Probate of the Will 1887 KA

33   Monumental Inscriptions, Herefordshire Family History Society AS88/224, Holme Lacy church guide (2007), photo album KA

34   Furniture inventory 1887 HAS AW15/2

35   *Burkes Peerage 1953*, Herefordshire Portraits (1908)

36   Skidmore, W., excerpt from Flashback (nd)

37   Monumental Inscriptions HAS AS88/224

38   Census Return 1891, Holme Lacy House History online, *Herefordshire Directory 1900*, Walford County Families 1892

39   Programme 1897 HAS L54/56, *Herefordshire Directory 1891*

40   *Country Life* July 1899 pp 80–84

41   TWNFC 1866 pp 318–319, 1867 p 216, the Monarch has fallen as seen 2018

42   *Burkes Peerage 1953*, Census Return 1901, *Herefordshire Directory 1902*

43   Holme Lacy photo album 1901 KA

44   Letter 1903 TNA Ladd/3762, St John's Hospital website, TNA H15/SJ

45   Charity Commission 1908 L54/49,Charity Commission Report 1819–1837, Monumental Inscriptions AS88/224. Benefactions Board in Holme Lacy church

46   Wye Free Fishery Case HAS AS58, Taylor, E., *Kings Caple in Archenfield* (1997) pp 311–319, Letter 1911 AS88/8/65, Fishing Case HAS BC79/15–16

47   Holme Lacy, Warner 1995, Probate of Will 1887 KA, *Country Life* June 1909, HCL and KA

48   *Country Life* adverts 1909 HAS K38/Cd/61 Box 3, Sale particulars and Plan 1909 KA also copies at HARC

49   Sale Agreement 1909 KA, undated newspaper cutting KA

50   Sale of Contents 1910 HAS AR21, Newspaper articles HAS M90/1

51   *Burke's Peerage 1953*, Sale of Contents of Beningbrough Hall 1958 KA, Beningbrough Hall, National Trust 1980 KA, *Burke's Landed Gentry 1972*

INDEX

Abergavenny 3, 5, 15, 73, 76, 77, 83, 106
Aconbury 33, 102, 108, *108*
Act of Uniformity 20, 198
Agincourt 12, 13
American War of Independence 53, 199

Baden-Powell, Robert 96, *97*
Ballingham 31, 107, 108, 112, 122, *123*, 124, 132, 135, 141, *141*, 155, 160, 172, 180, 184, 186, 188, 195
Bark stripping 47, *47*, 56, 87, 146, 163, 199
Bath 56, 123, 125, 145
Bear's paw 3, 84
Beaufort, Thomas (Earl of Dorset) 13
Beaufort, Duke of 52, 77, 161, 162, 191
Beer 62, 78, 138, 146, 166, 169
Beningbrough 100, *126*, 192
Bentham, George 75, 78
Bird, Thomas 53, 55, 56, 62, 65, 69, 173, 177, 179, 182, 183
Bird, William 76
Black Death 106
Bodenham, Thomas (& family) *111*, 112, 132
Bodenham, Sir Roger 122
Bolstone 106, 113, 122, *123*, 134, 154, 159, 162, 169, 172, 180, 184, 186, 188
Boultibrook (Presteigne) 67, *67*, 70, 71, 76, 82, 83, 87, 89, 96

Bower farm 102, 112
Bristol 70, 77, 132, 134, 158
Brydges family 33, 45, 51, 66, *66*, *67*, *68*, 89, 96, 120, 121, 141, 177
Buckinghamshire 17, 102, 108, 163, 177
Burton Farm *105*, *152*, 166
Bury Court 102, 106, 108, 112
Bye plot 25, 198

Caradoc (Sellack) 119, 120, *120*, 131, 135, 138-140, 146, 152, 160
Carmarthenshire 12, 13
Carpenter, Constance Primrose (*see Lucas-Scudamore, Connie*)
Castle Shane 79, 81, *82*, 84, 85, 87, 89, *90*, 91-95, *93*, 200, 201
Castle Shane fire 92–94, *93*
Catholics 20, 21, 25, 36, 38, 39, 66, 119, 121, 122, 163
Catholic faith (Catholicism) 8, 25, 29, 36, 116, 118, 127, 164
Cattle 12, 33, 62, 70, 106, 137, *137*, 145, 151
Cecil family 149, 150, 161
Chancery cases 42, 52, 56, 65, 66, 127, 173–175, 177, 200
Chantry 104, 105
Charcoal 29
Charities 40, 160, 191
Chepstow 39, 52, 69, 157

Church vaults 84, 118, 127, 146, 148, 154, 160, 163, 166, 175, 179, 200

Cider *vi*, 49, 51, 120, 135–137, *136*, 138, 145, 146, 154, 155, 169, 180, 183, 187, 199

Civil War (*1642*) 31–34, 121, 139, 140, 141, 146, 150, 199

Clog makers *87*

Coal 49, 62, 65, 69, 73, 83, 91, 138, 157, 184

Coat of arms 3, 92

Coningsby, Lord Thomas 120, 150, 152–154

Corn mills 21, 29, 46, 50, 56, 78, 132

Corras 1, 3–5, *4*, 15, 18, 20, 21, 25, 27, 31, *32*, 43, 46, 62, 69, 75,

Croft family 25, 110, 119, 120, 145, 154,

Cromwell, Thomas 110, 112

De Homme family 104, 106,

De Lacy family 101–103, *103*, 106, 113

Deer park 18, *19*, 45, 52, 70, 86, 114, 122, 155, 194

Devereux Court 102, 108, 112

Devereux family 102

Digby, Dir Kenelm 137

Digby family 145, 155–158, 160, 174, 175, 182

Dinedor 160, *160*, 169, 185

Dinmore 18

Dissolution (*1536*) 14, 17–20, 109, 110, 111, 113, 198

Domesday 1, 101, 191, 197

Donegan, John 81, 82

Donegan, Laura Adelaide (Scudamore/ Lucas) (known as Buzzy) (*1831–1912*) *75*, 75–79, 81, 85–87, 91, *91*, 200

Dore Abbey 1, 3, 10, 20, 102, *102*, 103, 110, 113, 134, 197

Dorstone 10, 139

Dublin 62, 87, 91

Duke of Norfolk (*see Howard, Charles*)

Eton College 66, 83, 91, 187

Ewyas Harold 1, 3, 21, 33, 76

Ewyas, Sir Robert 5

Farming 25, 49, 65, 103, 110, 135–138, 151, 155, 186

Ferries 31, 119, 120, 169, 184

First World War (*1914–18*) 91, 96, 201

Fishing 65, 83, 86, 151, 155, 191, 194, 195

Fitzroy, Charles 162

Fitzroy, Colonel Charles 161–163, 168, 173

Fitzroy, Lady Frances (known as Fanny, previously Duchess of Beaufort) (*1711–49*) *118*, 162, *162*, 163, 199

Foley family 36, 55, 125, 154, 157, 161,

Fords 1, 31, *32*, 119, 169, 184

Forest of Dean 29, 36, 65, 134, 137,

Fortune, Mr William (attorney-at-law) 43, 45, 46, 49

Fownhope 117, 166, *168*, 169, 170, 184, 187, 200

France 12, 13, 15, 77, 79, 82, 89, 96, 103, 108, 130, 132, 134, 137, 138, 140, 148, 150, 198, 199

Frances 2nd Viscountess 149–154

Frances 3rd Viscountess 155–160

Frizell, Richard 166, *181*, 199

Gardens 71, 76, 138, 151, *151*, 155, 158, 168, 171, 172, 182, 183, 187, *189*, 190, 200, 201

Garway *2*, 5, 15, 18, 20, 21, 27, 34, 40, *41*, 62, *63*, 69, 73, 77, 79, 86, 122,

Gentleman Pensioner 119, 120, 198

Gibbons, Grinling 100, 150, *150*, 167, 180, 195

Gibson, Matthew *102*, 129, 159

Gloucester 3, 55, *55*, *103*, *109*, 131, 140, *147*, 166, 169, 184

Glyndwr, Owain 3, *9, 11*, 12, 13, 79, 89, 197
Goodrich 10, 12, 33, 76, 199
Great pear tree 164–166, *165*, 172, 199
Grist mills 21, 43, 50, 56
Grosmont 8, 12, 13, 15, 21, 43, 47, *50*, 52, 62, 71, 73–75, 77, 78, 87, 88
Gunpowder Plot 25, 198
Guy's Hospital 45, 49

Harewood 18, 53, 146
Harley family 53, 55, 154
Hawking 122, 151
Hearth tax 34, 146
Hempsted 101, 111, *111*, 131, 134, 138, *147*, 148, 159, 162
Hereford 14, 21, 25, 31, 33, 37, 38, 40, 45, 47, 49, 51, 53, 55, 56, 59, 60, 62, 65, 76, 77, 101, *109*, 111, 120, 121, 139, 142, 154, 160, 162, 169
    Bishop of 20, 36, 37, 101–103, 106, 109, 110, 114, 121, 132, 140, 145, 155
    Cathedral 37, 60, 111, 120, 138, 140, 145, 146
    Cattle 137, *137*
    Infirmary 187
    Mayor of 5, 15, 53, 110
    Railway 73, 83, 184, *185*, 186, 200
Hereford Turnpike Trust 41, 160, 183, 199
Hereford family 53, 60
Highways 23, 25, 48, 75, 146, 183, 184
Hill, Miles 33, 199
Hoarwithy 159, 160, *160*, 168, 169, 183, 191
Hollington 15, *105*, 106–108, 111, 112, 172, 179, 197

Holme Lacy *vii*, 3, 15, 101–107, 112, 134-140, 136, 137, 142, 159, 160, 166, 168, 169, 172, 172, 175, 185, 194
    church 104–106, *104, 106*, 109, 113, 118, *118*, 125, 134, 135, *144, 152*, 154, *156*, 157, 160, *162*, 163, 166, 175, *176*, 177, 179, 186-188
    House and estate *viii*, 98, 100, 112-115, *114, 115*, 122, 127, 131, 138–140, 145, 146, 150–155, *153, 155, 159*, 161, 164–195, *165, 167, 170, 178, 179, 187, 189, 192, 193*, 198
    station 184, *185*
    Vicarage 112, 138, *146*, 146, 169, 199
Horse towing path 65, 66, *171*, 172, 184
Horse-drawn tram road 65, 73, 82
Horses 10, 15, 33, 50, 51, 62, 77, 86, 120, 121, 131, 132, 135, 137, 138, 140, 157, 159, 164, 172, 174, 194
Hoskyns family 53, 146, 170
Howard, Charles Duke of Norfolk 163–177, *164, 165, 169*, 180, 200
Howard, Frances Duchess of Norfolk (née Fitzroy) (*1749–1820*) 163–166, 164, 170, 173–177, *176*, 199
Howton 21, 22, 25, 27, 29, 31, 34, 39, 43, 46, 47, 56
Hunting 57, 60, 65, 86, 122, 151

Indian Mutiny 81, 200
Inns 8, *10*, 39, 55, 65, 70, *70*, 73, *73*, 74, 77, 83, 85, 132, 169, 199
Ireland 62, 79, 81, 82, 85–96, 132, 155, 200
Irish Civil War (*1922*) 96, 201
Iron forges *27, 28*, 29, 34–36, *35*, 43, 46, 47, 62, 65, 125, 132–134, *133*, 141, 142, 198, 199

Jack of Kent (John Kent) 7, 8, *9*, 13, 197
Jones-Brydges family (Sir Harford)
   66–70, *66*, *67*, *68*, 75

Keck, Anthony 53, 199
Kemble, Father John 36–38, *37*, 199
Kentchurch *vii*, 1–3, *2*, 5–8, 20, *22*, *24*,
   30, 34, 40, 43, 50, 73, 75, 85
      church and rectors 8, 15–17, 20, *26*,
         27, 29, 38, 40, 42, 60, 62, 83, *83*, 84,
         86, 89, 91, *92*
      Court and Park *vi*, *vii*, *viii*, *viii*, 2,
         5–8, *6*, *7*, *9*, 12–25, *19*, 29–53, *30*, *35*,
         42, *44*, *47*, *52*, 56–79, *57*, *59*, *68*, *69*,
         71, *74*, *77*, 82–91, *87*, 95–100, *97*, *98*,
         99, *112*, 182, 195, *196*, 197, 200, 201
      flood *99*, 100
      Rectory 76, *83*
      School 40
Kidwelly 12, 13
Kilpeck 20, 22, 34, 43, 47, 62, 86
King Charles I 29, 31, 33, 132, 137, 139,
   140, 167, 198, 199
King Charles II 34, 36, 145, 153, 155, 199
King Edward III 104, 106, 197
King Edward VI 114
King Edward VII 89, 191, 201
King Edward VIII 201
King George II 41, 163, 199
King George III 49, *51*, 65, 172, 199
King George IV 200
King George V 201
King George VI 201
King Henry I 197
King Henry II 197
King Henry III 103
King Henry IV 12, 13, 107, 197
King Henry V 13, 14, 197
King Henry VI 14
King Henry VII 14, 108, 198

King Henry VIII 17, 109, 112, 113, 118, 198
King James I 25, 121, 129, 131, 198
King James II 39, 155, 199
King Richard II 10, 14
King Richard III 198
King Stephen 3, 197
King William III (William of Orange)
   39, *39*, 145, 168, 199
King William IV 200
Kings Caple 49, *134*, 172,
Knights Hospitallers 15, 17, 18, 109,
   113, 198
Knights Templar 5, 109
Kyrle of Much Marcle 120, 125, 132, 134
Kyrle, John, Man of Ross 39, 146,
   158, 159
Kyrle family of Walford 33, 122

Land tax 62
Laud, Bishop William 129, 131, 132, 134,
   135, 137, 140
Ledbury 119, 169,
Lime kilns 56, 57, 70, 166
Linton 125
Llancillo 18, 22, 25, *27*, 28, 29, 32, 36, 43,
   46, 47, 56, 62, 92, 199
Llandovery *12*, 13, *13*
Llangarron 40, 119, 135,
Llangua 25, 43, 47, 50, 51, 56, 63, 73, 74,
   85–87, 89
Llangua Mill 50, *50*, 51, 62
Llanithog 15, 18, 20, 22, 25, 29, 46, 56,
   62, 78
Llanthony (Gloucestershire) 101, 111, 130,
   131, 138–140, *147*, 148, 173
Llywelyn ap Gruffydd Fychan 13
Lollards 9

London 12, 25, 37, 43, 47, 49, 51–55, *54*, 59, 62, 66, 71, 76, 79, 81, 85, 87, 88, 106, 131, 135, 137–140, 143, 146, 148, *153*, 155, 160, 161, 163, 166, 167, 173, 174, 177, 186, 188, 190, 191, 199

Lucas, Fitzherbert Dacre 79–81, *80*

Lucas, Rt Hon. Edward 79–84, *82*

Lucas-Scudamore, Charlotte (*1949–*) 100

Lucas, Scudamore, Connie (Carpenter) 96, 98

Lucas-Scudamore, Edward (known as Eddie) (*1853–1917*) 83–92, *85*, *88*, *92*, 200

Lucas-Scudamore, Geraldine (known as Gill) 89, *90*, 94, 96, 97

Lucas-Scudamore, John (*1953–*) 100

Lucas-Scudamore, John (known as Jack) (*1902–1976*) 89, *90*, *92*, *95*, 95–100, 195, 201

Lucas-Scudamore, Lady Patricia (Scudamore-Stanhope) *97*, 100, 195

Lucas-Scudamore, Oriel 91, 92, 96

Lucas-Scudamore, Sybil (Webber) 87–100, *88*, *90*, *94*, 97

Lunacy 40, 166, 173, 174

Militia 34, 49, *49*, 51, 55, 57, 59, 76, 79, 81, 121, 199

Militia assessment 34

Misericords 105

Monaghan 79, 81, 85, 87, 89, 91

Monmouth 12, 13, 25, 31, 39, 45, 47, 55, 63, 65, 69, 73, 75, 85, 157, 166, 171

Monmouth Cap 63, 72–74, *73*, 77, 83, 90

Monnow River 1, 2, 8, 20, 21, 22, 25, 29, 31, 34-36, *35*, 51, 73, 83, 86, 198

Morgan, George (steward) 95, 96

Mortimer's Cross 14

MPs (Member of Parliament) 14, 21, 51, 59, 62, 65, 76, 79, 89, 109, 119, 121, 131, 141, 149, 150, 153, 155, 162, 164, 188

Mynors family 18, 108, 109

Nash, John 45, 59–61, 200

Noble, Charlie (carpenter) 94, 95

Norfolk, Duke of (*see Howard, Charles*)

Oates, Titus 36, 199

Oke family 12

Oxford 8, 29, 66, 83, 84, *95*, 96, 114, 119, 129, 138, 139, 145, 149, 155, 159, 186, 187

Parliament 10, 31, 33, 39, 52, 62, 65, 110, 123, 129, 139, 140, 142, 164

Payne Knight family (of Downton Castle) 53, 59, 170

Perry 166, 172

Petty France (London) 138–140

Pleasure grounds 151

Poaching 55, 73

Pontrilas 29, 72–76, 72, *74*, 83, *84*, 85, 200

Court 77, 78, 83, *83*, 85, 89, 92, *95*, 96

Forge 34, *35*, 36, 199

Pope, Alexander 158–161, 199

Porter, Sir Arthur 111, 130

Poston (Vowchurch) 5, 13

Pound Farm 180–182, *181*, *182*, 185, 188, 191, 194

Powell, Joseph 62

Price, Uvedale 170, 171

Priests 8, 20, 21, 25, 36, 105, 106, 108, 109, 113, 119, 127, 132, 134,

Queen Anne 40, 155, 199
Queen Elizabeth I 14, 21, 23, 119, 120,
    127, 198
Queen Elizabeth II 201
Queen Mary 116, 127, 198
Queen Victoria 89, 188, 191, 200

Radnor 85
Railway 73, 79, 82, 83, 184, *185*, 186, 200
Rea, William 157
Rectors of Kentchurch (*see Kentchurch
    church and rectors*)
Recusants 22, 25, 121
Redstreak apple *136*, 137, 145, 146, 199
Rees, Daisy (nanny) 100
Reformation 17, 20, 111, 114, 116
Religious houses 17, 105, *109*, 111, 113
Restoration 145, 146, 199
Richardson, Samuel 48, 53
River navigation 49, 55, 65, 154, 155, 172,
    184, 199
River Wye 31, 39, 48, 55, 65, 66, 101, 106,
    113, 114, 119, 132, *133*, 134, 139, 142, 151,
    154, 155, 157–159, *159*, 163, 166, 168, 169,
    171, *171*, 172, *172*, 184, 188, 191, 199,
    200, 201
Road acts 48, 168
Ross *38*, 39, 47, 55, 73, 85, 110, 112, 119,
    139, 140, 158, 159, 166, 184, *185*, 200
Rowlestone 4, 5, 15, 17, 18, 21, 22, 25, *32*,
    34, 39, 42, 43, 45–47, 50–52, 56, 62, 63,
    76, 92, 106, 108
Rudhall 39, 42, 47, 117

Scudamore, Alice 3, 12, 13
Scudamore, Barnabas 121, 139, 141
Scudamore, Col John (*1727–96*)
    45–61, 199
Scudamore, James (*1489*) 15, 17, 198
Scudamore, Jane 149, 154

Scudamore, Joan (*1521*) 17, 18, 198
Scudamore, John (*1584*) 20–22 ,198
Scudamore, John (*1757–96*) 61–65, 199
Scudamore, Philip (*1382*) 106, 107, 197
Scudamore, Philip (*1521*) 17, 18, 198
Scudamore, Ralph (*1086*) 1, 3, 197
Scudamore, Reginald (*1120*) 1, 197
Scudamore, Richard of Rowlestone
    42, 45
Scudamore, Rowland of Caradoc 120,
    131, 135
Scudamore, Sarah Laura (Jones-
    Brydges) 67, *67*, 69, 76–78, 82
Scudamore, Sir James 120–127
Scudamore, Sir John 6th (*1386*)
    10–13, 197
Scudamore, Sir John 7th (*1430*)
    13–15, 197
Scudamore, Sir John (*1541–1623*)
    119–127, 198
Scudamore, John (*1616*) 25, 26, 198
Scudamore, John (*1624–1704*) 31–40, 198
Scudamore, John 1st Viscount (*1600–71*)
    129–148, 198
Scudamore, John 2nd Vis. (*1649–97*)
    148–154, 199
Scudamore, John 3rd Vis. (*1684–1716*)
    154–157, 199
Scudamore, John Lucy (*1798–1875*) 65,
    66, 69, 71, 73, 75–78, 85, 200
Scudamore, Sir Walter (*1148*) 3, 197
Scudamore, Thomas (*1607*) 22, 25, 198
Scudamore, Vincent (*1281*) 3, 4, 5
Scudamore, William (*1680–1741*) 40,
    42, 199
Scudamore, William of Ballingham
    132, 141
Scudamore-Stanhope, Sir Edward 12th
    Earl of Chesterfield 100, 195

Scudamore-Stanhope, Sir Edwyn 10th Earl of Chesterfield (*1854–1933*) 187, 190–194, 200

Scudamore-Stanhope, Sir Edwyn Frances (*1793–1874*) 180, 184, 186, 200

Scudamore-Stanhope, Hon. Harry 11th Lord Chesterfield 88

Scudamore-Stanhope, Sir Henry 9th Earl of Chesterfield (*1821–87*) 186, 187, 200

Second World War 96, 98, 201

Sellack 33, 107, 119, 120, 131, 135, 139, 152, 160

Sequestration 33, 140

Shelton, Mary 119

Shipbuilding 39, 49, 157

Shooting 57, 65, 86,

Shropshire Light Infantry 87, 89

Skenfrith 12, 31, 91

Smyth, George 43, 45, 47, 158,

Strangford 117

Talbot, Earl William 162

Tanyards 47,

Thomas, Francis (builder) 53, 62

Timber trade 23, 39, 49, 50, 52, 56, 61, 66, *68*, 68–70, 76, 83, 87, 133, 134, 154, 155, 157, 163, 172, 195, 199

Treaddow 108

Treason Act 110

Treworgan 135

Tudor, Jasper and Owen 14

Tudor, Thomas (land agent) 69–71, 73, 74, 75, 200

Turnpikes 41, 42, 48, 49, 55, 62, 73, 75, 77, 159, 160, *160*, 168, 169, 183, 199

Upton Scudamore (Wiltshire) 1

Vaughan family 20, 109, 113, 118

Wages 10, 13, 51, 62, 67, 71, 110, 138, *153*, 163

Wales 8, 12, 13, 20, 53, 55, 85, 91, 98, 114, 116, 122, 123

Waller, Sir William 139

Walwyn family 53, 61, 62, 119, 175, 179

Wars of the Roses 14, 108, 197

Watkins, Revd Morgan 86, 89

Webbe, Thomas (carpenter) 39

Webber, Col George 88

Webber, Sybil (*see Lucas-Scudamore, Sybil*)

Weirs 1, 22, *22*, 34, 50, 104, 106, 142, 154

Welsh Newton 36, *37*, 38

Westfaling family 39, 42, 43, 45, 47

White Castle 13

White, George 52

Whitsun riots 121, 198

Wilton 31, 33, 39, 112, 113, 119–121, *120*, 141

Wine 13, 56, 62, 137, 138, 169, 173, 187

Wood Court 102, 106, 112

Woodhouse, James 49, 52, 55, 56

Woodlands 45, 56, 101, 120, 182

Worm Brook 29, 34

Wye Free Fishery case 191, 194, 201

Wye River (*see River Wye*)

Also from Logaston Press (www.logastonpress.co.uk)

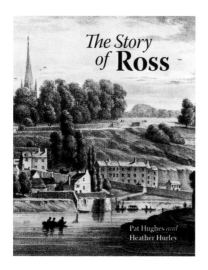

The Story of Ross
Pat Hughes & Heather Hurley
192 pages, 260 × 205 mm
170 B+W illustrations
ISBN: 978-1-906663-25-4
Paperback, £12.95

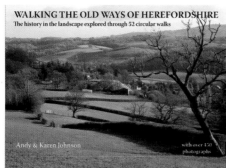

Walking the Old Ways of Herefordshire
Andy & Karen Johnson
384 pages, 148 × 210 mm
Over 450 colour photographs and 53 maps
ISBN: 978-1-906663-86-5
Paperback, £12.95

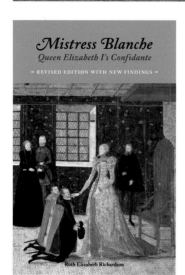

Mistress Blanche
Queen Elizabeth I's Confidante
(revised edition with new findings)
Ruth Elizabeth Richardson
224 pages, 234 × 157 mm
26 colour and 8 b&w illustrations
ISBN: 978-1-910839-28-7
Paperback, £12.95